Competitive Seed Science and Technology

About the Authors

Dr. K. Vanangamudi, Former Dean (Agriculture) and Seed Scientist, graduated B.Sc., (Ag.) in 1975 from Agricultural College and Research Institute, Tamil Nadu Agricultural University, Coimbatore; M.Sc., (Ag.) and Ph.D. in Seed Science and Technology, respectively in 1977 and 1981 from TNAU; and Post Doctoral Fellow (1988-1990) at Mississippi State University, USA. He joined Department of Seed Science and Technology, TNAU as Assistant Professor in 1982 and served the University for 32 years as Associate Professor (1986-1988) at Agricultural Research Station, Bhavanisagar; Professor (1992-2001) at Forest College & Research Institute, Mettupalayam; Professor and Head (2001-2003) of Department of Seed Science and Technology; Dean, Adhiparasakthi Agricultural College (2003-2006), Kalavai; and Dean (Agriculture), Agricultural College and Research Institute, TNAU, Coimbatore (2006-2009). He retired from service on August 31, 2013

He has undergone Post Doctoral Programme in Tree Seed Technology at Mississippi State University, USA from 1988-1990 and visited USA, Japan and Canada in connection with Forestry education and research under USAID-Winrock International program. He underwent training on e-learning and web based teaching at UC, Davis and Cornell University, USA during 2017.

Dr. Vanangamudi's significant contributions in Agricultural Education are 1. starting B.Tech (Bioinformatics), B. Tech (Agricultural Information Technology) and BS (Agribusiness Management) degrees at AC&RI, Coimbatore, and B.Sc (Horti.) degree at AP Agricultural College; 2. He introduced e-education and online examination; 3. Under NAIP project on "Development of e-courses for B.Sc., (Ag) degree program as Co.PI, he developed e-learning materials for all the 50 courses and hosted in TNAU and ICAR websites; and 4. Video streaming of lecture presentation by the teachers in the classroom (video filming, editing and publishing).

He has prepared course materials for 90 courses for Industrial Training Institute (ITI) program in Agriculture, Horticulture, Agricultural Engineering, Animal husbandry, Poultry, Food processing under "Modular Employment Skills" and "Centre of Excellence" funded by National Instructional Media Institute, Ministry of Labour & Employment, GOI, Chennai, for the students and instructors of ITI all over India.

As a researcher, he was the Principal Investigator of 11 research projects funded by ICAR-NIAP, ICAR-World bank, ICFRE-World bank, Tamil Nadu Forest department, Ministry of Labour and Employment (GOI), CIDA-Gulpeh, Canada and Private agencies.

Dr. Vanangamudi has published 2 review papers, 35 research papers in International journals, 112 research papers in National journals, 29 popular articles in English and 53 in Tamil. He has written 40 books in English and 10 in Tamil. He has also written 11 technical bulletins in English and 29 in Tamil.

In recognition of his contribution in Agriculture Education, Research and Extension, he was awarded with Best PG teacher award in 1998 and Best scientist award in 1999 by TNAU; Best PG Teacher award 2000 by Madras Agricultural Students Union (MASU), Coimbatore; Best Seed Scientist award in 2003 by Hisar Agricultural University (HAU), Hisar; Tamil Nadu Scientist award in 2006 by Tamil Nadu Council for Science and Technology (TNCST), Chennai; Best Research Paper award in 2005 by Indian Society of Seed Technology (ISST), New Delhi and Bharat Ratna Dr. C. Subramaniam Best Teacher award in 2006 by Indian Council of Agriculture Research (ICAR), New Delhi.

He is a recognized guide of Bharathiar University, Coimbatore; Bharathidasan University, Trichy and Forest Research Institute, Dehradun.

He was a Research and Technical Consultant to Little's Orientals Balm and Pharmaceuticals Ltd., Chennai for seed priming, seed film coating and setting up of Seed Research Lab; to a farmer for 200 acres of farm land development; to a EU-KKID-Peace trust project for end term evaluation; and to a Kerala Forest Department project (World Bank) for developing training course syllabi and establishment of seed processing and testing units. He served as Senior Advisor and Consultant to Dr Mohan's Health care Products Ltd., Chennai.

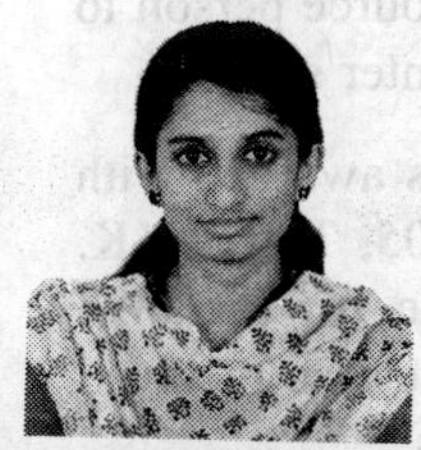

Ms. Shyni. P, graduated B.Sc., (Agriculture) in 2018 from Agricultural College & Research Institute, Kudumiyanmalai, Pudukkottai district, a constituent college of Tamil Nadu Agricultural University. She worked as Junior Research Fellow in the scheme "Restoration of genetic Quality of Dr. Mohan's High Fibre rice (DMHFR) using rapid generation advance method" funded by Dr. Mohan's Health Care Products Pvt Ltd, Chennai, from Sep 2018- May 2019. At present, she is working as Junior Research Fellow in the Production of sufficient and nutritious forage for university dairy farm and production of quality nucleus, breeders and truthfully labeled seeds/ planting materials of forage crops, (VCS-V60 AE) scheme at the Department of Forage Crops, TNAU, Coimbatore.

She has served as Entertainment Secretary during 2014-2016 and Dramatic Secretary during 2016-2017 in students' club of Agricultural College & Research Institute, Kudumiyanmalai, Pudukkottai.

Dr. S. Kavitha graduated B.Sc., (Agri.), M.Sc., (Agri.) and Ph.D. in Seed Science and Technology, respectively in 1999, 2002 and 2005 from Agricultural College and Research Institute, Tamil Nadu Agricultural University, Coimbatore. She was awarded with Senior Research Fellowship for doctoral research. She joined as Assistant Professor in the Department of Seed Science and Technology in 2009 and worked as a programme coordinator, KVK, Ramanathapuram since April 2018. Now, she is working in the Department of Plant Genetic Resources, TNAU, Coimbatore since November, 2019. She has got ten years of experience in teaching, research and extension.

She has authored three books, 23 book chapters and 22 popular articles and published 14 research articles in national and international journals. She has excellent research experience by heading eight research projects as Principal Investigator and 10 research projects as Co - Principal Investigator funded by various agencies.

She has attended two International conferences, two International workshops, 20 National trainings, two 21 days trainings, seven National seminars and five workshops. She also conducted and co-ordinated various On Farm trials (OFT), Front Line Demonstrations (FLD), Farmers Field School (FFS), Integrated Farming System (IFS), Entrepreneur Development Programme (EDP), 88 on campus trainings, 32 off campus trainings, 3 vocational trainings, 6 seminars, 26 exhibitions, three sponsored trainings and delivered 78 special lectures as resource person to farmers and extension functionaries. She organized one ICAR winter school.

She has guided two M.Sc. (Ag) students as chairperson. She was awarded with Dr.M. Balakumarasamy award for the best Ph.D. student in 2005, Thiru. V.K. Kumarasamy award and Coimbatore Seed Corporation prize for the best M.Sc.,(Agri.) student in Seed Science and Technology in 2002 and also received best paper (oral) presentation and best poster presentation awards.

Dr. K. Raja, Associate Professor (Seed Science and Technology) working in the prestigious Tamil Nadu Agricultural University, Coimbatore for the past 14 years. He has vast experience in seed production, teaching, research and extension activities. He has received the Best Seed Production Scientist and Best Paper Presentation Awards. With several international and national articles to his credit, he has authored two books that have been well received by the peer community. Presently he is working in the Department of Seed Science and Technology, Tamil Nadu Agricultural University, Coimbatore.

Competitive Seed Science and Technology

K. Vanangamudi
Former Dean (Agriculture)
Former Professor and Head (Seed Science and Technology)
Tamil Nadu Agricultural University
Coimbatore 641 003, Tamil Nadu

P. Shyni
Junior Research Fellow
Department of Forage Crops
Tamil Nadu Agricultural University
Coimbatore 641 003, Tamil Nadu

S. Kavitha
Assistant Professor (Seed Science and Technology)
Department of Plant Genetic Resources
Tamil Nadu Agricultural University
Coimbatore 641 003, Tamil Nadu

K. Raja
Associate Professor
Department of Seed Science and Technology
Tamil Nadu Agricultural University
Coimbatore 641 003, Tamil Nadu

New Delhi – 110 034

A Paperback Division of

NEW INDIA PUBLISHING AGENCY

101, Vikas Surya Plaza, CU Block, LSC Market
Pitam Pura, New Delhi 110 034, India
Phone: + 91 (11) 27 34 17 17 Fax: + 91 (11) 27 34 16 16
Email: info@nipabooks.com
Web: www.nipabooks.com

Feedback at feedbacks@nipabooks.com

ISBN 978-93-89547-98-6

Composed and Designed by NIPA

Preface

Production and bumper crops and food security begin with high quality seeds. Seed producers and processor's must provide these high quality genetically pure seeds to farmers and consumers every year. This is a challenging work, as it requires that seeds be clean, free from weed seeds and other contaminants. Seeds for sale must also be checked 1to make sure they have a good vigour and viability.

The importance of improved seed associated with genetic, physical, physiological and health qualities warrants thorough knowledge on seed biology, production of genetically pure seeds, post harvest management of seeds, seed quality enhancement techniques, seed legislation and certification, seed testing and seed industry and marketing. The question of man power development in Seed Science and Technology arises in early 70's among the policy makers to fulfil the above gaps. During fifth five year plan, the National Commission of Agriculture (1971-76), recommends teaching of Seed Science and Technology in Agricultural Universities and ICAR Institutes. Now, the students and graduates of agriculture, horticulture and forestry specializing in Seed Science and Technology are taking up competitive examinations at State and National levels for job opportunities and higher education.

Considering the need of the students and graduates including teachers, the book on "Competitive Seed Science and Technology" is prepared. I hope that this book can cater the requirements of students, graduates and teachers.

I welcome your suggestions and comments for improvement of the book.

November, 2019

K. VANANGAMUDI

Contents

UNIT-3 : SEED PROCESSING

UNIT-4 : SEED CERTIFICATION

UNIT-5 : SEED STORAGE

UNIT-6 : SEED HEALTH

UNIT-7 : SEED INDUSTRY AND MARKETING

UNIT - 1

FLORAL AND SEED BIOLOGY

1

Floral Biology

I. FILL UPS

1. A _____ is an unbranched, indeterminate inflorescence with pedicellate flowers along the axis.
2. A _____ is a type of raceme with flowers that do not have a pedicel.
3. An _____ is a type of raceme with a short axis and multiple floral pedicels of equal length that appear to arise from a common point.
4. Indeterminate simple inflorescences are generally called _____.
5. Determinate simple inflorescences are generally called _____.
6. A compound raceme is often called a _____.
7. _____ are umbels in which the single flowers are replaced by many smaller umbels called umbellets.
8. _____ is the pollen producing part of a flower, usually with a slender filament supporting the anther.
9. _____ is the part of the stamen where pollen is produced.
10. _____ is the ovule producing part of a flower.
11. The part of the pistil where pollen germinates is _____.
12. The enlarged basal portion of the pistil where ovules are produced is _____.
13. The mode (method) of arrangement of ovules in the ovary is called _____.
14. Ovules attached to the roof of the ovary is called as _____.
15. The arrangement of ovules few or one at the base of the ovary is called as _____.
16. The stamen has the anther and the _____.
17. The stamen has the _____ and the filament.
18. The _____ has the anther and the filament.
19. Anther is the part of the stamen where _____ is produced.

20. Pistil is the _____ producing part of a flower.
21. A compound _____ is often called a panicle.
22. A _____ is an ovary attached to the receptacle above the attachment of other floral parts.
23. An _____ lies below the attachment of other floral parts.
24. Flowers have both male (androecium) and female (gynoecium) reproductive structures are known as _____ flowers.
25. Flowers have both _____ and female (gynoecium) reproductive structures are known as bisexual or perfect flowers.
26. Flowers that contain both androecium and gynoecium are called _____.
27. Reproductive structure that is either functionally male or functionally female is called as _____ flowers.
28. Flowers with an androecium, but no gynoecium is termed as _____.
29. Flowers with a gynoecium, but no androecium is defined as _____.
30. _____ is an individual that has both male and female reproductive units.
31. _____ refers to a plant population having separate male and female plants.
32. Plants producing male flowers only are named as _____.
33. Plants producing female flowers only are known as _____.
34. _____ has both hermaphrodite and female structures.
35. _____ has both hermaphrodite and male structures.
36. Gynomonoecious has both _____ and female structures.
37. Andromonoecious has both _____ and male structures.
38. Gynomonoecious has both hermaphrodite and _____ structures.
39. Andromonoecious has both hermaphrodite and _____ structures.
40. The filaments are fused together to form one group and anthers are free, which is known as _____.
41. Filaments are fused to form two bundles as in pea, which is named as _____.
42. Filaments are fused to form many bundles as in lemon, which is termed as _____.

II. TRUE OR FALSE

1. The main kind of racemose inflorescence is the raceme.
2. A raceme is a type of raceme with flowers that do not have a pedicel.

3. A spadix is a spike of flowers densely arranged around it, enclosed or accompanied by a highly specialised bract called a spathe.
4. A flower head or capitulum is a much contracted raceme in which the single sessile flowers share is borne on an enlarged stem.
5. The pollen producing part of a flower is called as pistil.
6. The enlarged basal portion of the pistil where ovules are produced is named as ovule.
7. The mode (method) of arrangement of ovules in the ovary is called placentation.
8. A compound raceme is often called an umbel.
9. A superior ovary is an ovary attached to the receptacle above the attachment of other floral parts.
10. A superior ovary is an ovary attached to the receptacle below the attachment of other floral parts.
11. An inferior ovary lies above the attachment of other floral parts.
12. Flowers have both male (androecium) and female (gynoecium) reproductive structures is known as Bisexual or perfect flowers.
13. Flowers with an androecium, but no gynoecium is termed as Staminate or male.
14. Flowers with a gynoecium, but no androecium is defined as Pistillate, carpellate or female.
15. Flowers with an androecium, but no gynoecium is termed as Pistillate, carpellate or female.
16. Flowers with a gynoecium, but no androecium is defined as Staminate or male.
17. Monoecious is an individual that has both male and female reproductive units.
18. Dioecious refers to a plant population having separate male and female plants.
19. Dioecious is an individual that has both male and female reproductive units.
20. Monoecious refers to a plant population having separate male and female plants.
21. The stamen has the anther and the filament, which connects the anther to the floral axis or another organ.
22. Syncarpous is a type of gynoecium which has multiple carpels fused into a single structure.

23. Hermaphrodite flower has only unisexual reproductive unit.
24. Polysepalous or polypetalous flowers have free sepals or petals.
25. The filaments are fused together to form one group and anthers are free and this is known as diadelphous.

III. MATCH THE FOLLOWING

(i)

1.	Rice	A Raceme
2.	Red gram	B Cymes
3.	Sunflower	C Panicle
4.	Castor	D Axillary raceme
5.	Durian	E Capitulum

(ii)

1.	Mango	A Raceme
2.	Castor	B Spathe
3.	Black gram	C Cyme
4.	Date palm	D Panicle
5.	Brinjal	E Axillary raceme

(iii)

1.	Onion	A Spike
2.	Amaranthus	B Raceme
3.	Cauliflower	C Spadix
4.	Beetroot	D Spike
5.	Coconut	E Umbel

(iv)

1.	Arecanut	A Spadix
2.	Cashew nut	B Cyme
3.	Pepper	C Cymose
4.	Clove	D Spike
5.	Curry leaf	E Indeterminate panicle

(v)

1.	Ginger	A Solitary corymb
2.	Mustard	B Spike
3.	Anthurium	C Raceme
4.	Amaryllis	D Spadix
5.	Rose	E Umbel

ANSWER KEYS

I. FILL UPS

1. Raceme	2. Spike	3. Umbel
4. Racemose	5. Cymose	6. Panicle
7. Compound umbels	8. Stamen	9. Anther
10. Pistil	11. Stigma	12. Ovary
13. Placentation	14. Apical placentation	15. Basal placentation
16. Filament	17. Anther	18. Stamen
19. Pollen	20. Ovule	21. Raceme
22. Superior ovary	23. Inferior ovary	24. Bisexual or perfect
25. Male (androecium)	26. Androgynoecious or hermaphrodite	27. Unisexual
28. Staminate or male	29. Pistillate, carpellate or female	30. Monoecious
31. Dioecious	32. Androecious	33. Gynoecious
34. Gynomonoecious	35. Andromonoecious	36. Hermaphrodite
37. Hermaphrodite	38. Female	39. Male
40. Monoadelphous	41. Diadelphous	42. Polyadelphous

II. TRUE OR FALSE

1. True	11. False	21. True
2. False	12. True	22. True
3. True	13. True	23. False
4. True	14. True	24. True
5. False	15. False	25. False
6. False	16. False	
7. True	17. True	
8. False	18. True	
9. True	19. False	
10. False	20. False	

III. MATCH THE FOLLOWING

(i)	(ii)	(iii)	(iv)	(v)
1. C	1. D	1. E	1. A	1. B
2. D	2. A	2. D	2. E	2. C
3. E	3. E	3. B	3. D	3. D
4. B	4. B	4. A	4. C	4. E
5. A	5. C	5. C	5. B	5. A

IV. AT A GLANCE

1. Inflorescence types

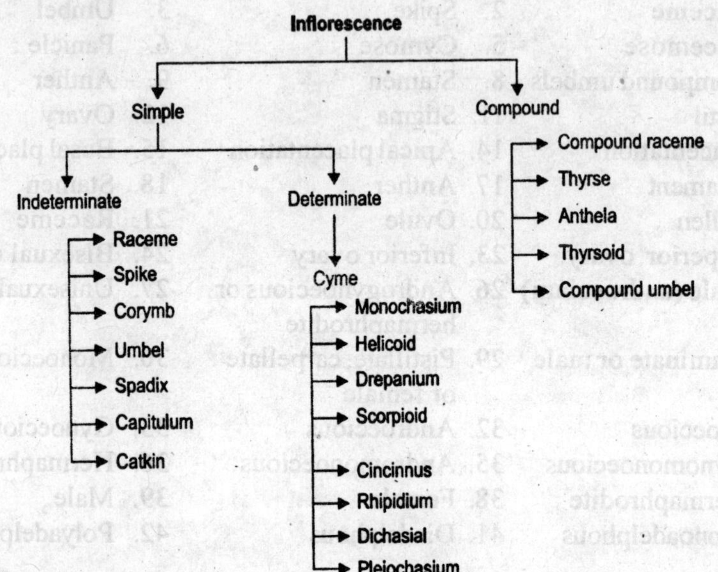

2. Sex expression in plants

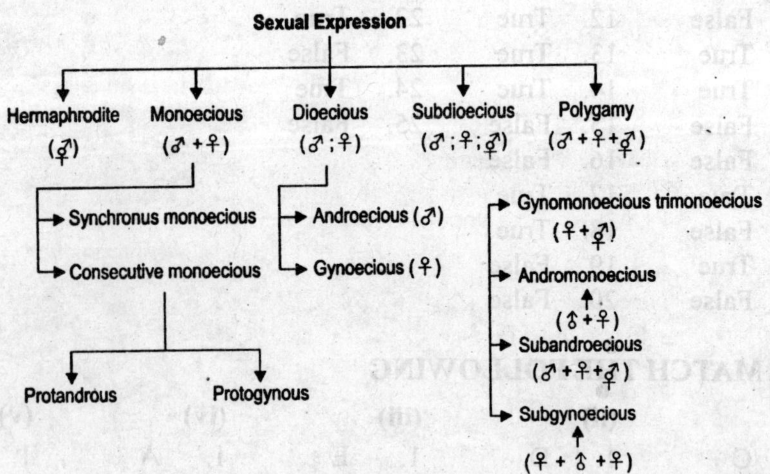

3. Floral biology in different crops

S.No.	Crops	Inflorescence	Flower
I. Agricultural Crops			
1. Cereals	Rice	Panicle	Perfect
	Wheat	Panicle	Perfect
2. Millets	Pearl millet	Panicle	Perfect
	Maize	Male inflorescence: Tassel Female inflorescence: Silk	Monoecious
	Finger millet	Panicle	Perfect
	Foxtail millet	Panicle	Perfect
	Little millet	Panicle	Perfect
	Kodo millet	Pancile	Perfect
	Proso millet	Panicle	Perfect
	Sorghum	Panicle	Perfect
3. Pulses	Red gram	Axillary receme	Bisexual
	Black gram	Axillary raceme	Bisexual
	Green gram	Racemose	Bisexual
	Bengal gram	Solitary	Bisexual
	Soybean	Solitary	Perfect
4. Oilseeds	Groundnut	Solitary	Bisexual
	Sesame	Receme	Bisexual
	Sunflower	Capitulum	Perfect
	Castor	Raceme	Monoecious
5. Fibre crops	Cotton	Solitary	Perfect
2. Horticultural Crops			
1. Fruits			
Tropical fruits	Mango	Panicle	Hermaphrodite
	Banana	Flowering stalk / spathe	Unisexual / monoecious
	Sapota	Solitary	Bisexual / hermaphrodite
	Guava	Solitary	Bisexual
	Citrus	Cluster cyme / solitary	Bisexual
	Papaya	Branched inflorescence	Dioecious or hermaphrodite
	Jack fruit	Cauliflorous	Monoecious / Dioecious
Sub tropical fruits	Pineapple	Compound	Bisexual
	Custard apple	Solitary	Hermaphrodite
	Pomegranate	Solitary in clusters	Andromonoecious
	Avocado	Panicle	Bisexual
	Durian	Cyme	Bisexual
	Grapes	Panicle	Dioecious
	Fig	Synchonium	Monoecious / Gynomonoecious
	Litchi	Branched panicle	Male / female / hermaphrodite
	Mangosteen	Solitary flowers in clusters	Monoecious / male / hermaphrodite

	Longan	Compound raceme	Male / female / hermaphrodite
	Loquat	Panicle	Bisexual
	Passion fruit	Solitary	Bisexual
	Persimmon	Solitary flowers in clusters	Dioecious / Monoecious
	Strawberry	Solitary	Bisexual
	Date palm	Spathe	Dioecious
Temperate fruits	Almond	Solitary clusters	Bisexual
	Apple	Solitary	Hermaphrodite
	Plum	Solitary / umbel like clusters	Bisexual
	Peach	Solitary	Hermaphrodite
	Pear	Corymbose	Hermaphrodite
Temperate nuts	Pecans	Catkins	Monoecious
	Pistachios	Axillary raceme / panicle	Unisexual / dioecious
2. Vegetables			
Tropical vegetables	Tomato	Racemose cyme	Hermaphrodite
	Brinjal	Cyme	Hermaphrodite
	Bhendi	Solitary	Hermaphrodite
	Chilli	Solitary	Hermaphrodite
	Pumpkin	Solitary	Monoecious
	Bitter gourd	Solitary	Monoecious
	Ribbed gourd	Solitary	Monoecious / andromonoecious, hermaphrodite
	Snake gourd	Solitary	Unisexual / monoecious
	Ash gourd	Solitary	Monoecious
	Bottle gourd	Solitary	Monoecious
	Onion	Umbel	Perfect
	Sponge gourd	Solitary	Monoecious
	Amaranthus	Spike	Perfect
	Sweet potato	Solitary axillary	Bisexual
Sub tropical vegetables	Cabbage	Terminal raceme	Perfect
	Cauliflower	Raceme	Perfect
	Knol kohl	Racemose corymb	Hermaphrodite
	Turnip	Raceme	Hermophrodite
	Carrot	Umbel	Bisexual
	Beetroot	Spike	Perfect
	Radish	Racemose	Bisexual
	Cucumber	Axillate	Unisexual
	Chow–chow	Cluster solitary	Monoecious
	Radish	Racemose	Monoecious
	Lettuce	Corymbose panicle	Bisexual
	Potato	Terminal inflorescence	Perfect
	Yam	Axillary panicle	Dioecious
3. Plantation crops			
	Coconut	Spadix	Monoecious
	Arecanut	Spadix	Monoecious

	Palmyrah	Axillary spadices	Dioecious
	Coffee	Axillary clusters	Hermaphrodite
	Tea	Solitary or cluster	Bisexual
	Rubber	Panicles of small cymes	Unisexual, Monoecious
	Cashew nut	Indeterminate panicle	Polygamomonoecious
	Cocoa	Cauliflorous	Hermaphrodite
4. Spices			
	Allspice	Umbel	Hermaphrodite / polygamodioecious
	Aniseed	Umbel	Hermaphrodite
	Pepper	Spike	Monoecious / dioecious / hermaphrodite
	Cardamom	Panicle	Hermaphrodite / bisexual
	Celery	Compound umbel	Bisexual
	Chicory	Axillary cluster	Bisexual
	Clove	Cymose	Bisexual
	Nutmeg	Axillary paniculate	Dioecious
	Cinnamon	Terminal or axillary panicle	Bisexual
	Coriander	Compound umbel	Bisexual, Protandrous
	Cumin	Umbel	Bisexual
	Curry leaf	Cyme	Bisexual
	Dill	Umbel	Bisexual
	Fennel	Compound umbel	Hermaphrodite
	Fenugreek	Compound umbel	Bisexual
	Garcinia	Solitary	Androdioecious
	Ginger	Spike	
	Mustard	Raceme	Bisexual
	Nutmeg	Axillary umbellate	Hermaphrodite
	Turmeric	Spike	Bisexual
	Vanilla	Raceme	
5. Flower crops			
	Anthurium	Spadix	
	Amaryllis	Umbel	
	Aster	Head	
	Bird of paradise	Spike	
	Carnation	Cyme	Bisexual
	Gerbera	Solitary	Protandrous
	Gladiolus	Spike	Protandrous
	Golden rod	Corymboid	
	Freesia	Spike	Actinomorphic
	Lilium	Raceme / umbel	
	Liatris	Cymose	
	Orchids	Racemose	
	Rose	Solitary corymb	
	Tulip	Solitary	

2

Anthesis and Pollination

I. FILL UPS

1. _____ is the period during which a flower is fully open and functional, in terms of pollen maturation and dispersal.
2. Flowers with _____ anthesis generally have brightly coloured flowers to attract insects, such as butterflies.
3. Flowers with _____ anthesis generally have white or less colourful flowers.
4. _____ is the mechanism, in which the stamens and pistil of a flower mature at different times.
5. The best example for protandry is _____.
6. _____ is the mechanism in which the stigma become receptive before pollen release.
7. _____ is the process by which plant pollen is transferred from the male reproductive organs to the female reproductive organs to form seeds.
8. In Bengal gram, the method of pollination is _____.
9. Red gram is _____ pollinated crop.
10. Maize is _____ pollinated crop.
11. Ground nut is _____ pollinated crop.
12. Bottle gourd is _____ pollinated crop.
13. The pollination brought about by the mediation of water is called _____.
14. Cross pollination brought about by wind is called _____.
15. In water hyacinth, the pollination brought about by _____.
16. In pearl millet, cross pollination brought about by _____.
17. Cross pollination brought about by the agency of insects is called _____.
18. In sunflower, cross pollination brought about by _____.
19. The petals are brightly coloured to attract _____ for cross pollination.
20. When insects like bees visits flowers to collect _____, cross pollination is brought about.

21. Pollination brought about by the mediation of birds is called ______.
22. In bombax, pollination is brought about by ______.
23. Pollination by means of the wasp is called ______.
24. The maturation of anthers and stigma at different times is called ______.
25. When anthers mature earlier than the stigma of the same flower, the condition is called ______.
26. When stigma matures earlier than the anthers of the same flower, the condition is called ______.
27. Having the male and female reproductive organs on different parts of the same plant rather than on separate plants (of the same species) is named as ______.
28. Having the male and female reproductive organs on separate plants (of the same species) rather than different parts of the same plant is known as ______.
29. In brinjal, cross pollination is aided by ______.
30. Pollination takes place between two different plants of allied genome is termed as ______.
31. Producing both bisexual and male flowers on the same plant is known as ______.
32. Plant species having each individual bearing both female and hermaphrodite flowers is known as ______.
33. Plants having separate male, female and hermaphrodite flowers on the same plant is known as ______.
34. The best example for the plants producing both bisexual and male flowers on the same plant is ______.
35. The best example for the plants having separate male, female and hermaphrodite flowers on the same plant is ______.

II. TRUE OR FALSE

1. Flowers with nocturnal anthesis generally have brightly coloured flowers to attract diurnal insects, such as butterflies.
2. Flowers with nocturnal anthesis generally have white or less colourful flowers, that contrast more strongly with the night.
3. Protandry refers to the flowers in which the anthers mature and release pollen after the stigmas are receptive.
4. Protogyny refers to the flowers in which the stigmas become receptive before pollen release.

5. The pollen grains can be carried from an anther to the stigma of the same flower is known as self pollination.
6. The pollen grains can be carried from an anther to the stigma of the same flower is known as homogamy.
7. In cleistogamous flowers, the pollens are shed within the closed flowers so that cross-pollination is obligatory.
8. Fertilization by transfer of pollen from the anthers of one flower to the stigma of another is named as allogamy.
9. The pollination brought about by the mediation of water is called hydrophily.
10. Cross pollination of flowers by means of the beetles on the pollen or on some of juicy tissues of the flower is known as canthophily.
11. Waspophily is the name of the syndrome by which flowers attract butterflies.
12. Chirotophily refers to pollination by means of the bats result in the production of the large, showy, white or light coloured flowers.
13. The maturation of anthers and stigma at different times is called protandry.
14. Self-sterile is used for describing plants which fail to set self-seed when they are grown in isolation or when they are self-pollinated.
15. Tomato is the example for heterostyly.
16. Cotton is an often cross pollinated crop.
17. The transfer of pollen grains of the anthers to the stigma of different flowers of same plant is referred to as geotenogamy.
18. Gynomonoecious refers to plant species having each individual bearing both male and hermaphrodite flowers.
19. Castor is an example for Andromonoecious.
20. In rice hybrid seed production, synchronous flowering is a problem.

III. MATCH THE FOLLOWING

(i)

1.	Autogamy	A	Pollination in closed flower
2.	Allogamy	B	Pollination between different flowers in different plants
3.	Geotenogamy	C	Pollination of different flowers in same plant
4.	Xenogamy	D	Cross pollination
5.	Cleistogamy	E	Self pollination

(ii)

1.	Homogamy	A	Coconut
2.	Cleistogamy	B	Hydrilla
3.	Chasmogamy	C	Rice
4.	Hydrophily	D	Ground nut
5.	Anemophily	E	Wheat

(iii)

1.	Sunflower	A	Waspophily
2.	Bombax	B	Entomophily
3.	Mango	C	Ornithophily
4.	Carrot	D	Canthophily
5.	Coriander	E	Symphytophily

(iv)

1.	Sunflower	A	Chirotophily
2.	Onion	B	Palenophily
3.	Castor	C	Psycophily
4.	Dianthus	D	Myophily
5.	Kapok	E	Mitophily

(v)

1.	Wheat	A	Cross pollination
2.	Pearl millet	B	Self pollination
3.	Sesame	C	Cross pollination
4.	Sunflower	D	Self pollination
5.	Jute	E	Often cross pollination

(vi)

1.	Cotton	A	Self pollination
2.	Groundnut	B	Often cross pollination
3.	Bhendi	C	Cross pollination
4.	Cabbage	D	Often cross pollination
5.	Onion	E	Cross pollination

(vii)

1.	Rice	A	1-4 am anthesis
2.	Black gram	B	5.30-7.30 am anthesis
3.	Brinjal	C	8-10 am anthesis
4.	Potato	D	4.30-6.30 am anthesis
5.	Moringa	E	8-10 am anthesis

ANSWER KEYS

I. FILL UPS

1. Anthesis	2. Diurnal	3. Nocturnal
4. Dichogamy	5. Maize	6. Protogyny
7. Pollination	8. Cleistogamy	9. Self
10. Cross	11. Often cross	12. Cross
13. Hydrophily	14. Anemophily	15. Water
16. Wind	17. Entomophily	18. Insects
19. Insects	20. Nectar	21. Ornithophily
22. Birds	23. Waspophily	24. Dichogamy
25. Protandry	26. Protogyny	27. Monoecious
28. Dioecious	29. Heterostyly	30. Xenogamy
31. Andromonoecious	32. Gynomonoecious	33. Trimonoecious
34. Sorghum/sunflower	35. Banana/castor	

II. TRUE OR FALSE

1. False	11. False
2. True	12. True
3. False	13. False
4. True	14. True
5. True	15. False
6. False	16. True
7. False	17. True
8. True	18. False
9. True	19. False
10. True	20. True

III. MATCH THE FOLLOWING

(i)	(ii)	(iii)	(iv)	(v)
1. E	1. C	1. B	1. A	1. B
2. D	2. D	2. C	2. B	2. A
3. C	3. E	3. D	3. C	3. E
4. B	4. B	4. E	4. D	4. C
5. A	5. A	5. A	5. E	5. D

(vi)	(vii)
1. D	1. E
2. A	2. A
3. B	3. B
4. E	4. C
5. C	5. D

IV. AT A GLANCE

1. Pollination

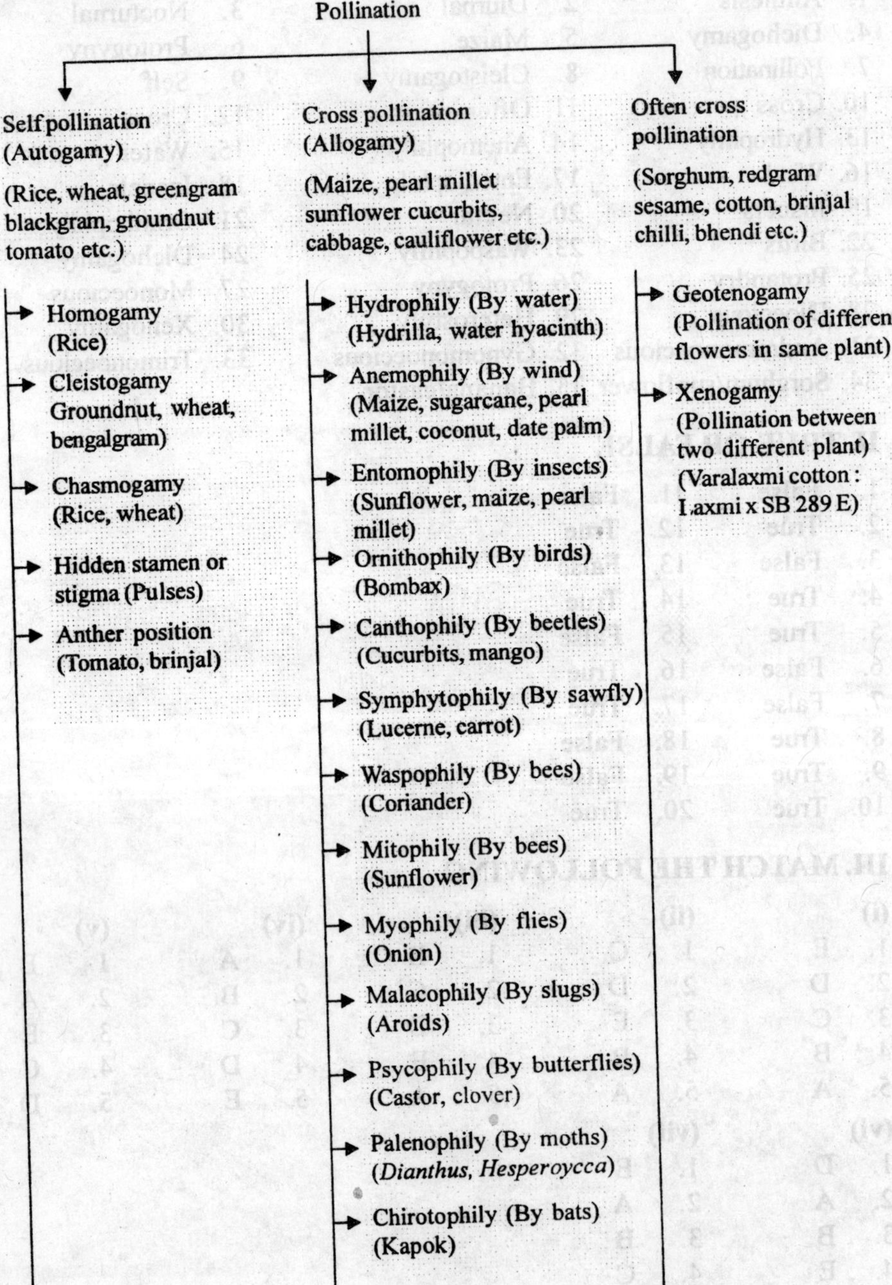

2. Pollination behaviour and anthesis in agricultural and horticultural crops

S. No.	Crop	Pollination behavior	Anthesis time	Stigma receptivity
1	**AGRICULTURAL CROPS**			
i	**Cereals**			
	Rice	Self	8-10 am	3 days from the time of anthesis
	Wheat	Self		
ii	**Millets**			
	Ragi/finger millet	Self	1–5 am	
	Barley	Self		
	Oats	Self		
	Maize	Cross	Extends 2-14 days	For 24 hours
	Pearl millet	Cross		2-3 days after emergence
	Pearl millet			
	Sorghum	Often cross	8 pm -2 am	Up to 2 days before blooming
iii	**Pulses**			
	Black gram	Self	1–4 am	
	Green gram	Self		
	Bengal gram	Self	3–9 am	
	Soybean	Self		
	Red gram	Often cross		
iv	**Oilseeds**			
	Groundnut	Self		Commences at 6 am and continues up to 8 am
	Sesame	Often cross	Between 5 and 7 am	
	Sunflower	Cross	5–8 am	2-3 days
	Castor	Cross		5-6 days
v	**Fibre crops**			
	Cotton	Often cross		
	Jute	Self		
2	**HORTICULTURAL CROPS**			
i	**Vegetables**			
	Tomato	Self	6–11 am	1–6 days after anthesis
	Bhendi	Often cross	6.30–10.30 am	
	Chilli	Often cross	6- 9 am	Receptive on day of anthesis
	Brinjal	Often cross	5.30 -7.30 am	2 days before anthesis and continues up to 8 days
	Cowpea	Self	7–9 am	
	Cabbage	Cross	8-10 am	5 days before and 4 days after anthesis
	Carrot	Cross	In morning hours	Become receptive on fifth day after flower open and remain active for 8 days
	Cucurbits	Cross		
	Pumpkin	Cross	Completed by 10 am	1 day
	Onion	Cross	7–1 pm	Last for 34 hrs
	Garlic	Cross		
	Moringa	Cross	4.30–6.30 am	A day before flower opening and continuous to be receptive on the day of opening

	Amaranthus	Cross		
	Radish	Cross	9–10 am	At the time of anthesis and last till 4 days after anthesis
	Beetroot	Cross		
	Potato	Self	8–10 am	2-3 days before anthesis
	Yam		Male flower-12.30 pm Female flower-1–2 pm	
ii	**Fruits**			
	Mango	Cross	Between 9–10 am	Upto 72 hours after anthesis
	Sapota	Cross		
	Pomegranate	Cross	Between 11 am & 2 pm	Viable for 92 days
	Banana	Cross		
	Citrus	Self	9.00 am – 12.00 noon	Starts 2-3 days earlier to anthesis and lost 4 days after anthesis
	Almond	Cross		
	Grapes	Self	Between 6 and 9 am	Day prior to anthesis and remains so a day after
	Guava		5 and 6.30 am	For 2 days
	Papaya	Self		
	Pear	Cross		
	Peach		10 am and all are open by noon	For 3 days
	Strawberry	Self		
iii	**Plantation crops**			
	Coconut	Cross		1 to 3 days
	Arecanut	Cross		
	Cocoa	Cross		
	Tea	Cross		
	Coffee	Self		
	Cashew	Cross		
	Rubber	Cross		
iv	**Spices**			
	Aniseed	Cross		
	Pepper	Self		2 days
	Cardamom	Cross		
	Nutmeg	Cross		
v	**Flower crops**			
	Cut flowers			
	Anthurium	Cross	6.30–10.00 am	8-15 days
	Amaryllis	Cross		
	Aster	Cross		
	Gerbera			3-4 days after flowering
	Gladiolus		8.00–9.30 am	24 h
	Golden rod	Cross		
	Freesia	Cross		6 weeks
	Lilium	Cross		
	Liatris	Cross		
	Tulip	Cross		

3

Fruits and their Structures

I. FILL UPS

1. Mango fruit is a _____.
2. _____ is a fleshy fruit with a single seed enclosed by a hard, stony endocarp or pit.
3. Apple fruit is a _____.
4. _____ fruit is a drupe.
5. Grape fruit is a _____.
6. Cucumber fruit is a _____.
7. Citrus fruit is a _____.
8. Sesamum fruit is a _____.
9. Bhendi fruit is a _____.
10. Sunflower fruit is a _____.
11. Almond fruit is a _____.
12. Sorghum fruit is a _____.
13. Maple fruit is a _____.
14. Carrot fruit is a _____.
15. Strawberry fruit is a _____.
16. Pineapple fruit is a _____.
17. Jute fruit is a _____.
18. Cotton fruit is a _____.
19. Castor fruit is a _____.
20. Brinjal fruit is a _____.
21. Cabbage fruit is a _____.
22. Amaranthus fruit is a _____.
23. Papaya fruit is a _____.

24. Arecanut fruit is a _____.
25. Cocoa fruit is a _____.
26. Coffee fruit is a _____.
27. Pepper fruit is a _____.
28. Orchid fruit is a _____.
29. Gladiolus fruit is a _____.
30. Tulip fruit is a _____.

II. TRUE OR FALSE

1. Fruit is a part of a flowering plant that derives from specific tissues of the flower, mainly one or more ovaries.
2. Fruit is a part of a flowering plant that derives from specific tissues of the flower, mainly one or more ovules.
3. Drupe is a simple fleshy fruit with a single seed enclosed by a hard, stony endocarp, or pit.
4. Sandal wood fruit is an example for drupe.
5. Mango is an example for pome.
6. Sapota is an example for berry.
7. Carambola is an example for hesperidium.
8. Follicle splits along one side.
9. Follicle splits along two sides.
10. Bhendi is an example for capsule.
11. A large, indehiscent achene, commonly one-seeded is known as nut.
12. Achene is a dry fruit that does not split at maturity.
13. Raspberry is an example for multiple fruit.
14. An example for pepo is pumpkin.
15. Orchid is a monocot.
16. Cardamom is a dicot.
17. Almond is a monocot.
18. Almond is a monocot.
19. Barley is a monocot.
20. Arecanut is a monocot

III. MATCH THE FOLLOWING

(i)

1.	Barley	A Boll
2.	Cotton	B Pod
3.	Soybean	C Siliqua
4.	Sesame	D Schizocarp
5.	Castor	E Caryopsis

(ii)

1.	Chilli	A Pepo
2.	Bhendi	B Aggregate
3.	Pumpkin	C Pod
4.	Beetroot	D Capsule
5.	Radish	E Berry

(iii)

1.	Sapota	A Berry
2.	Banana	B Drupe
3.	Guava	C Capsule
4.	Peach	D Berry
5.	Cardamom	E Fruit

(iv)

1.	Coconut	A Pod
2.	Cowpea	B Nut
3.	Orchid	C Berry
4.	Tomato	D Capsule
5.	Bengal gram	E Pod

ANSWER KEYS

I. FILL UPS

1. Drupe	2. Drupe	3. Pome
4. Mango	5. Berry	6. Pepo
7. Hesperidium	8. Siliqua	9. Capsule
10. Achene	11. Nut	12. Caryopsis
13. Samara	14. Schizocarp	15. Aggregate
16. Multiple	17. Pod	18. Boll
19. Schizocarp	20. Berry	21. Siliqua
22. Utricle	23. Berry	24. Nut/Drupe
25. Pod	26. Drupe	27. Berry
28. Capsule	29. Pod	30. Capsule

II. TRUE OR FALSE

1.	True	11.	True
2.	False	12.	True
3.	True	13.	False
4.	False	14.	True
5.	False	15.	True
6.	False	16.	False
7.	True	17.	True
8.	True	18.	True
9.	False	19.	True
10.	True	20.	True

III. MATCH THE FOLLOWING

(i)		(ii)		(iii)		(iv)	
1.	E	1.	E	1.	D	1.	B
2.	A	2.	D	2.	E	2.	A
3.	B	3.	A	3.	A	3.	D
4.	C	4.	B	4.	B	4.	C
5.	D	5.	C	5.	C	5.	E

IV. AT A GLANCE

1. Fruit and seed types in agricultural and horticultural crops

Crops	Fruit type	Seed type
AGRICULTURAL CROPS		
Cereals		
Rice	Caryopsis	Monocot
Wheat	Kernel/Caryopsis	Monocot
Millets		
Sorghum	Caryopsis	Monocot
Barley	Caryopsis	Monocot
Pearl millet	Caryopsis	Monocot
Maize	Caryopsis	Monocot
Fibre crops		
Cotton	Boll	Dicot
Jute	Pod	Dicot
Pulses		
Bengal gram	Pod	Dicot
Green gram	Pod	Dicot
Soybean	Pod	Dicot
Red gram	Pod	Dicot

Black gram	Pod	Dicot
Oilseeds		
Groundnut	Pod	Dicot
Sesame	Siliqua	Dicot
Sunflower	Achene	Dicot
Castor	Schizocarp	Dicot
HORTICULTURAL CROPS		
Vegetables		
Tomato	Berry	Dicot
Brinjal	Berry	Dicot
Chilli	Berry	Dicot
Bhendi	Capsule	Dicot
Cowpea	Pod	Dicot
Cucurbits	Pepo	Dicot
Pumpkin	Pepo	Dicot
Carrot	Schizocarp	Dicot
Beetroot	Aggregate	Dicot
Cabbage	Siliqua	Dicot
Cauliflower	Siliqua	Dicot
Amaranthus	Utricle	Dicot
Radish	Pod	Dicot
Fruit crops		
Mango	Drupe	Dicot
Sapota	Berry	Dicot
Banana	Fruit	Monocot
Pomegranate	Berry	Dicot
Apple	Pome	Dicot
Citrus	Hesperidium	Dicot
Almond	Drupe	Monocot (nut)
Grapes	Berry	Dicot
Guava	Berry	Dicot
Papaya	Berry	Dicot
Pear	Pome	Dicot
Peach	Drupe	Dicot
Plantation crops		
Coconut	Fibrous drupe–Nut	Monocot
Arecanut	Drupe–Nut	Monocot
Cocoa	Pod	Dicot
Tea	Berries	Dicot
Coffee	Drupe	Dicot
Spices		
Pepper	Berry	Diocot
Cardamom	Capsule	Monocot
Flower crops		
Gladiolus	Pod/capsule	Monocot
Orchid	Capsule	Monocot
Tulip	Capsule	Monocot

4

Seed and its Structure

I. FILL UPS

1. A seed is defined as a _____ or a reproductive unit formed from fertilized ovule, consisting of an embryo, reserve food and a protective cover.
2. A seed is defined as a mature ovule or a reproductive unit formed from _____ consisting of an embryo, reserve food and a protective cover.
3. A seed is defined as a mature ovule, or a reproductive unit formed from fertilized ovule, consisting of an _____, reserve food and a protective cover.
4. A seed is defined as a mature ovule or a reproductive unit formed from fertilized ovule, consisting of an embryo, _____ and a protective cover.
5. Seed acts as a carrier of _____.
6. Seed must ensure high _____ (true to type).
7. Seed must be viable and have good _____ capacity.
8. Seed must be free from pests and _____.
9. Seed must be free from _____ and diseases.
10. In _____, the seed coat and fruit coat are fused to form pericarp.
11. In caryopsis, the _____ and fruit coat are fused to form pericarp.
12. In caryopsis, the seed coat and _____ are fused to form pericarp.
13. In caryopsis, the seed coat and fruit coat are fused to form _____.
14. The embryo is minute and confined to one end of the seed and is viable with _____ number of chromosome.
15. The _____ is minute and confined to one end of the seed and is viable with 2n number of chromosome.
16. The embryo is minute and confined to one end of the seed and is _____ with 2n number of chromosome.
17. The storage tissue is known as _____ and is non-viable with 3n number of chromosome.

18. The storage tissue is known as endosperm and is _____ with 3n number of chromosome.
19. The storage tissue is known as endosperm and is non-viable with _____ number of chromosome.
20. The single cotyledon of the monocot is known as _____.
21. The single _____ of the monocot is known as scutellum.
22. _____ layer is a protein body which remains at the periphery of the endosperm.
23. Aleurone layer is a _____ body which remains at the periphery of the endosperm.
24. Monocot seeds are known as _____ or endospermous seeds.
25. _____ seeds are known as albuminous or endospermous seeds.
26. The _____ consists of radicle and plumule which are enclosed in coleorhiza and coleoptile, respectively.
27. The embryo consists of _____ and plumule which are enclosed in coleorhiza and coleoptile, respectively.
28. The embryo consists of radicle and _____ which are enclosed in coleorhiza and coleoptile, respectively.
29. The embryo consists of radicle and plumule which are enclosed in _____ and coleoptile, respectively.
30. The embryo consists of radicle and plumule which are enclosed in coleorhiza and _____, respectively.
31. The _____ seeds consist of a primary axis and a living storage tissue, the cotyledons which combinely form the embryo of the seed.
32. The dicot seeds consist of a _____ and a living storage tissue, the cotyledons which combinely form the embryo of the seed.
33. The dicot seeds consist of a primary axis and a living storage tissue, the _____ which combinely form the embryo of the seed.
34. _____ has well developed endosperm.
35. _____ has well developed perisperm.
36. _____ develops from the 2 integuments of ovule.
37. Seed coat develops from the 2 _____ of ovule.
38. Outer layer of the seed coat which smooth and rough is known as the _____ and is formed from the outer integument.

39. Outer layer of the seed coat which smooth and rough is known as the testa and is formed from the outer _____.
40. The inner layer of the seed coat is called the _____ and is formed from inner integument.
41. The inner layer of the seed coat is called the tegmen and is formed from inner _____.
42. Embryo is a _____ plant consisting of plumule, radicle and cotyledon.
43. _____ is a miniature plant consisting of plumule, radicle and cotyledon.
44. Embryo is a miniature plant consisting of _____, radicle and cotyledon.
45. Embryo is a miniature plant consisting of plumule, _____ and cotyledon.
46. Embryo is a miniature plant consisting of plumule, radicle and _____.
47. The single cotyledon of the monocot is known as _____.
48. The single _____ of the monocot is known as scutellum.
49. Endosperm develops from the endosperm nuclei which is formed by the two _____ nuclei and one sperm nuclei.
50. _____ develops from the endosperm nuclei which is formed by the two polar nuclei and one sperm nuclei.
51. Endosperm develops from the endosperm nuclei which is formed by the two polar nuclei and one _____ nuclei.
52. In paddy, the bract tip was elongated in to the _____.
53. Hilum is the scar mostly white in colour present on the lateral side of the _____ seed.
54. _____ is the scar mostly white in colour present on the lateral side of the seeds of pulses.
55. Caruncle is the white spongy outgrowth of the micropyle end in _____.
56. _____ is the white spongy outgrowth of the micropyle end in castor.
57. _____ is coloured fleshy mass present on the outside of nutmeg seed.
58. Aril is coloured fleshy mass present on the outside of _____ seed.
59. Hairs are minute thread like appendages present on the surface of the seed of _____.
60. _____ are minute thread like appendages present on the surface of the seed of cotton.
61. _____ are papery structure attachment to the side of the seed coat either to a specific side of the seed coat or to all sides of moringa seeds.

62. Wings are papery structure attachment to the side of the seed coat either to a specific side of the seed coat or to all sides of _____ seeds.
63. The part of the plant growing underground from the seed/embryo is known as _____.
64. The _____ of embryo develops into root.
65. The part of the plant growing above the ground is known as _____.
66. Shoot develops from the _____ of the embryo.
67. _____ is the portion of the shoot above the cotyledons.
68. _____ is the region of shoot below the cotyledon and above the root.
69. The fruit of rice is _____.
70. The fruit of maize is _____.
71. The fruit of sorghum is _____.
72. The fruit of pearl millet is _____.
73. The fruit of finger millet is _____.
74. _____ has a papery seed coat.
75. _____ seed is a achene.
76. _____ seed has a coiled cotyledon.
77. The embryo of _____ is curved.
78. The embryo of _____ is spirally twisted.
79. Cotton seed has a _____ cotyledon.
80. Safflower seed is a _____.

II. TRUE OR FALSE

1. A seed is defined as a 'mature ovule' or a reproductive unit formed from fertilized ovule, consisting of an embryo, reserve food and a protective cover.
2. A seed is defined as a 'mature ovary' or a reproductive unit formed from fertilized ovary, consisting of an embryo, reserve food and a protective cover.
3. Respiration rate and other physiological and biological processes should be kept at high level during storage.
4. In monocot seeds, the seed coat and fruit coat are fused to form epicarp.
5. The embryo is minute and confined to one end of the seed and is viable with 2n number of chromosome.

6. The storage tissue is known as endosperm and is non-viable with 2n number of chromosome.
7. Aleurone layer is a protein body which remains at the periphery of the endosperm.
8. Aleurone layer is a protein body which remains at the periphery of the cotyledons.
9. Monocot seeds are known as ex-albuminous or endospermous seeds.
10. In monocots, the endosperm is living tissue.
11. The scar mostly white in colour present on the lateral side of the seed is known as caruncle.
12. The white spongy outgrowth of the micropyle end is called as caruncle.
13. The thorn like projection in the tip of the seeds in paddy is called as aril.
14. The appendages of seed or fruit sometimes help in dispersal of seeds, but not in identification of genotypes.
15. The portion of the shoot above the cotyledons is known as epicotyls.
16. The region of shoot below the cotyledon and above the root is called as epicotyls.
17. Aleurone layer is the thin layer present above the pericarp.
18. The pod of groundnut typically contains two seeds, each with a papery seed coat.
19. The pod of groundnut typically contains two seeds, each with a papery fruit coat.
20. In cotton seed, embryo is present inside the twisted cotyledon.
21. In tomato, embryo is linear and curved or coiled.
22. In tomato, embryo is linear and folded.
23. Onion is a monocotyledonous albuminous seed.
24. In onion, embryo is spirally twisted and cylindrical in shape.
25. The embryo of onion seed is spirally folded and linear in shape.
26. In pine, the storage tissue is mega gametophyte.
27. In pine, the mega gametophyte is an embryonic tissue.
28. The cotton seed is a hard seed coated in nature.
29. Cowpea seed is oblong shaped.
30. The shape of cowpea seed varies from globular and kidney shaped.

III. MATCH THE FOLLOWING

(i)

1.	Seed	A	Integument 1
2.	Fruit	B	Integument 2
3.	Testa	C	Fertilized egg
4.	Tegmen	D	Fertilized polar nuclei
5.	Embryo	E	Matured ovule
6.	Endosperm	F	Matured ovary

(ii)

1.	Seed	A	True to type
2.	Genetic purity	B	Inert matter
3.	Physical purity	C	Optimum moisture
4.	Health quality	D	Carrier of new technology
5.	Seed storage	E	Germination
6.	Physiological quality	F	Seed borne pathogen

(iii)

1.	Maize	A	Single cotyledon
2.	Scutellum	B	2n
3.	Embryo	C	3n
4.	Endosperm	D	Protein body
5.	Single cotyledon	E	Caryopsis
6.	Aleurone layer	F	Monocot

(iv)

1.	Monocot	A	Coleorhiza
2.	Endosperm	B	Coleoptile
3.	Aleurone layer	C	Nucellus
4.	Perisperm	D	Living tissue
5.	Plumule	E	Non living tissue
6.	Radicle	F	Albuminous

(v)

1.	Cotyledon	A	Integuments
2.	Seed coat	B	Living tissue
3.	Dicot	C	Protective part
4.	Embryonic axis	D	Cotyledon
5.	Embryo	E	Primary axis
6.	Seed coat	F	Miniature plant

(vi)

1.	Radicle	A	Primary shoot
2.	Plumule	B	Primary root
3.	Paddy	C	Hilum
4.	Cowpea	D	Nutmug
5.	Castor	E	Awn
6.	Aril	F	Caruncle

(vii)

1.	Hairs	A	Below the cotyledon
2.	Moringa	B	Seed and fruit coat fused
3.	Above the cotyledon	C	Rice
4.	Caryopsis	D	Epicotyle
5.	Pearl millet	E	Wings
6.	Hypocotyle	F	Cotton

(viii)

1.	Sorghum	A	Folded cotyledon
2.	Papery seed coat	B	Cotton
3.	Endosperm	C	Safflower
4.	Achene	D	Castor
5.	Cotton	E	Caryopsis
6.	Hard seed coat	F	Groundnut

(ix)

1.	Spirally curved embryo	A	Bhendi
2.	Brinjal	B	Onion
3.	Folded cotyledon	C	Tomato
4.	Carrot	D	Spirally curved embryo
5.	Spirally twisted	E	Exalbuminous
6.	Onion	F	Bristly hard

ANSWER KEYS

I. FILL UPS

1. Mature ovule	2. Fertilized ovule	3. Embryo
4. Reserve food	5. New technology	6. Genetic purity
7. Germination	8. Diseases	9. Pests
10. Caryopsis	11. Seed coat	12. Fruit coat
13. Pericarp	14. 2n	15. Embryo

16. Viable
17. Endosperm
18. Non-viable
19. 3n
20. Scutellum
21. Cotyledon
22. Aleurone
23. Protein
24. Albuminous
25. Monocot
26. Embryo
27. Radicle
28. Plumule
29. Coleorhiza
30. Coleoptile
31. Dicot
32. Primary axis
33. Cotyledon
34. Castor/Fenugreek
35. Pepper
36. Seed coat
37. Integuments
38. Testa
39. Integument
40. Tegmen
41. Integument
42. Miniature
43. Embryo
44. Plumule
45. Radicle
46. Cotyleldon
47. Scutellum
48. Cotyledon
49. Endosperm
50. Polar
51. Sperm
52. Awn
53. Pulses
54. Hilum
55. Castor
56. Caruncle
57. Aril
58. Nutmeg
59. Cotton
60. Hairs
61. Wings
62. Moringa
63. Root
64. Radicle
65. Shoot
66. Plumule
67. Epicotyl
68. Hypocotyl
69. Caryopsis
70. Caryopsis
71. Caryopsis
72. Caryopsis
73. Caryopsis
74. Groundnut
75. Sunflower
76. Cotton
77. Tomato
78. Onion
79. Folded
80. Achene

II. TRUE OR FALSE

1. True
2. False
3. False
4. False
5. True
6. False
7. True
8. False
9. False
10. False
11. False
12. True
13. False
14. False
15. True
16. False
17. False
18. True
19. False
20. False
21. True
22. False
23. True
24. True
25. False
26. True
27. False
28. True
29. False
30. True

III. MATCH THE FOLLOWING

(i)		(ii)		(iii)		(iv)		(v)	
1.	E	1.	D	1.	E	1.	F	1.	B
2.	F	2.	A	2.	A	2.	E	2.	A
3.	A	3.	B	3.	B	3.	D	3.	D
4.	B	4.	F	4.	C	4.	C	4.	E
5.	C	5.	C	5.	F	5.	B	5.	F
6.	E	6.	D	6.	D	6.	A	6.	C

(vi)		(vii)		(viii)		(ix)	
1.	B	1.	F	1.	E	1.	C
2.	A	2.	E	2.	F	2.	D
3.	E	3.	D	3.	D	3.	A
4.	C	4.	C	4.	C	4.	F
5.	F	5.	B	5.	A	5.	B
6.	D	6.	A	6.	B	6.	E

IV. AT A GLANCE

1. Type of seed and chemical composition

Crops	Cotyledons	Storage tissue	Special features		
			Protein (%)	Oil (%)	Carbohydrates (%)
Cereals					
Wheat, Barley, Rye	Monocot	Endosperm (non-embryonic)	10-14	2-3	75-77
Maize	Monocot	Endosperm (non-embryonic)	10-12	5-6	80-82
Oat	Monocot	Endosperm (non-embryonic)	12-14	6-10	60-65
Pulses/legumes					
Pea, broad bean	Dicot	Cotyledon (embryonic)	22-26	1-6	50-56
Soybean	Dicot	Cotyledon (embryonic)	35-40	15-20	25-30
Oil seeds					
Rape seed	Dicot	Endosperm (non embryonic)	20-22	45-50	18-22
Castor	Diocot	Endosperm (non embryonic)	18-20	60-66	Trace
Gymnosperms					
Pine	Monocot	Non embryonic (mega gametophyte)	35	48	6

5

Vegetative Propagation

I. FILL UPS

1. _____ is the method of propagating plants with the use of organs other than the seed and spore.
2. The word asexual, which means _____.
3. In asexual, the _____ of the male and female sexual gametes (fertilization) is not a requisite to the production of new plants.
4. In vegetative propagation, the union of the male and _____ sexual gametes (fertilization) is not a requisite.
5. _____ without fertilization is known as vegetative propagation.
6. In vegetative propagation, _____ cell division takes place.
7. Onion is propagated by _____.
8. Elephant foot yam is propagated by __________
9. A _____ is used for propagation of banana.
10. _____ is a vegetative popagule for turmeric.
11. Potato is propagated by _____.
12. A _____ is used for propagation of strawberry.
13. _____ is a vegetative popagule for chlorophytam.
14. An _____ is used for propagation of pineapple.
15. Gerbera is propagated by _____.
16. _____ is a vegetative popagule for agave.
17. _____ propagation is a rule in rice.
18. In sugarcane, _____ is a rule for propagation.
19. _____ grafting is the method of propagation in sapota.
20. The method of propagation in pomegranate is _____ layering.
21. _____ budding is the method of propagation in citrus.

22. In grapes, _____ cutting is mostly followed for propagation.
23. _____ cutting is the method of propagation in jasmine.
24. The method of propagation in tea is _____ cutting.
25. _____ cuttings is the method of propagation in pepper.
26. In jatropha, _____ cutting is mostly followed for propagation.
27. The most common methods of propagation in neem are _____.
28. _____ is propagated by bulbs.
29. The corm is a vegetative popagule for _____.
30. The method of propagation in _____ is suckers.
31. In _____, rhizome is mostly followed for propagation.
32. The most common method of propagation in _____ is tuber.
33. Offshoot is the method of propagation in _____.
34. _____ is propagated by crown.
35. The most common method of propagation in _____ is bulbil.
36. Veneer grafting is the method of propagation in _____.
37. In _____, tip layering is used for propagation.
38. Stooling is the method of propagation in _____.
39. _____ is propagated by crown by division.
40. Epicotyl grafting is the method of propagation in _____.

II. TRUE OR FALSE

1. Asexual propagation is the union of the male and female sexual gametes (fertilization).
2. Asexual propagation is the method of propagating plants with the use of organs other than the seed and spore.
3. In asexual reproduction, meiosis cell division.
4. In sexual reproduction, mitosis cell division.
5. In sexual reproduction, the offspring is genetically identical.
6. In asexual reproduction, the offspring is genetically identical.
7. Bulbs are used for propagation of ginger.
8. Turmeric is propagated by rhizome.
9. Corm is used for propagation of banana.

10. Banana is propagated by suckers.
11. Tuber is commonly recommended for propagation of dahlia.
12. Tuber is commonly recommended for propagation of potato.
13. Runner is a specialized stem which is the vegetative propagule to propagate gooseberry.
14. Jamun is multiplied by both seeds and grafting.
15. Nutmeg is propagated by both seeds and grafting.
16. Hardwood cutting is commonly recommended for propagation of cut rose.
17. In jasmine, hardwood cutting is commonly recommended for propagation.
18. Rooted cuttings is used for propagation of pepper.
19. Cocoa is sexually propagated.
20. Asexual is the common practice in rubber.

III. MATCH THE FOLLOWING

(i)

1.	Maize	A	Sexual
2.	Rice	B	Asexual
3.	Sugarcane	C	Seed
4.	Mango	D	Sucker
5.	Citrus	E	Budding
6.	Banana	F	Grafting

(ii)

1.	Sapota	A	Stooling
2.	Pomegranate	B	T' budding
3.	Almond	C	Hardwood cutting
4.	Grapes	D	Seed
5.	Peach	E	Air layering
6.	Guava	F	Approach grafting

(iii)

1.	Gerbera	A	Nut
2.	Anthurium	B	Softwood cutting
3.	Jasmine	C	Offshoots
4.	Orchid	D	Crown
5.	Balsam	E	Division
6.	Coconut	F	Seed

ANSWER KEYS

I. FILL UPS

1. Vegetative propagation or asexual propagation	2. Without sex or not sexual	3. Union
4. Female	5. Reproduction	6. Mitosis
7. Bulbs	8. Corm	9. Sucker
10. Rhizome	11. Tuber	12. Runner
13. Stolon	14. Offshoot	15. Crown
16. Bulbil	17. Sexual	18. Asexual
19. Approach	20. Air	21. Patch
22. Hardwood	23. Softwood	24. Stem
25. Rooted	26. Stem	27. Seed and stem cutting
28. Onion/lily/garlic	29. Gladiolus/colocasia/ elephant foot yam	30. Chrysanthemum/ ixora/banana
31. Ginger/Turmeric	32. Dioscorea/dahlia/ potato	33. Date palm/Pineapple
34. Strawberry/ Gerbera	35. Begonia/agave	36. Mango
37. Apple	38. Guava	39. Orchid
40. Cashew nut		

II. TRUE OR FALSE

1. False	11. True
2. True	12. True
3. False	13. False
4. True	14. True
5. False	15. True
6. True	16. True
7. False	17. False
8. True	18. True
9. False	19. True
10. True	20. True

III. MATCH THE FOLLOWING

(i).		(ii)		(iii)	
1.	C, A	1.	F	1.	D
2.	C, A	2.	E	2.	C
3.	B	3.	D	3.	B
4.	F	4.	C	4.	E
5.	E	5.	B	5.	F
6.	D	6.	A	6.	A

IV. AT A GLANCE

1. Propagation methods and propagules in agricultural and horticultural crops

S.No.	Crops	Propagation method	Propagules
1.	**AGRICULTURAL CROPS**		
a	**Cereals**		
	Rice	Sexual	Seed
	Wheat	Sexual	Seed
b	**Millets**		
	Maize	Sexual	Seed
	Sorghum	Sexual	Seed
	Pearl millet	Sexual	Seed
	Barley	Sexual	Seed
	Oats	Sexual	Seed
c	**Pulses**		
	Black gram	Sexual	Seed
	Green gram	Sexual	Seed
	Bengal gram	Sexual	Seed
	Soybean	Sexual	Seed
	Redgram	Sexual	Seed
d	**Oilseeds**		
	Groundnut	Sexual	Seed
	Sesame	Sexual	Seed
	Sunflower	Sexual	Seed
	Castor	Sexual	Seed
	Mustard	Sexual	Seed
e	**Fiber crops**		
	Cotton	Sexual	Seed
	Jute	Sexual	Seed
f	**Sugar crops**		
	Sugarcane	Asexual	Sett
	Sugarbeet	Sexual	Seed

2.	**HORTICULTURAL CROPS**		
i	**Vegetables**		
	Tomato	Sexual	Seed
	Bhendi	Sexual	Seed
	Chilli	Sexual	Seed
	Brinjal	Sexual	Seed
	Cowpea	Sexual	Seed
	Cucurbits	Sexual	Seed
	Amaranthus	Sexual	Seed
	Radish	Sexual	Seed
	Cabbage	Sexual	Seed
	Carrot	Sexual	Seed
	Cauliflower	Sexual	Seed
	Beetroot	Sexual	Seed
ii	**Fruits**		
	Mango	Asexual	Veneer grafting
	Sapota	Asexual	Approach grafting
	Pomegranate	Asexual	Air layering
	Banana	Asexual	Sucker
	Apple	Asexual	Tip layering
	Citrus	Asexual	Patch budding
	Almond	Sexual	Seed
	Grapes	Asexual	Hardwood cutting
	Guava	Asexual	Stooling
	Papaya	Sexual	Seed
	Pear	Asexual	Hardwood cutting
	Peach	Asexual	'T' budding
	Plum	Asexual	'T' budding
	Apricot	Sexual	Seed
	Pineapple	Asexual	Offset
	Walnut	Sexual	Seed
	Jackfruit	Sexual	Seed and grafting
iii	**Flower crops**		
a.	**Cut flower**		
	Cut rose	Asexual	Hardwood cutting
	Carnation	Asexual	Softwood cutting
	Gerbera	Asexual	Crown
	Anthurium	Asexual	Offshoots
b.	**Loose flowers**		
	Jasmine	Asexual	Softwood cutting
	Crossandra	Asexual	Softwood cutting
	Chrysanthemum	Asexual	Softwood cutting
	Gladiolus	Asexual	Corms
	Orchid	Asexual	Division
c.	**Ornamentals**		
	Bauhinia	Asexual	Softwood cutting
	Forest jasmine	Both sexual and asexual	Seed and cutting

	Fire bush	Sexual	Seed
	Ixora	Asexual	Stem cutting
	Clerodendron	Asexual	Cutting
	Duranta	Asexual	Semi hardwood cutting
	Nerium	Asexual	Cutting
	Thuja	Asexual	Hardwood cutting
	Aster	Asexual	Rooted cutting
	Balsam	Sexual	Seed
iv	**Plantation crops**		
	Coconut	Sexual	Nut
	Arecanut	Sexual	Nut
	Tea	Asexual	Stem cutting
	Coffee	Sexual	Seed
	Cocoa	Sexual	Seed
	Rubber	Asexual	Green budding, brown budding and crown budding
	Cashew nut	Asexual	Softwood grafting, air layering and epicotyl grafting
v	**Spices and condiments**		
	Pepper	Asexual	Rooted cutting
	Cardamom	Asexual	Seedling/sucker
	Clove	Sexual	Seed
	Turmeric	Asexual	Rhizome
	Coriander	Sexual	Seed
	Nutmeg	Both sexual and asexual	Seed or graft
	Ginger	Asexual	Rhizome
	Cinnamon	Asexual	Seedling or rooted cutting
	Garlic	Asexual	Bulb
3.	**SILVICULTURAL CROPS**		
	Mahua	Asexual	Cutting and layering
	Jamun	Sexual and asexual	Seed, 'T'- budding and patch budding
	Tamarind	Sexual and asexual	Seed and cutting
	Jack fruit	Sexual	Seed and grafting
	Pungam tree	Sexual and asexual	Seeds and stem cutting
	Jatropha	Asexual	Stem cutting
	Acacias	Sexual	Seed
	Subabul	Sexual	Seed
	Teak	Sexual	Seed
	Neem	Sexual and asexual	Seed and stem cutting
	Albizias	Sexual	Seed
	Terminalias	Sexual	Seed
	Sandal wood	Sexual	Seed
	Paradise tree	Sexual and asexual	Seed and stem cutting
	Himalayan pine	Sexual	Seed
	Silver oak	Sexual	Seed
	Kapok	Sexual	Seed
	Punnai	Sexual	Seed

6

Apomixis, Parthenocarpy and Polyembryony

I. FILL UPS

1. Development of seed without fertilization is called _____.
2. _____ is the substitution for any sexual nuclear fusion.
3. Apomitic seed will have genetic material only from the _____ plant.
4. In _____ apomixis type, the megaspore cell undergoes the usual meiotic division and forms a haploid embryo sac.
5. The process of seed formation without sexual fusion is known as_____.
6. _____ is defined as the development of embryo from some other cell of embryo sac other than egg.
7. Haploid embryo arises from the egg without fertilization is called_____.
8. Formation of haploid embryo from some other cell of the female gametophyte other than egg is called _____.
9. _____ parthenogenesis is found in Solanum nigrum.
10. In _____ type of apomixes, embryo sac arise from a cell of archesporium (or) other parts of nucleus.
11. In _____ apomixis type, all the nuclei of embryo sac are diploid.
12. Development of diploid embryo sac from egg without fertilization is called _____.
13. Development of diploid embryo sac from some other cell of gametotype is called _____.
14. Adventive embryony is otherwise called _____.
15. In citrus, _____ adventive embryos are formed.
16. In _____ type of apomixes, the embryo does not arise from the cells of gametophyte.

17. In _____ apomixis type, embryo arise from the nucleus (or) the integument.
18. Parthenocarpy literally means _____.
19. Natural (or) artificial induced production of fruit without fertilization of ovules is called as _____.
20. Parthenocarpy otherwise known as _____.
21. An example of parthenocarpy _____.
22. Fruit production by pollination (or) stimulation without fertilization is called _____.
23. Hormones induced fruit formation is called _____.
24. Fruit production without pollination (or) fertilization is called _____.
25. Occurrence of more than one embryo is known as _____.
26. _____ type of polyembryony develops due to splitting (or) cleavage of the proembryo.
27. Occurrence of more than one embryo sacs found in _____.
28. _____ is an example for the development of embryos from the cells of embryo sac other than egg.
29. Two (or) more embryos are formed in the seed by the cleavage of zygote (or) proembryo is called _____.
30. An example for adventives embryony is _____.

II. TRUE OR FALSE

1. All apomitic seed have genetic material only from the female plant.
2. In recurrent apomixis type all the nuclei of the embryo sac are diploid.
3. In non-recurrent apomixis, megaspore cell undergoes meiotic division to form haploid embryo sac.
4. Seedless watermelon is an example for vegetative parthenocarpy.
5. Seedless cucumber is an example of stenospermocarpy.
6. The embryo arises from the nucellus (or) integument in adventive embryony.
7. Plants produced by non-recurrrent apomixis are usually fertile.
8. Heterozygous types may be obtained from haploid parthenogenesis.
9. Hormones induced fruit formation is called artificial parthenocarpy
10. Fruit production by pollination (or) stimulation is called artificial parthenocarpy

11. Cleavage polyembryony is widespread in angiosperms.
12. Occurrence of more than one embryo in a seed is called polyembryony.
13. When a single cultivar is grown, pineapple produces seedless fruit because they are self-fertile.
14. Adventive embryony is otherwise known as sporophytic budding.
15. *Allium* is an example of apogamy.
16. *Solanum nigrum* is an example for haploid parthenogenesis.
17. 'Thompson seedless' is the commercial seedless grape cultivar produced by parthenocarpy.
18. Parthenocarpy is a method of asexual reproduction.
19. The plant equivalent of parthenogenesis is apomixis.
20. Plant that do not require pollination (or) other stimulation to produce parthenocarpic fruit have artificial parthenocarpy.

III. MATCH THE FOLLOWING

(i)

1.	Haploid parthenogenesis	A	Seedless cucumber
2.	Apogamy	B	Citrus
3.	Adventive embryony	C	Seedless watermelon
4.	Vegetative parthenocarpy	D	*Solanum nigrum*
5.	Stenospermocarpy	E	*Allium*

(ii)

1.	Parthenocarpy	A	*Mangifera*
2.	Cleavage polyembryony	B	Pomegranate
3.	Polyembryony	C	Gymnosperms
4.	Artificial parthenocarpy	D	Angiosperms
5.	Additional embryo sac	E	Plant hormones

IV. ONE WORD ANSWER

1. Give an example for non-recurrent apomixis.
2. Give any two examples for apogamy.
3. Types of parthenocarpy.
4. What is the reason for seedless grape cultivar 'Thompson seedless'?
5. Give one example for vegetative parthenocarpy and stenospermocarpy.

ANSWER KEYS

I. FILL UPS

1. Apomixis
2. Apomixis
3. Female
4. Non-recurrent apomixis
5. Apomixis
6. Apogamy
7. Haploid parthenogenesis
8. Apogamy
9. Haploid parthenogenesis
10. Recurrent apomixis
11. Recurrent
12. Diploid parthenogenesis
13. Diploid apogamy
14. Sporophytic budding
15. Thirteen
16. Adventive embryony
17. Adventive embryony
18. Virgin fruit
19. Parthenocarpy
20. Antennaria
21. Taraxoeum
22. Stimulative parthenocarpy
23. Artificial parthenocarpy
24. Vegetative parthenocarpy
25. Polyembryony
26. Cleavage polyembryony
27. *Mangifera*
28. Argemone
29. Cleavage polyembryony
30. Citrus

II. TRUE OR FALSE

1. True
2. True
3. True
4. False
5. False
6. True
7. False
8. False
9. True
10. False
11. False
12. True
13. False
14. True
15. True
16. True
17. False
18. False
19. True
20. False

III. MATCH THE FOLLOWING

(i)		(ii)	
1.	D	1.	D
2.	E	2.	C
3.	B	3.	B
4.	A	4.	E
5.	C	5.	A

IV. ONE WORD ANSWER

1. *Solanum nigrum*
2. *Allium, Antennaria*
3. i) Stimulative
   ii) Vegetative
   iii) Artificial
4. Stenospermocarpy
5. Vegetative-seedless cucumber
   Stenospermocarpy - seedless watermelon

V. AT A GLANCE

S.No.	Types	Causes and examples
1	Apomixis	Formation of seed without fertilization
a	Non-recurrent apomixis	Haploid parthenogenesis E.g. *Solanum nigrum*
b	Apogamy	Embryo formation from cells other than embryo sac E.g. *Allium*
c	Recurrent	Development of embryo sac from archesporial cell
d	Adventive	Embryo sac formation from nucellus or integument E.g. Citrus
2	Parthenocarpy	Fruit production without fertilization by natural or artificial means E.g. Alehemilia
a	Stimulative parthenocarpy	Fruit production by pollination without fertilization or other stimulation
b	Vegetative parthenocarpy	No pollination or stimulation to produce fruit
c	Artificial parthenocarpy	Hormones induce fruit formation
3	Polyembryony	Occurrence of more than one embryo E.g. Pomegranate
a	Cleavage polyembryony	Splitting of proembryo E.g. Most gymnosperms
b	Embryo from embryosac cells	Development of embryos from the cells of embryo sac other than egg E.g. *Argemone*
c	Additional embryosac	Occurrence of more than one embryo sac E.g. *Mangifera, Hydrilla*
d	Induced	Formation of embryo sac from nucellus or integuments

7

Somatic Embros and Synthetic Seed

I. FILL UPS

1. Somatic embryo encased with artificial endosperm and protective cover is called _____.
2. The term artificial seed was coined by_____.
3. The artificial seed technology was patented by_____.
4. The most common gelling agent used for artificial seeds is_____.
5. In desiccated system, the artificial seeds are coated with _____.

II. TRUE OR FALSE

1. Artificial seeds have also been referred to as synthetic seeds.
2. Somatic embryos enclosed with hydrated gel in the dessicated system.
3. The most common gelling agent used is Polyethylene Glycol (PEG).
4. Synthetic seeds help to supply beneficial adjuvents.
5. Alginate hydrogel was used frequently because of high viscosity & low spinnability of solution.

III. MATCH THE FOLLOWING

1.	Dessicated system	A	Produced by tissue culture
2.	Hydrated system	B	Encapsulated artificially
3.	Synthetic seed	C	Encapsulated with Hydrated gel
4.	Artificial seed technology	D	Artificial seed
5.	Somatic embryo	E	Redenbaugh

IV. ONE WORD QUESTION

1. Give some examples of gelling agent.
2. Types in synthetic seed production system.

ANSWER KEYS

I. FILL UPS

1. Synthetic seed
2. Murashige
3. Redenbaugh
4. Sodium alginate
5. Polyethylene glycol

II. TRUE OR FALSE

1. True
2. False
3. False
4. True
5. False

III. MATCH THE FOLLOWING

1. B
2. C
3. D
4. E
5. A

IV. ONE WORD ANSWER

1. **Sodium alginate, agar, carboxymethyl cellulose, carageenan.**
2. **Dessicated system, Hydrated system.**

V. AT A GLANCE

1. Somatic embryo	Produced by tissue culture from an explant. Similar to zygotic embryo.
2. Synthetic seed	An artificial seed. Somatic embryo encased with artificial endosperm and protective cover. Coined by Murashige (1977). Patented by Redenbaugh and Co-workers (1988).
3. Production method	
Desiccated	Hardened somatic embryo encapsulated artificially.
Hydrated	Somatic embryo enclosed with hydrated gel.
4. Encapsulation	
method / Dropping	Dropping somatic embryos in hydrogel. *E.g.* sodium alginate and then coated seeds in complexation solution. *E.g.* Calcium nitrate
Molding	Mixing somatic embryos in gelrite and get coated while temperature lowers
5. Gelling agent	Sodium alginate, agar, Carboxy Methyl Cellulose (CMC), carragenan, gelrite, guar gum

8

Terminator Seed

I. FILL UPS

1. _____ is a technology that eliminates or reduces the germination capacity of the following seed germination.
2. _____ technology offers a means of preventing the unwanted flow of genes from genetically modified organisms.
3. Terminator technology is technically known as _____.
4. _____ technology is used to protect the transgenes from being pirated by researches elsewhere.
5. _____ is a inducer used to initiate the terminator gene interaction.

II. TRUE OR FALSE

1. Terminator technology will stop genetically modified crop contamination.
2. Genetic use restriction technology will produce fertile seeds at harvest
3. To protect useful transgenes from being pirated, gene protection technology is used.
4. To initiate terminator gene interactions, a chemical inducer is used.
5. Terminator technology is relevant to pure lines and open pollinated variety.

III. MATCH THE FOLLOWING

1.	Terminator technology	A	Tetracycline
2.	Gene I	B	Recombinase gene
3.	Gene II	C	Repressor gene
4.	Gene III	D	Gene protection technology
5.	Inducer	E	Toxin gene

IV. ONE WORD QUESTION

1. Which inducer is used to initiate the terminator gene?
2. What are the genes used in the terminator seed technology?

ANSWER KEY

I. FILL UPS

1. Terminator technology
2. Genetic seed sterilization technology
3. Genetic use restriction technology (GURT)
4. Gene protection
5. Tetracycline

II. TRUE OR FALSE

1. False
2. False
3. True
4. True
5. True

III. MATCH THE FOLLOWING

1. D
2. C
3. B
4. E
5. A

IV. ONE WORD ANSWER

1. Tetracycline
2. Repressor gene
   Recombinase gene
   Toxin gene

V. AT A GLANCE

Terminator genes in the absence of the inducer	**Terminator genes in the presence of the inducer**
Gene I: Repressor gene	
A repressor gene produces a repressor protein.	The same repressor protein is produced.
Gene II: Recombinase gene	
A recombinase gene is controlled by a promoter. Between the promoter and the recombinase gene, scientists place a DNA fragment which is a binding site for the repressor from Gene I.	
In the absence of the inducer, the repressor binds to the binding site and the plant cannot produce the recombinase protein, an enzyme that snips out pieces of DNA.	The inducer interferes with the repressor attachment to the binding site thus allowing Gene II to produce recombinase.
Gene III: Toxin gene	
A gene for a toxin lethal to embryos (Toxin gene) is controlled by a late promoter (LP), that is active only during the late stage of seed development when the embryo is developing. Between the late promoter and the toxin gene, the scientists place a piece of DNA called a Blocker, which interferes with the ability of the promoter to turn on the gene.	
Without the inducer, there is no recombinase to snip out the blocker.	Recombinase from Gene II snips out the blocker and allows the late promoter to turn on production of the toxin gene late in the season.
With the blocker in place, no toxin is produced.	
Thus, by withholding the inducer, seed companies can produce generations ofiable seeds.	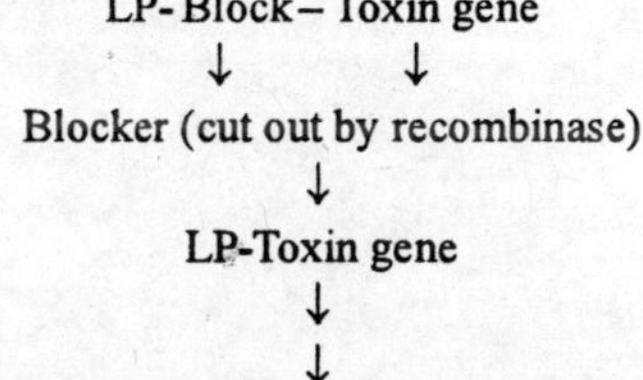 Toxin is produced and kills the embryo before the mature seeds are harvested.

1. Terminator seed

a) Genetically modified to produce sterile or non-viable seed.

b) Sowing of farm saved seed is prevented.

c) Useful for pure lines, varieties, but not hybrids.

2. Development of terminator seed

	Gene I	Gene II	Gene III	Remarks
	Repressor gene	Recombinase gene (place DNA fragment between induce and recombinase gene)	Toxin gene	
No inducer	Protein formed	No recombinase gene produced	No toxin produced	Seed company produces viable seed and sells to farmers
Inducer	Protein formed	Recombinase gene produced	Toxin produced	Farmers harvest sterile and non-viable seed which exists at late period of seed development

9

Embryo and Endosperm Formation

I. FILL UPS

1. The developing ovule is commonly attached to the placenta by the ______.
2. The scar on the ovule made where the funiculus detaches at maturity is known as the ______.
3. The point where the integuments meet at the nuclear apex is ______.
4. Opposite to the micropyle, the region of integumentary origin and attachment is called ______.
5. Between the chalaza and the hilum is an area called ______.
6. ______ is an example for species with developed perisperm.
7. ______ is an opening in the ovule through which the pollen tube grows to fertilize the egg cell of the female gametophyte.
8. ______ is the development of well defined nucellar (or) integumentary tissue in the micropylar region of the seed of certain species.
9. The period of flower development when the stigma is ready to receive the pollen is known as ______.
10. Microspores produced from reduction division undergoes two divisions known as ______.
11. Fertilization is otherwise known as ______.
12. Syngamy occurs in a dual fusion process known as ______.
13. Morphologically, micropyle is at the upper end of the ______.
14. Nutritive supply for growing embryo sac is provided by ______.
15. In angiosperms, endosperm is ______ in nature.
16. In gymnosperms, endosperm is ______ in nature.
17. During endosperm development, the nuclear division is accompanied by cell wall formation is known as ______.
18. ______ formation does not take place in nuclear endosperm development.

19. The outermost layer of the endosperm is known as _____ layer.
20. If the seed does not have endosperm, it is called as _____.

II. TRUE OR FALSE

1. Fruit is the matured ovule.
2. The raphae will be visible on the seed coat of all species.
3. The developing ovule is commonly attached to the placenta by raphae.
4. Sugar beet species have well developed perisperm.
5. In Umbelliferae family, the inner integuments does not persists.
6. Appendage arising from the seed coat over the area of raphae is known as strophiole.
7. Anthesis is the time when pollen begins to blow and pollinate the female flowers.
8. Fertilization can occur when both male and female gametophytes are immature.
9. Growing embryo sac requires a constant nutritive supply which is provided by micropyle.
10. The endosperm is the principle nutritive support for the embryo during both seed development and germination.
11. In cellular endosperm, nuclear division is unaccompanied by cell wall formation.
12. In nuclear endosperm, each nuclear division accompanied by cell wall formation.
13. Helobial endosperm is intermediate between the nuclear and cellular types.
14. Seeds with little (or) no endosperm is known as exalbuminous.
15. Haustoria functions as both storage tissue and for secretion of hydrolytic enzymes.

III. MATCH THE FOLLOWING

1.	Sugar beet	A	Embryo straight (or) curved
2.	Water lily	B	Operculum
3.	Acorus	C	Micropylar plug
4.	Syngamy	D	Well developed perisperm
5.	Torpedo stage	E	Dual fusion process

IV. ONE WORD QUESTION

1. Mention the different stages of embryo formation
2. Mention types of endosperm development

ANSWER KEY

I. FILL UPS

1. Funiculus
2. Hilum
3. Micropyle
4. Chalaza
5. Raphe
6. *Beta vulgaris*
7. Micropyle
8. Epitase
9. Anthesis
10. Microgameto-genesis
11. Syngamy
12. Double fertilization
13. Embryo sac
14. Chalaza
15. Triploid
16. Haploid
17. Cellular endosperm
18. Albuminous layer
19. Aleurone
20. Exalbuminous

II. TRUE OR FALSE

1. False
2. False
3. False
4. True
5. False
6. True
7. True
8. False
9. False
10. True
11. False
12. False
13. True
14. True
15. False

III. MATCH THE FOLLOWING

1. D
2. C
3. B
4. E
5 A

IV. ONE WORD ANSWER

1. i) Globular ii) Heart
   iii) Torpedo iv) Mature embryo
2. i) Cellular ii) Nuclear
   iii) Helobial

V. AT A GLANCE

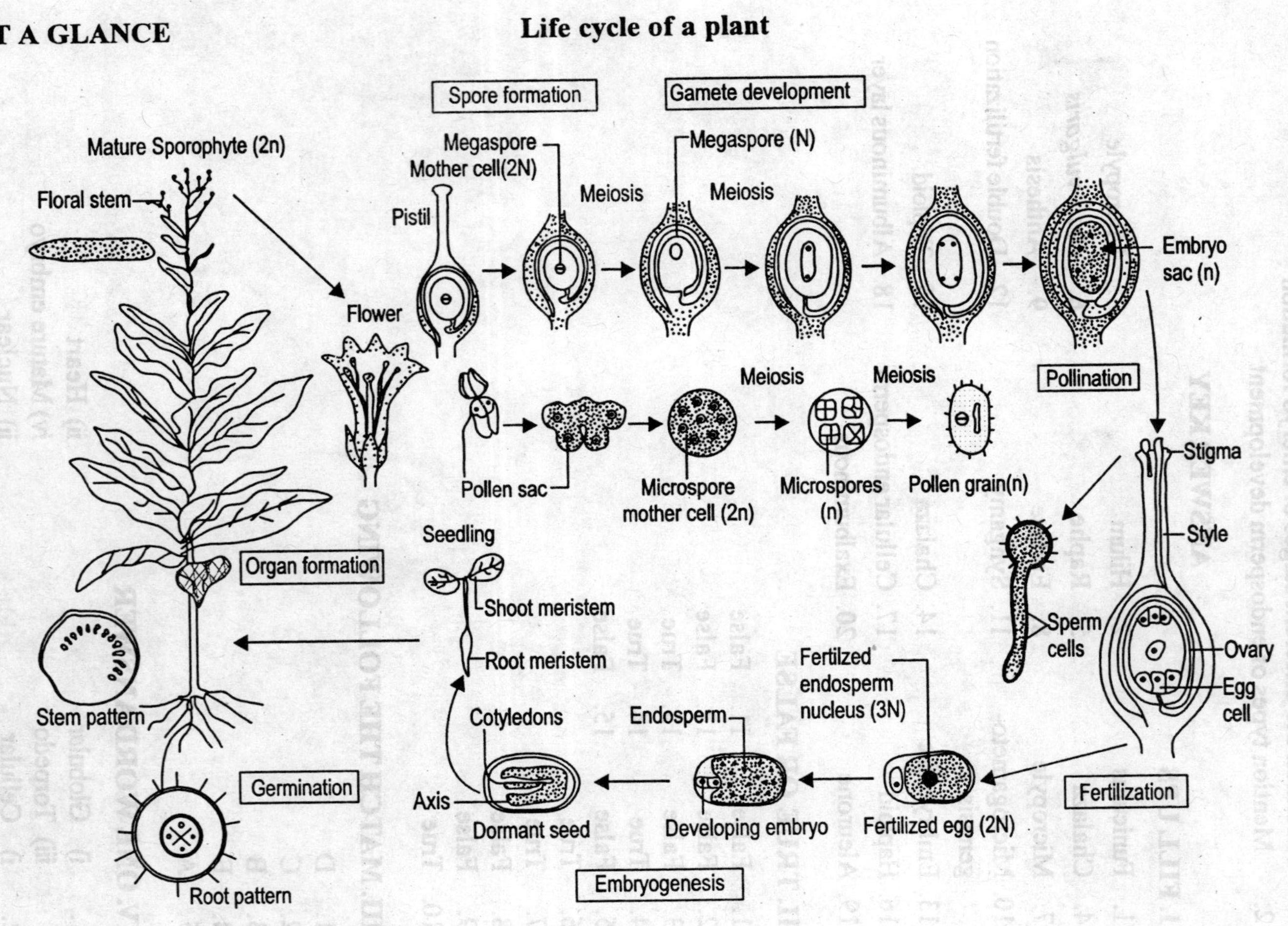
Life cycle of a plant
Spore formation
Gamete development
Mature Sporophyte (2n)
Floral stem
Flower
Pistil
Megaspore
Mother cell(2N)
Meiosis
Megaspore (N)
Meiosis
Embryo
sac (n)
Pollination
Pollen sac
Microspore
mother cell (2n)
Meiosis
Microspores
(n)
Meiosis
Pollen grain(n)
Stigma
Style
Sperm
cells
Ovary
Egg
cell
Fertilization
Fertilzed
endosperm
nucleus (3N)
Fertilized egg (2N)
Endosperm
Developing embryo
Embryogenesis
Cotyledons
Axis
Dormant seed
Seedling
Shoot meristem
Root meristem
Organ formation
Stem pattern
Germination
Root pattern

10

Changes during Seed Development and Maturation

I. FILL UPS

1. Ovule moisture content at the time of fertilization is approximately _____.
2. After sexual fusion, the developing seeds begin to _____ in weight as a result of nutrient accumulation.
3. _____ is the precursor substrate for starch formation in a seed.
4. In cereals, the walls of the dead cells of the mature starchy endosperm are composed of _____ and _____.
5. In coffee and ivory nut seeds _____ is deposited in the cell wall.
6. In cereal seeds, proteins are accumulated in the _____ layer.
7. _____ is associated with the synthesis process and also the arrest of embryo growth to avoid precocious seed germination while the seed remains attached to the parent plant.
8. _____ are important for cell expansion, activation of enzyme synthesis and to monitor reserve accumulation.
9. _____ assure the normal reserve assimilation that occurs during seed development.
10. First concept of physiological maturity was proposed by _____.
11. _____ has the greatest influence on seed size, seed germination and vigor.
12. _____ indicates maximum dry weight accumulation, high germination associated with vigorous seedling and low seed moisture.
13. Reduced light to the parent plant results in smaller seeds in crops such as _____.
14. In cereal crops, carbohydrates are polymerized in _____ part.
15. Sucrose entering the developing oil seed is used for the synthesis of storage _____ and _____.

II. TRUE OR FALSE

1. First stage of seed development is pollination followed by fertilization.
2. Ovule moisture content increases during maturation.
3. Seed size reduction in leguminous seeds is more obvious than in cereal seeds.
4. Starch is the only carbohydrate stored in the cereal and legume seeds.
5. Seed germination and vigor are adversely affected by exposure to low temperatures during development.
6. Oil seeds usually show reduced quantitative and qualitative changes in lipid reserves when high temperature occur during the later stages of maturation.
7. Low temperature are considered the principal reason for the "forced maturation" of soybean seeds.
8. Reduced light to parent plants results in smaller seeds.
9. Seed position in the inflorescence can affect the seed development rate.
10. Distal seeds in a wheat spike have higher growth rates and shorter seed filling periods than proximal seeds.

III. MATCH THE FOLLOWING

1.	Physiological maturity	A	60% moisture content
2.	Morphological maturity	B	Maximum dry weight accumulation
3.	Gibberellins	C	Anderson
4.	Coffee	D	Cell expansion
5.	Recalcitrant species	E	Galactomannans

IV. ONE WORD QUESTION

1. Give any two examples to verify that the light to the parent plant affects seed development.
2. Mention one major role of gibberellins hormone.
3. Mention the different phases of seed development.

ANSWER KEY

I. FILL UPS

1. 80%	2. Increase	3. Sucrose
4. Hemicellulose & glucans	5. Galactomannans	6. Aleurone
7. Abscisic acid (ABA)	8. Gibberellins	9. Auxin
10. R.H. Shaw and W.E. Loomis	11. Nitrogen	12. Physiological maturity
13. Carrot, soybean	14. Endosperm	15. Glycerol & protein

II. TRUE OR FALSE

1. True	6. False
2. False	7. False
3. True	8. True
4. False	9. True
5. True	10. False

III. MATCH THE FOLLOWING

1. B
2. C
3. D
4. E
5. A

IV. ONE WORD ANSWER

1. Carrot, soybean
2. Cell expansion
3. Phase I & Phase II – cell division and expansion
   a. Phase III- dry weight accumulation
   b. Phase IV – Moisture loss

V. AT A GLANCE

1. Steps in seed development

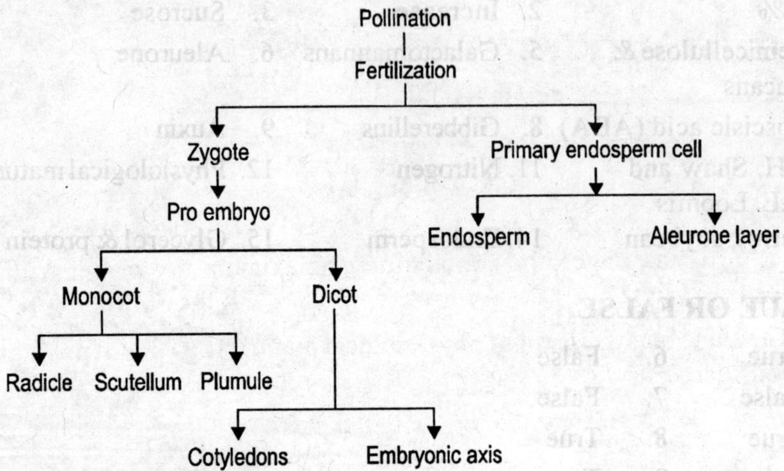

11

Seed Maturity

I. FILL UPS

1. _____ is the stage of accumulation of maximum dry matter within the seeds.
2. The stage of attainment of physiological maturity by 80% of population is considered as _____ stage.
3. In rice, during harvestable maturity the moisture content of long duration varieties will be _____.
4. For short and medium duration varieties of rice, the moisture content will be _____.
5. Rattling sound of kernel is the physiological maturity symptom of _____.
6. The harvestable maturity indices of cotton is _____.
7. The harvestable maturity indices of bhendi is _____.
8. The harvestable maturity indices of casuarina is _____.
9. In cassava during physiological maturity stage the carbohydrate content is _____.
10. The tamarind, the days to attain physiological maturity is _____.

II. TRUE OR FALSE

1. Change of schizocarp colour from green to brown is the harvestable maturity of coriander.
2. During harvestable maturity in ashwagandha the colour of capsule changes from deep orange in colour.
3. In radish, the pod turn brown and parchment like during physiological maturity stage.
4. The physiological maturity indices of beet root is that the middle portion of the inflorescence become brown.
5. Seeds of onion become black on ripening in silvery capsules during physiological maturity stage.

6. The harvestable maturity of minor millets occurs uniformly.
7. Drying of silk is one of the harvestable maturity indices of maize.
8. Formation of dunken layer spot on the aleurone layer is the physiological maturity indice of sorghum.
9. Harvestable maturity is the stage of accumulation of maximum dry matter within the seeds.
10. During harvestable maturity, the moisture content of the seed will be higher than the physiological maturity stage.

III. MATCH THE FOLLOWING

(i)

1.	Physiological maturity	A	Dark pigment strand beneath the embryo
2.	Wheat	B	Rattling sound
3.	Maize	C	Kapas bursting
4.	Groundnut	D	Maximum drymatter accumulation
5.	Cotton	E	Formation of milk line

(ii)

1.	Bhendi	A	Middle of inflorescence become brown
2.	Beetroot	B	Formation of ashy coat on the skin
3.	Ashgourd	C	Seeds produce rattling sound
4.	Pungam	D	Drying and browning of seed wings
5.	Dipterocarp	E	Formation of hairline cracks

IV. ONE WORD QUESTION

1. Mention the harvestable maturity indice of bhendi.
2. Formation of dunken layer is physiological maturity indice of which crops.
3. What is the harvestable maturity indice of maize crop?
4. How many days it will take for rice crop to attain physiological maturity?
5. What is the harvestable maturity indice of castor?

ANSWER KEYS

I. FILL UPS

1. Physiological maturity
2. Harvestable maturity
3. 17%
4. 20%
5. Groundnut
6. Kappas bursting
7. Formation of hairline cracks
8. Cone colour
9. Decrease
10. 285-300

II. TRUE OR FALSE

1.	True	6.	False
2.	False	7.	True
3.	True	8.	True
4.	False	9.	False
5.	True	10.	False

III. MATCH THE FOLLOWING

(i)		(ii)	
1.	D	1.	E
2.	A	2.	A
3.	E	3.	B
4.	B	4.	C
5.	C	5.	D

IV. ONE WORD ANSWER

1. Formation of hairline cracks.
2. Sorghum, maize, pearl millet.
3. Drying of silk.
4. 28 and 31 days after 50% of spikelet have flowered.
5. Capsules show signs of drying.

V. AT A GLANCE

1. Table showing the stage of physiological maturity in agricultural and horticultural crops

Day to physiological maturity	Cereals and millets	Pulses	Oilseeds	Fibre crops	Green manures	Vegetables	Fruits	Flowers	Medicinal plants	Trees	Spices	Tubers
15	-	-	-	-	-	-	Acidlime	-	-	-	-	-
18	-	-	-	-	-	-	-	-	*Ocimum sanctum*	-	-	-
21	-	-	-	-	Stylosanthus	-	-	-	-	-	-	-
22	-	-	-	-	-	-	-	-	*Ocimum basilicum*	-	-	-
24	-	Rice bean	-	-	-	-	-	-	-	-	-	-
25	-	Greengram	-	-	Vegetable cowpea	Amaranthus	-	Cosmos, Petunia	-	-	-	-
28	-	-	-	-	Deenanath grass	-	-	-	-	-	-	-
30						Onion	-	Balsam	*Ocimum gratissimum*	-	-	-
35	-	Field	Safflower, Niger, Kolingi, Guinea grass, *Solanum nigrum*	-	Butter pea	Ambrette	-	Marigold	Ashwagandha, Ambrettee			
36	Proso millet	-	Sunflower	-	-	-	-	-	-	-	-	-
40	-	Pea, Pole bean	Gingelly	-	Daincha Palmarosa	-	-	Gailardia Zinnia	Senna, Roselle, Periwinkle			
42	-	-	-	-	-	-	-	-	Sarpagantha	-	-	-

44	Sorghum African tall, Maize, Foxtail millet	-	-	-	-	-	-	-	-	-	-	-
45	Soybean	-	-	-	Manila agathi	-	-	-	Wild indigo, Mucana	-	-	-
46	-	Bengalgram	-	-	-	-	-	-	-	-	-	-
48	Finger millet	-	-	-	-	-	-	-	-	-	-	-
49	-	Lablab	-	-	-	Brinjal, Carrot, Cauliflower, Palak	-	-	-	-	-	-
50	-	-	-	-	-	Cluster bean	-	-	-	-	-	-
52	Barnyard millet	-	-	Cotton	-	-	-	-	-	-	-	-
60	-	-	Castor	-	-	-	-	-	-	-	-	Cassava
65	-	-	-	-	-	Bittergourd	-	-	-	-	-	-
70	-	-	-	-	-	Pumpkin, Moringa	-	-	-	-	-	-
77	-	-	-	-	-	Jamun	-	-	-	-	-	-
84	-	-	-	Kapok	-	-	-	-	-	-	-	-
85	-	-	-	-	-	-	-	-	Neem	-	-	-
90	-	-	-	-	-	-	-	-	-	*Ailanthus*	-	-
91	-	-	-	-	-	-	-	-	-	*Prosopis*	-	-
100	-	-	-	-	-	-	-	Gymnema	-	-	-	-
120	-	-	-	-	-	-	-	-	-	Hardwickia	-	-
126	-	-	-	-	-	-	-	-	-	Pungam, Casuarina	-	-
140	-	-	-	-	-	-	-	-	-	Cassia	-	-

20-25	-	Blackgram, cowpca	-	-	-	-	-	-	-	-	-	-
28-31	Rice	-	-	-	-	-	-	-	-	-	-	-
30-40	Pearl millet	-	-	-	-	-	-	-	-	-	-	-
30-35	-	Horsegram	-	-	-	-	-	-	-	-	-	-
40-50	-	Pigconpca	-	-	-	-	-	-	-	-	-	-
40-60	-	-	-	-	-	-	Cashew	-	-	-	-	-
42-63	-	-	-	Jutc	-	-	-	-	-	-	-	-
70-80	-	-	-	-	-	Ashgourd	-	-	-	-	-	-
84-91	-	-	-	-	-	-	Ber	-	-	-	-	-
90-100	-	-	-	-	-	-	-	-	Keelanelli	-	-	-
100-110	-	-	-	-	-	-	-	-	-	-	-	Coriander
126-133	-	-	-	-	-	-	Papaya	-	-	-	-	-
154-168	-	-	-	-	-	-	Amla	-	-	-	-	-
285-300	-	-	-	-	-	-	-	-	-	-	Tamarind	-

12

Chemical Composition of Seeds

I. FILL UPS

1. The major storage organ for cereals is _____.
2. The major storage organ for legumes is _____.
3. The major storage organ in pine is _____.
4. The average protein percent present in soybean is _____.
5. The average oil percent present in oilpalm is _____.
6. Starch occurs in 2 forms as _____ and _____.
7. Amylase comprises between _____ and _____.
8. _____ are the most abundant storage carbohydrate in plants next to starch and sucrose.
9. _____ is soluble in alcohol and has high proline content.
10. _____ is responsible for baking properties in bread wheat.
11. Fats and oils are organic compounds called _____.
12. If the chemical bonds between the carbon atoms of fat molecules can hold _____ hydrogen atom then the fat is monounsaturated.
13. If the chemical bond between the carbon atom of fat molecules can hold more additional hydrogen atom, then the fat is _____.
14. Seed lipid reserves are stored in the form of _____ within the cells of storage tissue.
15. Among oil seeds, coconut contain _____% oil.
16. Plant produced organic compounds that have no direct function of growth and development is _____.
17. _____ occurs in seed particularly in seed coat structure.
18. _____ serve as antifeedants and to protect the plant against microbes and fungi.
19. _____ is the major form of phosphorus storage in seeds.

20. _____ is necessary for developing embryo and endosperm.
21. _____ and _____ involves in respiration.
22. _____ involves in oxidation reduction during germination.
23. _____ is a substance strongly antagont to growth was isolated by addicott from young cotton fruits.
24. _____ was the first hormone extracted from axomycetous fungus *Fusarium monoliforme*.
25. _____ organic compound has a faint *Fusarium monoliforme* sweet and musky odour when pure.
26. _____ is the most potent native auxin.
27. _____ is recognized as a 6th class of plant hormones.
28. The most important member of auxin family is _____.
29. Sunflower contains _____ % oil.
30. _____ is present in embryo and aleurone layer.

II. TRUE OR FALSE

1. The major storage organ of rape is endosperm.
2. Starch and hemicelluloses are the major form of carbohydrate in seeds.
3. Waxy corn contain virtually all amylopectin.
4. Starches usually contain more amylase than amylopectin.
5. Cellulose is easily digested by amylase enzyme.
6. Sucrose is a disaccharide made of one glucose and one fructose molecule.
7. Albumin is insoluble in water.
8. Prolamin is available in oats and rice.
9. Fats and oils are esters with fairly low relative molecular masses.
10. Biotin is necessary for developing embryo and endosperm.

III. MATCH THE FOLLOWING

(i)

1.	ABA	A	Faint 'sweet and musky' odour
2.	Gibberellins	B	Young cotton fruits
3.	Ethylene	C	*Fusarium moniliforme*
4.	Ascorbic acid	D	Proline content
5.	Prolamin	E	Oxidation reduction

(ii)

1.	Fructan	A	Polypeptides
2.	Proteins	B	Ketose
3.	Glutelin	C	Triglycerides
4.	Albumin	D	Bread wheat
5.	Lipids	E	Sunflower

IV. ONE WORD QUESTION

1. What is extracted from the causal organism of foolish seedling of rice (or) bakane disease?
2. What is the role of thiamine?
3. What is the role of ascorbic acid?
4. Which hormone is extracted from young cotton fruits?
5. Which secondary metabolite which forms a soapy lather when shaken with water?
6. Saturated fatty acid.
7. Which storage protein is responsible for baking properties in bread wheat?
8. What is the basic structure of a fructan called?
9. Mention any two factors affecting chemical composition of seeds
10. Which is the most important member of the auxin?

ANSWER KEYS

I. FILL UPS

1. Endosperm	2. Cotyledons	3. Mega gametophyte
4. 37%	5. 49%	6. Amylase and amylopectin
7. 11 and 37%	8. Fructans	9. Prolamine
10. Glutelin	11. Triglycerides	12. One additional
13. Polyunsaturated	14. Spherosomes	15. 65
16. Secondary metabolites	17. Tannin	18. Saponins
19. Phytin	20. Thiamine	21. Biotin and ascorbic acid
22. Ascorbic acid	23. Abscisin II	24. Gibberellins
25. Ethylene	26. Indole 3 acetic acid	27. Brassinosteroid
28. IAA	29. 40-50	30. Globulin

II. TRUE OR FALSE

1.	False	6.	True
2.	True	7.	False
3.	True	8.	False
4.	False	9.	False
5.	False	10.	False

III. MATCH THE FOLLOWING

(i)		(ii)	
1.	B	1.	B
2.	C	2.	A
3.	A	3.	D
4.	E	4.	E
5.	D	5.	C

IV. ONE WORD ANSWER

1. Gibberellins
2. Developing embryo and endosperm
3. Involves oxidation reduction during germination
4. Abscisic acid
5. Saponin
6. When the chemical bonds between the carbon atoms of the fat molecules have saturated with hydrogen atom.
7. Glutellin
8. Ketose
9. Temperature, water stress
10. IAA (Indole – 3 – acetic acid)

V. AT A GLANCE

1. Chemical composition of crops

Crop	Average per cent composition			Major storage organs
	Protein	Oil	Carbohydrates	
Cereals				
Barley	12	3	76	Endosperm
Maize	10	5	80	Endosperm
Oats	13	8	66	Endosperm
Rye	12	2	76	Endosperm
Wheat	12	2	75	Endosperm
Legumes				
Broad bean	23	1	56	Cotyledons
Garden pea	25	6	52	Cotyledons
Peanut	31	48	12	Cotyledons
Soybean	37	17	26	Cotyledons
Others				
Castor bean	18	64	Negligible	Endosperm
Oil palm	9	49	28	Endosperm
Pine	35	48	6	Megagametophyte
Rape	21	48	19	Cotyledons

2. Storage protein

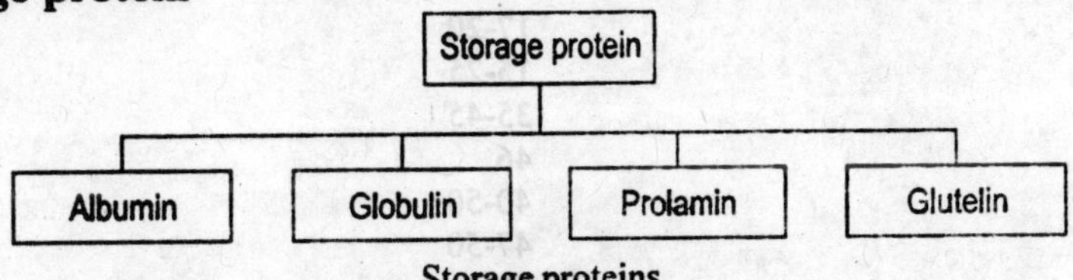

Storage proteins

3. Protein concentrations of some dicotyledonous seeds

Crop	Protein (%)	Protein type (% total N)			
		Albumin	Globulin	Prolamin	Glutelin
Castorbean	20	10	90	*	*
Cotton	20	*	90	*	10
Flax	30	*	Max.	*	much
Lupine	40	1	78	*	16
Soybean	30-50	*	85-95	*	*
Sunflower	30-35	*	Max.	*	*
Dry beans	25	*	90-95	*	*
Pea	-	21	66	12	*
Peanut	-	15	70	10	*

4. Lipids

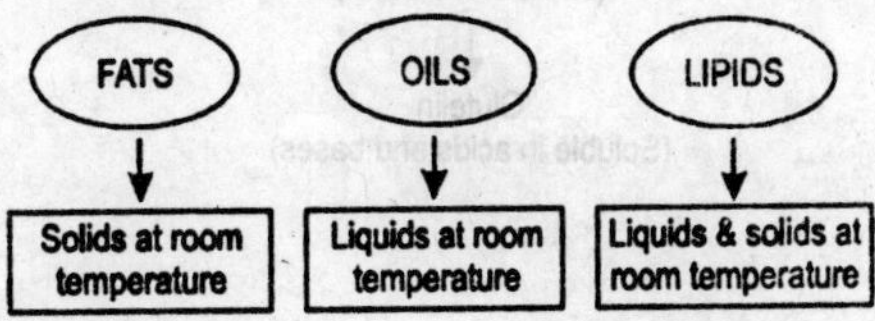

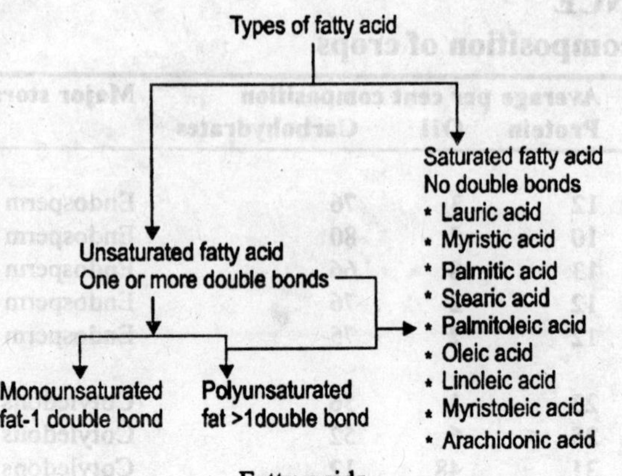

Fatty acids

5. Per cent oil present in different crops

Crop	Oil concentration (%)
Broad bean	1
Wheat	2
Maize	5
Soybean	17-20
Cotton	15-25
Rapeseed	35-45
Canola	46
Sunflower	40-50
Peanut	47-50
Palm kernel	50
Coconut	65

6. Different chemical composition of seeds

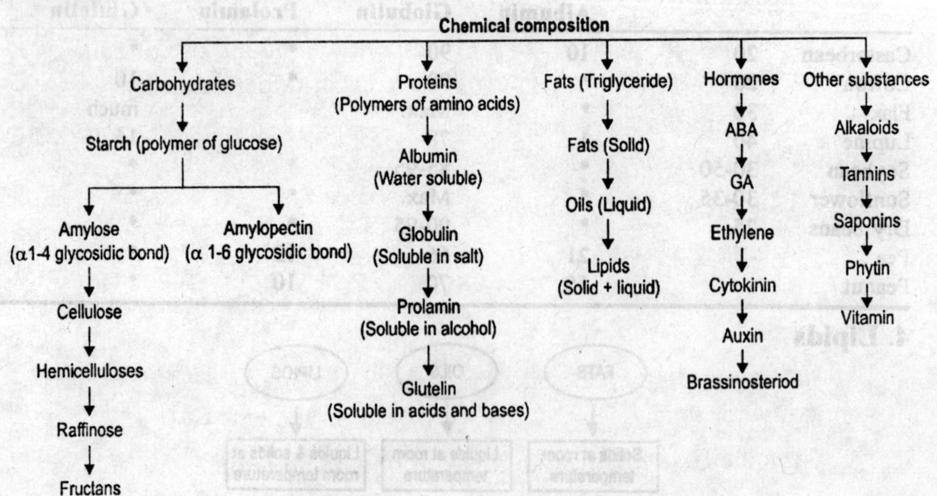

13

Seed Dormancy and its Breaking Treatments

I. FILL UPS

1. _____ refers to lack of growth due to any external or internal cause.
2. _____ refers to a state in which viable seeds fail to germinate even when given favourable environmental conditions.
3. _____ is a condition in which seed can germinate upon absorption of water.
4. _____ is otherwise known as primary dormancy.
5. A condition that develops to prevent germination after the seed has been detached from the plant is called _____.
6. Dormancy related to the embryo is called _____.
7. When two or more dormancy types occurs in a seed, that condition is called _____.
8. Any treatment may be physical or chemical that weakens or softens the seed coat is known as _____.
9. _____is subjecting the seeds to pretreatment by making use of animals and microorganisms for break down of seed coat impermeability.
10. _____ is a method of exposing imbibed seeds to lower temperature or higher temperature for a period of time.
11. _____ is a light substituting chemical.
12. _____ accumulate predominantly in liquid embryo.
13. Treatment of dormant seeds with _____ induced a high percentage of germination.
14. _____ is a toxin produced by the fungus *Fusicoccum amygdala* capable of breaking dormancy.
15. _____ was the first chemical to break dormancy in lettuce.
16. _____ is an active oxygen source able to diffuse into plant tissue.

17. _____ is an example for immature embryo.
18. _____ is an example for thermodormancy.
19. An example of chemical dormancy is _____.
20. Fruit and seed contain chemical inhibitory compounds that prevent the germination is called _____.

II. TRUE OR FALSE

1. H_2O_2 may facilitate dormancy breakage by supplying oxygen by cracking the hard coat.
2. Kinetin is a light supporting chemical.
3. Pre-chilling temperature for cold stratification is 20-25°C.
4. Mechanical scarification denotes rubbing or abrasion of seeds against hard surface.
5. Physical scarification is most effective for large leguminous seeds.
6. An example for mechanical dormancy is spinach.
7. Photo dormancy is the type of dormancy induced by high temperature.
8. Endogenous dormancy is otherwise known as seed coat dormancy.
9. Exogenous dormancy is otherwise known as embryo dormancy.
10. Secondary dormancy is otherwise known as induced dormancy.

III. MATCH THE FOLLOWING

(i)

1.	Primary dormancy	A Embryo dormancy
2.	Secondary dormancy	B Innate dormancy
3.	Endogenous dormancy	C Double dormancy
4.	Exogenous dormancy	D Induced dormancy
5.	Combined dormancy	E Seed coat dormancy

(ii)

1.	Mechanical dormancy	A Apples
2.	Chemical dormancy	B Poppy
3.	Morphological dormancy	C Olive
4.	Scarification	D Bitter gourd
5.	Mechanical scarification	E Malvaceae

(iii)

1.	KNO_{-3}	A	*Gossypium hirsutum*
2.	Fusicoccin	B	Giberellic acid
3.	*Ziziphus mauritiana*	C	*Casuarina equisetifolia*
4.	Hydrogen peroxide	D	*Zygophyllum gatarensis*
5.	Ethyl alcohol and ether	E	Camphor seeds

IV. ONE WORD QUESTION

1. Give an example for immature embryo.
2. Which was the first chemical used to break dormancy of lettuce?
3. How H_2O_2 can decrease ABA content and promote germination?
4. Acid scarification for Malvaceae seeds.
5. What is the insect used for bioscarification?

ANSWER KEYS

I. FILL UPS

1. Seed dormancy	2. Seed dormancy	3. Quiescendce
4. Innate dormancy	5. Induced dormancy	6. Endogenous or embryo dormancy
7. Double dormancy or combined dormancy	8. Scarification	9. Bioscarification
10. Stratification	11. Gibberellic acid	12. Cytokinin
13. Ethylene	14. Fusicocin	15. Thiourea
16. H_2O_2	17. *Gingko biloba*	18. Fagus, *Ficus Eucalyptus*
19. Drupes or pomes	20. Chemical dormancy	

II. TRUE OR FALSE

1.	True	6.	False
2.	False	7.	False
3.	False	8.	False
4.	True	9.	False
5.	True	10.	True

III. MATCH THE FOLLOWING

(i)		(ii)		(iii)	
1.	B	1.	C	1.	C
2.	D	2.	A	2.	D
3.	A	3.	B	3.	B
4.	E	4.	E	4.	E
5.	C	5.	D	5.	A

IV. ONE WORD ANSWER

1. *Gingko biloba*
2. Thiourea
3. By enhancing oxygen production
4. Use 100 ml H_2SO_4/kg of seeds for 2-3 minutes.
5. Termite

V. AT A GLANCE

1. Terminology

- **Quiescence:** Condition in which seed can germinate upon absorption of water. No internal germination barriers exist.
- **After-ripening:** Physiological processes that occur in the seed after harvest that enables germination to take place.
- **Primary dormancy:** Dormancy which develops when the seed is attached to the plant and exists when first harvested. It is also referred as innate dormancy.
- **Secondary dormancy:** A condition that develops to prevent germination after the seed has been detached from the plant and is exposed to specific unfavorable environmental conditions. It is synonyms to induced dormancy.
- **Endogenous dormancy:** Any cause of dormancy related to the embryo *e.g.* immature development or chemical inhibitors located in the embryo is collectively referred as endogenous dormancy or embryo dormancy.
- **Exogenous dormancy:** Mechanical resistance, physical impermeability, inhibitors or light sensitivity associated with seed coat is called as seed coat dormancy.
- **Double dormancy or combined dormancy:** It is defined that where two or more dormancy types occur in the seed *e.g.* fleshy fruits with chemical inhibitors combines with hard endocarp.
- **Thermo-dormancy:** Type of dormancy induced by high temperature.

- **Photo–dormancy:** Most seeds having photo-dormancy germinate only under light conditions. Such seeds are therefore also called light sensitive.

2. Light and germination

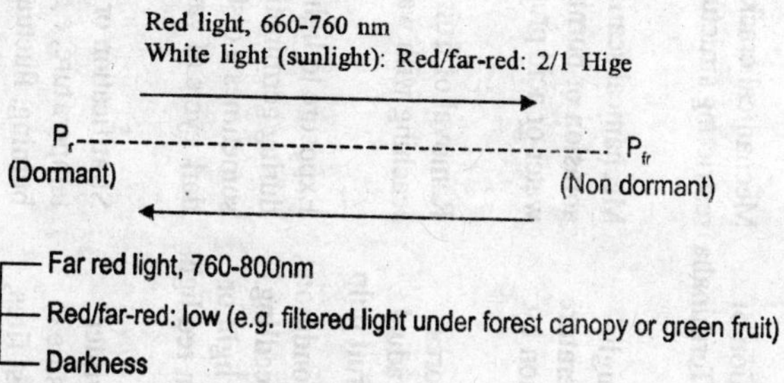

3. Acid scarification

Species	Duration of acid pretreatment
Acacia nilotica	>15 min
Albizia lebeck	40 min (85%)
Cassia fistula	45 min (75%)- 90 min (84%)
Delonix regia	3-6 h
Leucaena leucocephala	30 min (95%)
Prosopis juliflora	15-60 min (95-100%)

4. Summary of seed dormancy and its breaking treatments

Dormancy type	Characteristics	Example of occurrence	Dormancy breaking stimulus	
			Natural	Seed handling
Immature embryo	Seeds are physiologically immature for germination	*Fraxinus excelcior; Gingko biloba*	Post-dispersal development	After ripening
Mechanical dormancy	Embryo development physically restricted due to hard seed/fruit coat	*Pterocarpus, Terminalia* spp., *Melia volkensii*	Gradual deco-mposition of hard structures, *e.g.* Terminalia	Mechanical cracking of restricting structure
Physical dormancy	Imbibitions impeded because of impermeable seed coat or fruit	Leguminaceae, Myrtaceae	Abrasion by sand, high temperatures, temperature fluctuations, ingestion by animals or others	Mechanical scarification (*e.g.* abrasion or burning), boiling water or acid pretreatment
Chemical dormancy	Fruit and seed contain chemical inhibitory compounds that prevent the germination	Fleshly fruit such as berries, drupes and pomes and some dry seeds	Ingestion by frugivores, leaching by rain, gradual decomposition of fruit pulp	Removal of fruit pulp plus leaching with water.
Photo dormancy	Seeds fail to germinate unless exposed to appropriate light conditions/regimes. Is operated by a bio chemical phytochrome mechanism	Many temperate species, *e.g. Betula*. Humid tropical pioneer species *e.g. Spathodea* and some *Eucalyplus*	Exposure to light conditions likely to promote seedling survival viz.. white light or light relative rich in red light	Exposure to light, normally during germination, sometimes a distinct light and dark cycle of variable duration
Thermo dormancy	Germination low without pretreatment with appropriate temperatures	Most temperate species, *e.g. Fagus, Quercus, Pinus.* Dry zone tropical sub tropical pioneers *e.g. Hakea, Pinus, Eucalyptus, B. banksia,* humid tropical pioneers.	Exposure to low winter temperature, exposure to grass, bush or forest fires, diurnal fluctuating temperature in gaps	Stratification or chilling, high temperature, *e.g.* kiln or light burning, fluctuating temperature

14

Seed Germination

I. FILL UPS

1. The process whereby seeds sprout and begin to grow is known as _____.
2. During germination of a seed, the water is absorbed through _____.
3. _____ is the onset growth of a seed often following a period of dormancy.
4. _____ is a type of germination in which cotyledons and shoot are carried above the soil level.
5. _____ is a type of germination in which the cotyledon or comparable structure remain in the soil.
6. Water moves into the tissues and cells by _____.
7. The uptake of water by the seeds is called as _____.
8. The major means of fatty acid breakdown is by _____.
9. The phenomenon known that the radicle will always grow down into the soil _____.
10. pH above _____ is detrimental both to total number of germinating seeds and seedling survival.

II. TRUE OR FALSE

1. Aeration is closely connected to soil structure and moisture conditions.
2. Germinating seeds are vulnerable, especially during earlier phase of germination.
3. As seed enters into the second and third phase with structural changes, cell elongation and division. The germination process become reversible.
4. Cell division preceded cell elongation.
5. Enzyme activation phase is one of the most essential and dynamic phase in seed for embryonic axis elongation.

III. MATCH THE FOLLOWING

1.	Phase I	A. 12 ATP
2.	Phase II	B. Roots become function
3.	Phase III	C. Water imbibition
4.	α oxidation	D. Lag phase
5.	Krebs cycle	E. Sunflower

IV. ONE WORD QUESTION

1. Mention the types of germination.
2. Mention any two factors affecting seed germination.

ANSWER KEYS

I. FILL UPS

1. Germination 2. Micropyle 3. Germination
4. Epigeal germination 5. Hypogeal germination 6. Osmosis
7. Imbibition 8. β oxidation 9. Geotropism
10. 8.5

II. TRUE OR FALSE

1. True
2. False
3. False
4. False
5. True

III. MATCH THE FOLLOWING

1. C
2. D
3. B
4. E
5. A

IV. ONE WORD ANSWER

1. Epigeal and hypogeal
2. pH, orientation of seed sowing

V. AT A GLANCE

1. Steps in germination

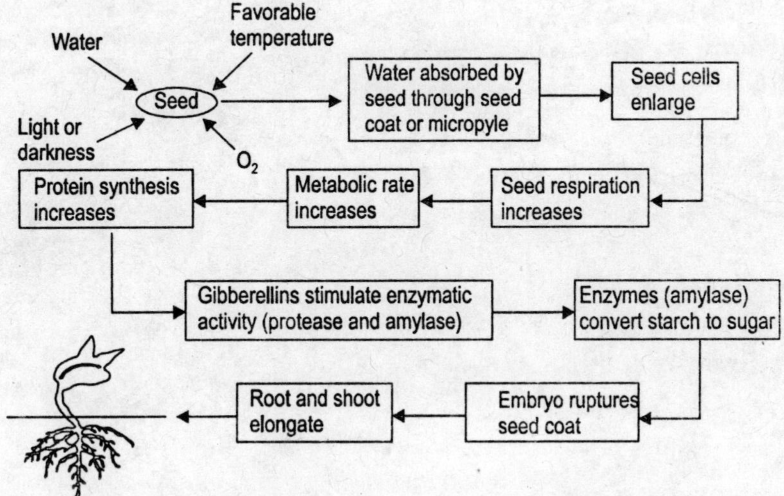

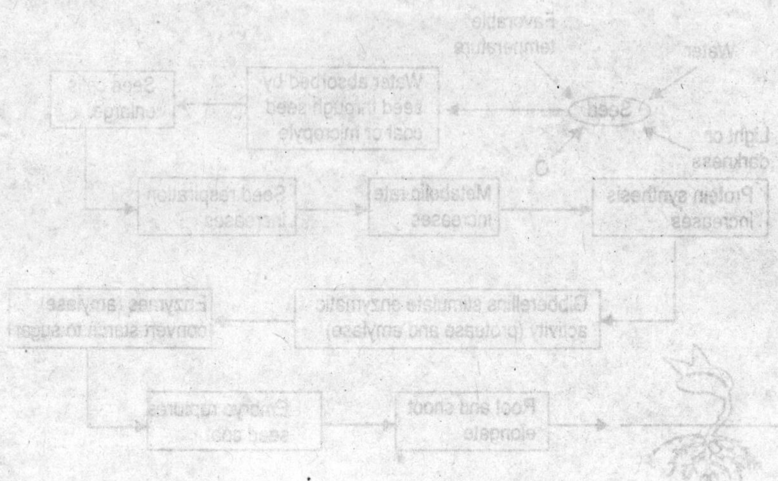

UNIT - 2

SEED PRODUCTION TECHNOLOGY

1

Breeding Techniques and Seed Production

I. FILL UPS

1. ______ is the process of bringing wild species under human management.
2. ______ is referred to as taking a genotype into new environments, where they were not being grown before.
3. Introduction of plants from a foreign country is called as ______.
4. Introduction from one state to another state is called as ______.
5. When the introduced variety is well suited to the new environment it is called as ______.
6. When the introduced variety is hybridized with local varieties it is known as ______.
7. An example for secondary introduction is ______.
8. ______ means to keep materials in isolation to prevent the spread of diseases, pests etc.
9. A process that leads to the adaptation of a variety to a new environment ______.
10. Evaluation of the growth of the plants on the basis of performance of their progenies is called as ______.
11. ______ is a progeny of a single, homozygous, self pollinated plant.
12. In ______ breeding method, a large number of plants of similar phenontype are selected and their seeds are mixed to constitute a new variety.
13. The matting (or) crossing of two plants (or) lines of dissimilar genotype is known as ______.
14. Parents belong to the same species are crossed then, it is called ______.
15. When more than two parents are crossed to produce a hybrid, it is called as______.

16. _____ is defined as the description of ancestors of an individual.
17. A modification of the bulk method is based on _____ selection in F2.
18. A cross between a hybrid and one of its parents is known as _____.
19. CMS is most commonly used in _____ to produce hybrid seed.
20. _____ are advanced generation seed mixture of an inter varietal cross.
21. An example for composites in maize is _____.
22. _____ is defined as the superiority of a F1 hybrid over both of its parents in terms of yield (or) some other character.
23. A group of plants produced from a single plant through asexual reproduction is called as _____.
24. _____ breeding method is done for both biotic and abiotic stresses.
25. A plants ability to reduce (or) overcome the possible injuries effect caused directly (or) indirectly by the presence of soluble salts in its root zone is called _____.
26. The term mutation was introduced by _____.
27. When mutations are induced for crop improvement, the entire operation of the induction and isolation of mutants is termed as _____.
28. _____ refers to induced chromosome manipulation.
29. Genomes identical with each other are called _____.
30. Best source of aneuploids are _____ plants.

II. TRUE OR FALSE

1. Introduction from one state to another is called exotic collection.
2. Lerma Rojo is introduced through primary introduction.
3. Mass selection is a uniform as purelines.
4. A pureline is the progeny of a single heterozygous self pollinated plant.
5. In inter specific hybridization, 2 species of same genus are crossed.
6. Pureline selection method is widely adopted.
7. Pureline selection variety is easily identified.
8. The recombination is limited to 2 (or) 3 generations.
9. Average reduction in fitness (or) of a character is due to inbreeding.
10. A synthetic variety is produced by crossing in all combinations.
11. Resistance breeding is done for abiotic stress only.

12. Best source of the aneuploids are tetrasomic plants.
13. Induced mutations occurs naturally without any apparent cause.
14. Clonal selection is the only method of selection applicable to clonal crops.
15. Heterosis results from the masking of harmful effects dominant alleles by their recessive alleles.

III. MATCH THE FOLLOWING

1.	Sonara 64	A	Secondary intro
2.	Sonalika	B	Primary intro
3.	*Oryza sativa var indica* x *Oryza porennis*	C	Sorghum
4.	Triticale	D	Inter specific
5.	CMS	E	Inter generic

IV. ONE WORD QUESTION

1. What is the concentration of colchicine treated to the growing shoot apices?
2. What is autoploidy?
3. What is spontaneous mutation?
4. Mention some composite varieties released in maize
5. Give one difference between pureline selection and mass selection.
6. Give one example for inter generic hybridization.
7. IW refers to?
8. EC refers to?
9. Give one example for variety released through primary introduction.
10. In which crop plants introduction leads to asexual reproduction.

ANSWER KEYS

I. FILL UPS

1. Domestication	2. Plant introduction	3. Foreign (or) exotic collection
4. Indigenous introduction	5. Primary introduction	6. Secondary introduction
7. Kalyan sona	8. Quarantine	9. Acclimatization
10. Progeny test	11. Pureline	12. Mass selection
13. Hybridization	14. Inter varietal hybridization	15. Complex cross
16. Pedigree method	17. Artificial	18. Back cross

19. Sorghum	20. Composites	21. Protina
22. Heterosis	23. Clone	24. Resistance
25. Salt tolerance	26. Hyode vries	27. Mutation breeding
28. Polyploidy breeding	29. Autoploidy	30. Triploid

II. TRUE OR FALSE

1.	False	6.	False	11.	False
2.	True	7.	True	12.	False
3.	False	8.	True	13.	False
4.	False	9.	True	14.	True
5.	True	10.	True	15.	False

III. MATCH THE FOLLOWING

1. B
2. A
3. D
4. E
5. C

IV. ONE WORD ANSWER

1. 0.001 to 1%
2. Genomes identical with each other.
3. Occurs naturally without any apparent cause
4. Sona, protina
5. Variety is easily identified
6. Triticale (cross between *Triticum sp.* and *Secale cereale*).
7. Indigenous wild collections
8. Exotic collections
9. Sonara 64, Lerma Roja
10. Sugarcane, potato

V. AT A GLANCE

1. Breeding methods

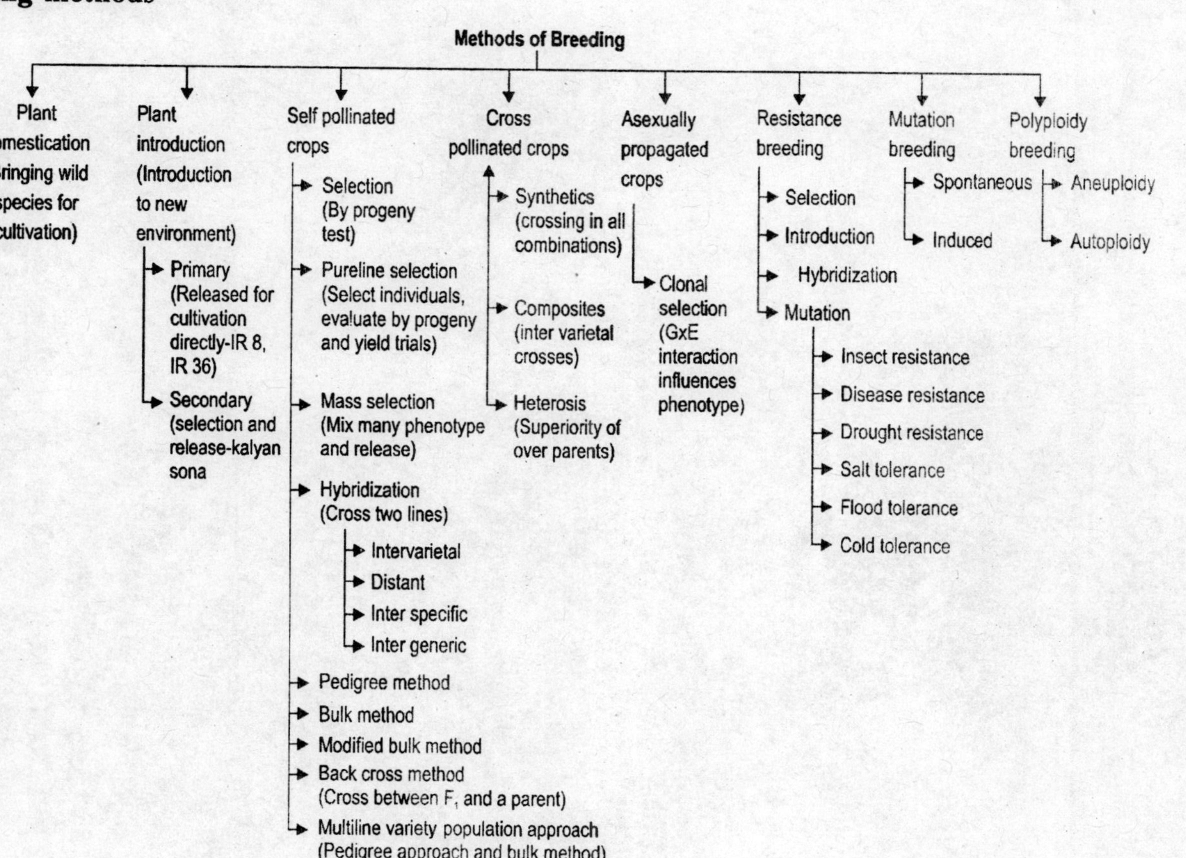

2

Heterosis and Hybrid Vigour

I. FILL UPS

1. _____ is the increased function of any biological quality in a hybrid offspring.
2. Heterosis is otherwise known as _____.
3. _____ is the reduced fitness in a given population as a result of breeding of related individuals.
4. In _____ heterosis type, naturally occurring mutants are sheltered.
5. The progeny posses superiority over parents in vegetative growth, but reduction in yield is known as _____.
6. Average heterosis is mathematically expressed as _____.
7. When heterosis is estimated over better parent, it is called as _____.
8. When heterosis is estimated over standard commercial hybrid , it is called as _____.
9. Standard heterosis is otherwise known as _____.
10. Any offspring resulting from the mating of two distinctly homozygous individuals is known as _____.
11. The cross between two different homozygous lines produced an F1 hybrid that is _____.
12. _____ result from the cross between one parent that is a F1 hybrid and the other is K, an inbred line.
13. The crossing of two different three way cross hybrids is called _____.
14. The cross between an inbred line and an open pollinated variety is known as _____.
15. Crossing between parents from two different species is known as _____.
16. Crossing between parents from the two different genera is known as _____.
17. _____ is a variety developed by mixing the seeds of various phenotypically outstanding lines.

18. In _____ type of hybridization, two parents from the same species are crossed.
19. An example of coconut synthetic variety is _____.
20. An example of maize composite variety is _____.

II. TRUE OR FALSE

1. A synthetic variety is developed by inter mating of inbreeds with good general combining ability (GCA).
2. Composite variety can be exactly reconstituted.
3. In synthetic variety, gca is evaluated.
4. In composite variety, gca is evaluated.
5. Triple cross hybrid results from the cross between one parent that is an F1 hybrid and other is K, an inbreed line.
6. Heterobeltiosis has practical importance in plant breeding.
7. Balanced heterosis has application in hybrid production.
8. The higher the genetic variation within a breeding population, the more likely it is to suffer from inbreeding depression.
9. Heterosis is otherwise known as hybrid vigor.
10. Comparison of hybrid to performance of best parent is called high parent heterosis.

III. MATCH THE FOLLOWING

(i)

1.	Pseudoheterosis	A (AxB)xC
2.	Economic heterosis	B (AxB) x (CxD)
3.	Relative heterosis	C Luxuriance
4.	Double cross	D Standard heterosis
5.	Three way cross	E Average heterosis

(ii)

1.	Synthetics	A Relative heterosis
2.	Composites	B ICMS 7703
3.	(F1-MP)/MPx100	C HB 3
4.	(F1-HP)/HPx100	D Outbreeding enhancement
5.	Heterosis	E High parent heterosis

IV. ONE WORD QUESTION

1. Mention the types of heterosis on basis of types of estimation.
2. How average heterosis is expressed?
3. How heterosis is expressed?
4. How standard heterosis is expressed?
5. How high parent heterosis is expressed?
6. Give any two examples for synthetic variety of pearl millet.
7. Give an example for composite variety of pearl millet.
8. Mention the synthetic variety of coconut
9. Give any two example for composite variety of maize.
10. Mention the type of heterosis on the basis of origin and nature.

ANSWER KEYS

I. FILL UPS

1. Heterosis
2. Outbreeding enhancement
3. Inbreeding depression
4. Mutational
5. Pseudoheterosis
6. (F1 – MP / MP) x 100
7. Heterobeltiosis
8. Standard heterosis
9. Economic heterosis
10. Hybrids
11. Heterozygous
12. Three way cross hybrid
13. Triple cross hybrids
14. Top cross hybrids
15. Interspecific hybridization
16. Intergeneric hybridization
17. Composite
18. Intervarietal
19. PCA SYN VAR 001
20. Sona

II. TRUE OR FALSE

1. True
2. False
3. True
4. False
5. False
6. False
7. True
8. False
9. True
10. False

III. MATCH THE FOLLOWING

(i)		(ii)	
1.	C	1.	B
2.	D	2.	C
3.	E	3.	A
4.	B	4.	E
5.	A	5.	D

IV. ONE WORD ANSWER

1. i. Average heterosis
   ii. Heterobeltiosis
   iii. Economic heterosis
2. (F1-MP/MP) x 100
3. (F1-BP/MP) x 100
4. (F1-SH/SH) x 100
5. (F1-HP/HP) x 100
6. MH-179, HB – 3
7. ICMS – 7703
8. PCA SYN VAR 001
9. Amber, Sona
10. i. Euheterosis
    ii. Mutational
    iii. Pseudoheterosis

V. AT A GLANCE

1. Heterosis and its expression

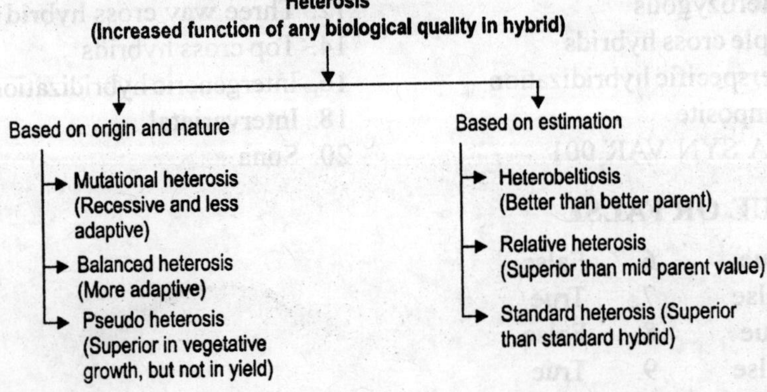

2. Measurement

Heterobeltiosis = $(F_1$ - BP) / BP x 100

Relative heterosis = $(F_1$ - MP) / MP x 100

Standard heterosis = $(F_1$ - SH) / SH x 100

Where, F_1 - F_1 Value

BP - Better parent value

MP - Mid parent value

SH - Standard hybrid value

3. Development of hybrids

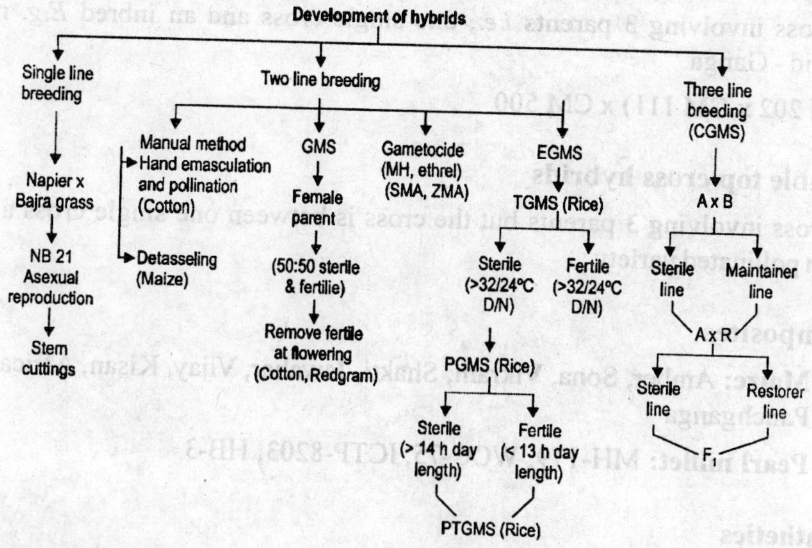

4. Types of hybrids

Intraspecific hybrids: Involving parents belong to the same (intervarietal hybrids) species, but between two varieties. *E.g.* CSH 5, CSH 9, K Tall, JKHY-1, Suguna.

Interspecific hybrids: Involving parents from entirely different species of a crop.

Eg. Cotton - Varalakshmi

Laxmi x SB 289 E

(*G. hirsutum*) x (*G. barbadense*)

DCH 32 or Jayalakshmi

D.S. 28 x SB (YF) 425

(*G. hirsutum*) x (*G. barbadense*)

Tomato - Pusa red pulp

L. esculentum x *L. pimpinellifolium*

Single cross hybrids

Involving only two parents *i.e.*, inbreds *E.g.* Maize COH1 – (UMI 29 x UMI 51).

Double cross hybrids

Involving 4 parents *i.e.*, inbreds of two single crosses *E.g.* Deccan maize. (CM 104 x CM 105) x (CM 202 x CM 201)

Three way cross hybrids

A cross involving 3 parents *i.e.*, one single cross and an inbred *E.g.* maize hybrid - Ganga.

(CM 202 x CM 111) x CM 500

Double top cross hybrids

A cross involving 3 parents but the cross is between one single cross and an open pollinated variety.

Composites

- **Maize:** Amber, Sona, Vikram, Shakti, Jawahar, Vijay, Kisan, African tall, Panchganga
- **Pearl millet:** MH-179, WCC-75, ICTP-8203, HB-3

Synthetics

- **Pearl millet:** ICMS-7703.

3

Development of Hybrids and Release of Varieties

I. FILL UPS

1. _____ is a crossing between two genetically dissimilar parents.
2. Detasseling is done in _____.
3. _____ is an example for chemical hybridizing agent.
4. _____ is called as pollen parent.
5. _____ is the fertile counter part of A line.
6. DUS stand for _____.
7. _____ is an example for interspecific hybrid in cotton.
8. _____ is an example for single cross hybrid in maize.
9. _____ is an example for double cross hybrid in maize.
10. _____ is an example for three way cross hybrid in maize.

II. TRUE OR FALSE

1. The degree of uniformity depends on the mode of reproduction.
2. Varieties of cross pollination species are more stable than varieties of self pollination.
3. Hybrids are stable.
4. DUS tests are conducted to establish whether or not a variety is sufficiently distinct from all other varieties and sufficiently uniform and stable.
5. Screening for biotic and abiotic stresses will be done at comparative yield trial stage.
6. Double top cross hybrid is a cross involving two parents.
7. B line is the maintainer line.
8. 100% male sterility can be maintained in three line breeding system.
9. Chemical hybridizing agents does not affect the pollen sterility.
10. 100% male sterility can be maintained in GMS.

III. MATCH THE FOLLOWING

(i)

1.	Single line breeding	A Jayalakshmi
2.	Two line breeding	B Sunflower
3.	Three line breeding	C CSH 5
4.	Intraspecific hybrid	D Maize
5.	Interspecific hybrid	E NB21 grass

(ii)

1.	Sodium methyl arsenate	A Double cross hybrid
2.	Maize CoH 1	B Three way cross
3.	Deccan maize	C 100% male sterility
4.	Ganga	D CHA
5.	Three line breeding	E Single cross hybrid

IV. ONE WORD QUESTION

1. Genetic male sterility is used in commercial production of which crops.
2. Hand emasculation and natural pollination is done in which crops.
3. Give an example for single line breeding in spice crop.
4. Why chemical hybridizing agents are used?
5. What does MLT and ART stands for?

ANSWER KEYS

I. FILL UPS

1. Hybrid
2. Maize
3. Maleic hydrazide (MH)
4. R line
5. B line
6. Distinctness, uniformity and stability
7. Varalakshmi
8. CoH(M)5
9. Deccan
10. Ganga

II. TRUE OR FALSE

1.	True	6.	False
2.	False	7.	True
3.	False	8.	True
4.	True	9.	False
5.	False	10.	False

III. MATCH THE FOLLOWING

(i)		(ii)	
1.	E	1.	D
2.	D	2.	E
3.	B	3.	A
4.	C	4.	B
5.	A	5.	C

IV. ONE WORD ANSWER

1. Redgram, castor, groundnut
2. Rice, maize, pearl millet, sorghum
3. Turmeric, pepper
4. To create male sterility
5. MLT – Multi location trial
   ART – Adaptive research trial

4

Deterioration of Varieties

I. FILL UPS

1. _____ is the most important source of varietal deterioration during seed production.
2. _____ in oats is caused due to mutation.
3. In peas, _____ is caused due to mutation.
4. _____ is another most important source of varietal deterioration due to introgression to genes from unrelated stocks.
5. _____ is the major source of genetic contamination and varietal deterioration in cross fertilized crop.

II. TRUE OR FALSE

1. Mutation is a serious factor of varietal deterioration.
2. In case of vegetatively propagated crops periodic increase of true to type stock would eliminate the deteriorating effects of mutations.
3. Pigeon pea is a cross pollinated crop.
4. Minor genetic variation is common in self pollinated crops.
5. Rabbit ear is present in oats.

III. MATCH THE FOLLOWING

1.	Fatuoids	A	Self pollinated
2.	Rabbit ear	B	Cross pollinated
3.	Pearl millet	C	Oats
4.	Cotton	D	Peas
5.	Ground nut	E	Often cross pollinated

IV. ONE WORD QUESTION

1. Give any two examples for varietal deterioration caused by mutation.
2. Mention any two varietal deterioration factors.

ANSWER KEYS

I. FILL UPS

1. Mechanical mixtures
2. Fatuoids
3. Rabbit ears
4. Natural crossing
5. Natural crossing

II. TRUE OR FALSE

1. False
2. True
3. False
4. False
5. False

III. Match the following

1. C
2. D
3. B
4. E
5. A

IV. ONE WORD ANSWER

1. i) Fatuoids in oats
   ii) Rabbit ear in peas
2. i) Mutations
   ii) Natural crossing

V. AT A GLANCE

1. Classification of crops on the basis of mode of pollination

Self pollinated crops	Often cross pollinated crops	Cross pollinated crops
Rice, wheat, black gram, chickpea, green gram, lentil, soybean, groundnut, potato, tomato, lettuce	Sorghum, pigeonpea, cotton, linseed, sesame, *Brassica* sp. (self compatible), brinjal	Maize, pearlmillet, sunflower, safflower, niger, castor, *Brassica* sp. (self incompatible), sugarcane, lucerne, cabbage, cauliflower, cucumber, musk melon and watermelon, pumpkin, Indian summer and winter squash, radish, onion, turnip and coriander

2. Deterioration factors

1. Developmental variation
   a) Variation due to difficult environment
2. Mechanical mixtures
   a) Admixtures during sowing and post harvesting
   b) Volunteer plants
   c) Varieties grown in nearby field
3. Mutations
   a) Roguing of mutants (Rabbit ear in peas)
4. Natural crossing
   a) Crossing with undesirable types, diseased plants and off-types
5. Minor genetic variation
   a) Common in often-cross pollinated crops
6. Influence of diseases
   a) Produce disease free breeder seed
7. Techniques of breeder
   a) Cytogenetical irregularities
   b) Premature release of varieties

5

Maintenance Breeding

I. FILL UPS

1. The initial handful of seeds obtained from selected individual plants of a particular variety is called as _____.
2. The panicles collected should be stored in a airtight drum under _____.
3. _____ is the original purified seed stock of a new variety in the hands of a plant breeder.
4. The seeds of a notified variety collected from the evolving institute with all the passport information is considered as _____.
5. Nucleus seed is produced by _____.

II. TRUE OR FALSE

1. Genetic drift should be avoided during collection of panicle.
2. Breeder can select large number of individual plants from foundation seed production plot for maintenance breeding.

ANSWER KEYS

I. FILL UPS

1. Nucleus seed
2. Dehumidified cold room
3. Breeder's stock seed
4. Basic nucleus seed
5. Plant breeder

II. TRUE OR FALSE

1. True
2. False

6

Seed Generation System

I. FILL UPS

1. _____ is the progeny of nucleus seed.
2. Genetic purity of breeder seed is _____.
3. Physical purity of breeder seed is _____.
4. The colour of tag for breeder seed is _____.
5. _____ is the progeny of breeder seed.
6. Genetic purity of foundation seed is _____.
7. Tag colour for foundation seed is _____.
8. _____ is the progeny of foundation seed.
9. Seeds are stored with _____ tags.
10. Registered seeds are stored with _____tags.
11. _____ is the category of seed produced by private seed companies.
12. Truthfully labeled seeds are stored in bags with _____ tag.
13. In seed production, _____ is voluntary.
14. _____ is applicable to both notified and released varieties.
15. _____ is applicable to notified kinds only.

II. TRUE OR FALSE

1. Nucleus seed has 100% genetic purity and physical purity.
2. For truthful labeled seed, seed certification officer alone can take samples.
3. For certified seeds, labelling is compulsory.
4. Registered seeds are stored in bags with purple colour tags.
5. Certified seed produced from paddy and wheat is eligible for certification by NSC upto 2 generations from foundation seed.

III. MATCH THE FOLLOWING

1.	TFL	A	Golden yellow tags
2.	Certified seed	B	White colour tags
3.	Registered seed	C	Azure blue tags
4.	Foundation seed	D	Opal green colour tags
5.	Breeder seed	E	Purple colour tags

IV. ONE WORD QUESTION

1. Mention the different classes of seeds
2. Mention two differences between certified seed and truthfully labelled seed.
3. What is three generation system?

ANSWER KEYS

I. FILL UPS

1. Breeder seed
2. 100%
3. 98%
4. Golden yellow
5. Foundation seed
6. 99.5%
7. White colour
8. Certified seed
9. Purple colour
10. Azure blue colour
11. Truthfully labelled seeds
12. Opal green colour
13. Certification
14. Truthfully labelled seed
15. Certified seed

II. TRUE OR FALSE

1. True
2. False
3. True
4. True
5. True

III. MATCH THE FOLLOWING

1. D
2. C
3. E
4. B
5. A

IV. ONE WORD ANSWER

1. i) Nucleus seed
   ii) Breeder seed
   iii) Foundation seed
   iv) Registered seed
   v) Certified seed

2.

Certified seed	TFL seed
i) Certification is voluntary	i) Truthful labelling is compulsory for notified kinds or varieties.
ii) Applicable to notified kinds only	ii) Applicable to both notified and released varieties.

3. i) Breeder seed
   ii) Foundation seed
   iii) Certified seed

V. AT A GLANCE

1. Seed generation system

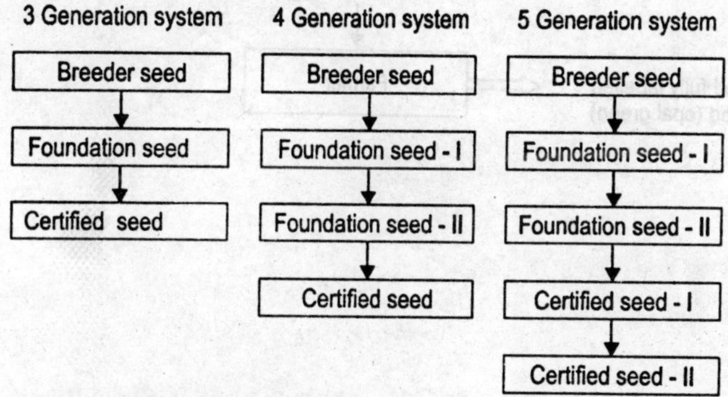

- Five generation system is followed only when multiplication is very poor
- There should be heavy demand
- Should be of self - pollinated crop

2. Differences between certified seed and truthfully labelled seed

Certified seed	Truthful labelled seed
- Certification is voluntary	- Truthful labelling is compulsory for notified kinds or varieties
- Applicable to notified kinds only	- Applicable to both notified and released varieties
- It should satisfy both minimum field and seed standards	- Tested for physical purity and germination
- Seed certification officer, seed inspectors can take samples during inspection	- Seed inspectors alone can take samples for checking the seed quality.

3. Production and quality control of different classes of seed

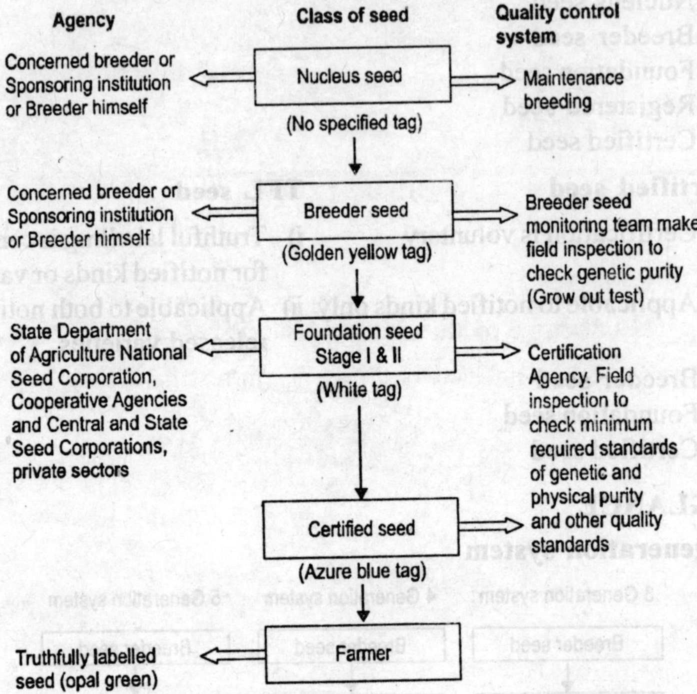

7

Seed Quality

I. FILL UPS

1. _____ is a matured ovule usually developed after fertilization.
2. Seed can also be defined as the _____ in resting stage.
3. _____ of seeds refers to the trueness to type.
4. Pure live seed is calculated by _____
5. _____ is the most crucial factor in the maintenance of seed germination and viability during storage.
6. _____ refers to the sum total of all the attributes that give effective plant stand in the field.

II. TRUE OR FALSE

1. Seed is a matured ovary usually developed after fertilization.
2. Physical purity has direct effect on ultimate yields.
3. The health of seed refers to the presence or absence of disease causing organisms/insect pests on the seeds.
4. Seed must be dried to safe moisture content.
5. The seeds should have low physical vigour and stamina.

III. MATCH THE FOLLOWING

1.	Genetic purity	A	Matured ovule
2.	Physical purity	B	Trueness to type
3.	Seed moisture	C	Physical composition of seed lots
4.	Seed	D	Pure seed % x Germination %
5.	Pure live seed	E	Viability

IV. ONE WORD QUESTION

1. Mention any two advantages of quality seed.
2. What is the genetic purity of certified seed?

3. What is the physical purity of bhendi and carrot?
4. What are the physiological quality of seed?
5. Which is called as a basic tool for secured food supply?

ANSWER KEYS

I. FILL UPS

1. Seed
2. Embryonic plant
3. Genetic purity
4. Pure seed % x Germination %
5. Seed moisture
6. Seed vigour

II. TRUE OR FALSE

1. False
2. False
3. True
4. True
5. False

III. MATCH THE FOLLOWING

1. B
2. C
3. E
4. A
5. D

IV. ONE WORD ANSWER

1. i. Plants stand will be uniform
   ii. There will be greater resistance to stress and diseases.
2. 98%
3. Bhendi – 99%
   Carrot – 95%
4. Seed germination and vigor
5. Seed

V. AT A GLANCE

1. Quality seed concepts

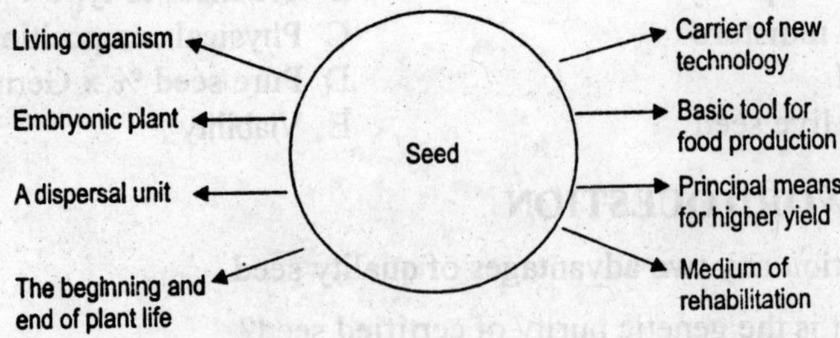

2. Characteristics of good quality seed

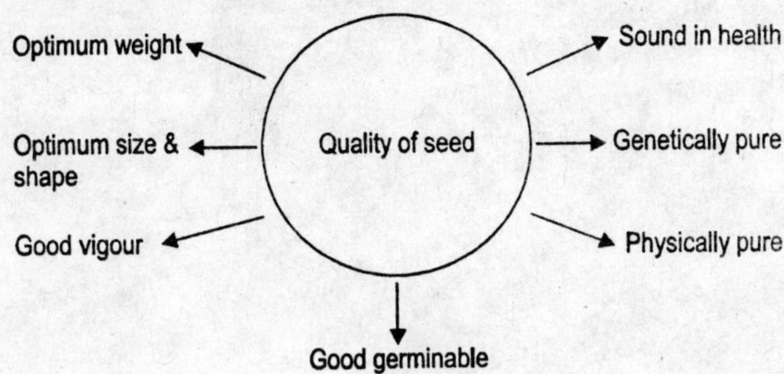

3. Genetic purity

Breeder / nucleus seed	:	100 %
Foundation seed	:	99.5 %
Certified seed	:	99.0 %

4. Physical purity

All crops	:	98 %
Carrot	:	95 %
Bhendi	:	99 %
Other crops	:	98 %
Sesame, soybean, jute	:	97 %
Groundnut	:	96 %

5. Designated inseparable other crop seeds

Crop	Designated inseparable other crop seeds
Barley	Wheat, Oats and Gram
Oats	Wheat, Gram and Barley
Wheat	Oats, Gram and Barley

2. Characteristics of good quality seed

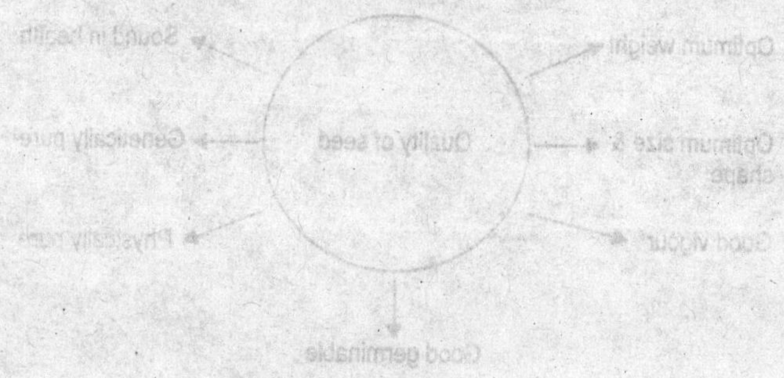

3. Genetic purity

Breeder / nucleus seed	100 %
Foundation seed	99.5 %
Certified seed	99.0 %

4. Physical purity

All crops	98 %
Carrot	95 %
Bhendi	99 %
Other crops	98 %
Sesame, soybean, jute	97 %
Groundnut	96 %

5. Designated inseparable other crop seeds

Crop	Designated inseparable other crop seeds
Barley	Wheat, Oats and Gram
Oats	Wheat, Gram and Barley
Wheat	Oats, Gram and Barley

8

Seed Policy

I. FILL UPS

1. The Seeds Act was passed in the year _____
2. Seed Control Order was passed in the year _____
3. The New Policy on Seed Development was passed in the year _____
4. Seed Act came into force in _____
5. In _____ year, Seed Rules were formed.
6. In _____ year, Seed Certification Agencies and Central Seed Certification Board were formed.
7. National Seed Corporation was started in the year _____
8. Essential Commodities Act & Consumer Protection Act was passed in the year _____
9. Plant Variety Act was passed in the year _____
10. Protection of Plant Varieties and Farmers Right was passed in the year _____
11. Protection of Plant Varieties and Farmers Rights Act was passed in the year _____
12. National Seed Policy was formulated in the year _____
13. In _____ year, PPV & FRA was implemented in India.
14. In the year _____ New Seed Bill was submitted.
15. NSC stands for _____
16. SFCI stands for _____
17. National Seed Project was implemented in the year _____
18. National Seed Project was launched by GOI in _____
19. From _____ year, NSP is functioning as NSP (Crops) and dealing with seed production and research related to development of seed industry.
20. NSP stands for _____

II. TRUE OR FALSE

1. National Seed Corporation plays an important role in formation of Seed Act and Rules.
2. National Seed Policy was formulated in the year of 1974.
3. SFCI has regional office at state level to perform its function.
4. Seed Rules was passed in 1966.
5. In the year, 2001 PPV & FRA was implemented in India.

III. MATCH THE FOLLOWING

1.	Seed Act	A 2002
2.	Seed Rules	B 2001
3.	PPV & FRA	C 1968
4.	New Seed Bill	D 1966
5.	National Seed Policy	E 2004

IV. ONE WORD QUESTION

1. Mention any two Multinational Seed Companies in India.
2. Three phases of NSP.
3. Mention any two agencies involved in seed quality control system

ANSWER KEYS

I. FILL UPS

1. 1966	2. 1983	3. 1988
4. 1969	5. 1968	6. 1972
7. 1963	8. 1986	9. 1993
10. 1999	11. 2001	12. 2002
13. 2003	14. 2004	
15. National Seed Corporation	16. State Farm Corporation of India	17. 1975-76
18. 1974	19. 2003	20. National Seed Project

II. TRUE OR FALSE

1.	True	2.	False
3.	False	4.	False
5.	True		

III. MATCH THE FOLLOWING

1. D
2. C
3. B
4. E
5. A

IV. ONE WORD ANSWER

1. i) Monsanto
   ii) Syngenta
2. i) Phase I (1976-1981)
   ii) Phase II (1981-1986)
   iii) Phase III (1987 to till date)
3. i) Seed certification agency
   ii) Seed testing laboratory

V. AT A GLANCE

1. Seed policy

Year	Events
1966	Seeds Act passed (came into force in 1969).
1968	Seed Rules.
1972	Seed Certification Agencies and Central Seed Certification Board formed.
1983	Seed Control Order.
1986	Essential Commodities Act, Consumer Protection Act.
	Breeder Seed Supply Policy. Before 1986, Breeder seed was supplied by NSC only for production of foundation seed, which was send to private sector.
1988	A New Seed Policy to encourage import of seed and planting material was announced.
1993	Plant Variety Act
1999	Protection of Plant Varieties and Farmers' Right.
2001	Protection of Plant Varieties and Farmers Rights Act.
2001-02	National Seed Policy
2003	PPV&FRA implemented in India
2004	New Seed Bill submitted

2. Structure of seed industry as per Seed Act (1966)

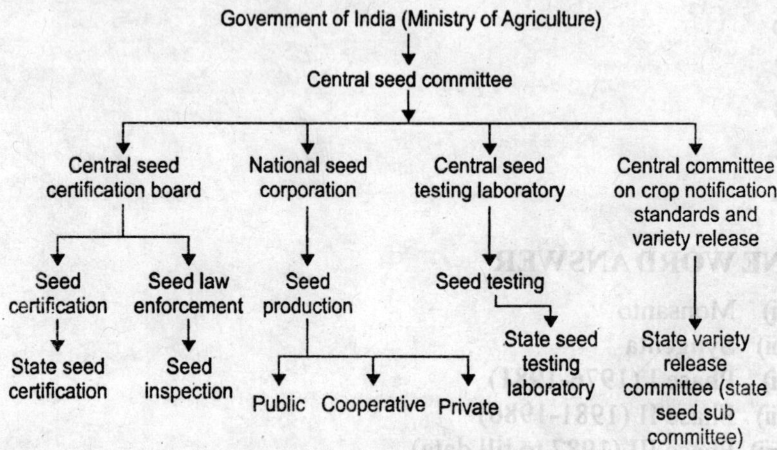

3. Multinational seed companies in India

Rank	Company name	Country
1	Monsanto (US)+ Seminis	USA
2	Dupont/Poineer	USA
3	Syngenta	Switzerland
4	Groupe Limagrain	France
5	KWS AG	Germany
6	Land O' Lakes	USA
7	Sakata	Japan
8	Bayer Crop Science	Germany
9	Taikii	Japan
10	DLF-Trifolium	Denmark

4. Indian seed organisation

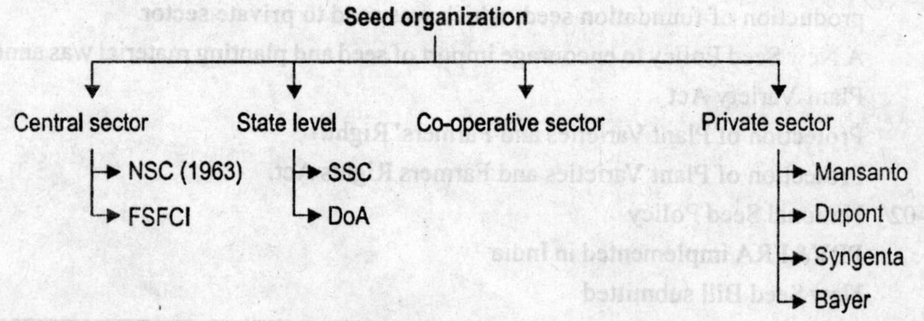

5. Seed production and research

ICAR - NSP started in 1974, renamed as NSP (Crops) in 2003

i) Phase I : 1976 - 1981

ii) Phase II : 1981 - 1986

iii) Phase III : 1987 - till date

9

Seed Planning

I. FILL UPS

1. _____ is basically a critical assessment of effective seed requirement.
2. _____ is the ratio of seed yield per seed generation.
3. The quantity of quality seed that have replaced the actual seed requirement of the location is _____.
4. SRR for hybrid seeds is _____
5. Seed multiplication ratio for groundnut _____

II. TRUE OR FALSE

1. The seed supply must keep pace with seed demand in terms of quantity, quality and price.
2. Seeds of cross–pollinating varieties should be replaced in 3 to 4 years.
3. In demand forecasting, losses and benefits at all production stages should not be considered.
4. Seed multiplication ratio for cotton is : 46.
5. Seed renewal period for sorghum is 3 times.

III. MATCH THE FOLLOWING

1.	Groundnut	A	Area x seed rate
2.	Quantity of seed	B	1:8
3.	SMR	C	3-4 years
4.	Paddy	D	Seed yield /Seed rate
5.	Self pollinating varieties	E	152

IV. ONE WORD QUESTION

1. Give the basic formula used in planning area to be covered.
2. What is the formula for seed multiplication ratio?
3. Seed multiplication ratio for groundnut.

ANSWER KEYS

I. FILL UPS

1. Demand forecast
2. Seed multiplication ratio
3. Seed replacement rate
4. 100%
5. 1:8

II. TRUE OR FALSE

1. True 2. False
3. False 4. True
5. True

III. MATCH THE FOLLOWING

1. B
2. A
3. D
4. E
5. C

IV. ONE WORD ANSWER

1. $\text{Area to be covered} = \dfrac{\text{Quantity of seeds required}}{\text{Seed yield}}$

2. $\text{SMR} = \dfrac{\text{Seed yield}}{\text{Seed rate}}$

3. $\text{SMR for groundnut} = \dfrac{800}{100} = 8 = 1:8$

V. AT A GLANCE

1. Demand forecast

Requirements

- Total acreage
- Seed yield
- Seed rate
- In case of cotton, ginning percentage
- In case of tomato, brinjal, cucurbits etc., seed recovery percentage

- Seed renewal period
  Self pollinating varieties: 3-4 years
  Hybrid : Every season/year
- Cultivar preference

2. SMR

SMR = $\frac{\text{Seed yield}}{\text{Seed rate}}$

E.g. SMR for groundnut = $\frac{800}{100} = 8 = 1:8$

SRR = $\frac{\text{Quality seed sown}}{\text{Quality seed needed}} \times 100$

E.g. For varieties = 15-20 %

For hybrids = 100 %

3. Multiplication ratio, seed renewal period and seed multiplication stages

S. No.	Seed crop	Multiplication ratio	Seed renewal period (times)	Seed multiplication stages		
				BS	FS	CS
1.	Paddy	152	4	1	1	2
2.	Wheat	49	4	1	1	2
3.	Barley	26	4	1	1	2
4.	Maize hybrid	248	1	1	1	1
5.	Maize variety	115	3	1	1	1
6.	Sorghum hybrid	179	1	1	1	1
7.	Sorghum variety	94	3	1	1	1
8.	Pearl millet hybrid	380	1	1	1	1
9.	Pearl millet variety	175	3	1	1	1
10.	Finger millet	420	4	1	1	2
11.	Gram and pea	24	3	1	1	2
12.	Pigeon pea	150	3	1	1	1
13.	Other pulses	125	3	1	1	1
14.	Groundnut	18	5	1	2	2
15.	Brassicas	200	3	1	1	1
16.	Sesamum	200	3	1	1	1
17.	Linseed	42	4	1	1	2
18.	Other oil crops	73-100	3	1	1	1
19.	Cotton	46	3	1	1	1
20.	Jute	120	3	1	1	1
21.	Fodder	75	3	1	1	1

10

Seed Village

I. FILL UPS

1. Seed village is also known as _____.
2. ITC with Zeneca stands for _____.
3. ITC Zeneca has recently changed name to _____.
4. CENSAR stands for _____.
5. _____ is a compact area approach in which the whole village involved in seed production.
6. The concept of seed village is a _____.
7. Seed village concept was started in_____.
8. _____ has guided the experiment in wheat.
9. _____ is a milestone in green revolution.
10. CAPART stands for _____.

II. TRUE OR FALSE

1. There is no operational difficulties in seed village project.
2. In seed village mechanization is easier.
3. AID stands for Association of India Department.
4. Seed village acts as an empowerment of farm women and livelihood security.
5. Seed village is not convenient for inspection and there is isolation problem.

III. ONE WORD QUESTION

1. Mention one advantage of seed village.
2. Mention one disadvantage of seed village.
3. What is the concept of seed village?

ANSWER KEYS

I. FILL UPS

1. Compact area approach
2. India Tobacco Company
3. Advanta India
4. Center for Sustainable Agriculture and Rural Development
5. Seed village
6. Win-win model
7. 1964
8. Dr. M.S. Swaminathan
9. Seed village project
10. Council for Advancement of People's Action and Rural Technology

II. TRUE OR FALSE

1. False
2. True
3. False
4. True
5. False

III. ONE WORD ANSWER

1. Mechanization is easier
2. Operational difficulties may arise
3. Win – win model

11

Principles of Seed Production

I. FILL UPS

1. _____ is required during raising of a seed crop to avoid contamination due to natural crossing.
2. _____ is another potent source of genetic contamination i.e., the plants differing in their characteristics from the seed variety.
3. Removal of off types is referred as _____.
4. _____ is the distance maintained between the seed crop and source of contaminant.
5. The isolation distance for cotton foundation seed production is _____.
6. The isolation distance for paddy is _____.
7. An example for wind pollinated crop is _____.
8. Blossom end rot of tomato is caused by _____ deficiency.
9. Whiptail of cauliflower is caused by _____ deficiency.
10. _____ is responsible for filling and lusture of the crops.
11. _____ deficiency causes bleaching in peas.
12. _____ spray will be given to the seed field to arrest flower shedding.
13. _____ spray at flowering stage produces bolder seeds in pulses.
14. _____ is the ratio to be maintained between the female and male lines in order to have good amount of pollen grains.
15. _____ aids in exertion of panicle.

II. TRUE OR FALSE

1. Application of urea or DAP is a technique for achieving uniformity.
2. In sunflower, female and male are raised in separate blocks and hence called block system.
3. Multi picking is done in cotton.

4. The rogues may be of physical or genetic contaminants.
5. Copper deficiency leads to sterility.
6. Line sowing is advisable for seed crop.
7. Bacterial wilt inoculum available in most of the soils will infect solanaceous vegetables.
8. Sesbania is grown for artificial barrier isolation.
9. Wind pollination improves seed setting in highly cross pollinated crops.
10. Off type plants may arise due to presence of some recessive genes in homozygous condition.

III. MATCH THE FOLLOWING

(i)

1.	Boron	A	Whiptail in cauliflower
2.	Manganese	B	Blossom end rot in tomato
3.	Molybdenum	C	Blotching in tomato
4.	Calcium	D	Hollow / heart in garden pea
5.	Potassium	E	Marsh spot in pea

(ii)

1.	K	A	Poor embryo growth
2.	Zn	B	Germination in onion
3.	Cu	C	Sterility
4.	Fe	D	Fertilization
5.	Selenium	E	Filling and lusture of crops

(iii)

1.	Paraguat	A	Avoids flower shedding
2.	Atrazine	B	Physical contaminant
3.	2% DAP	C	Post emergence
4.	40 ppm NAA	D	Pre emergence
5.	Volunteer plants	E	Improves seed quality

IV. ONE WORD QUESTION

1. What are pollen shedders?
2. Mention supplementary pollination in rice crop.
3. Mention supplementary pollination in sunflower crop.

4. What are the techniques followed to achieve uniformity?
5. Mention any two physical contaminant rogues.
6. 2% DAP improves seed quality, justify.
7. Mention any two post emergence herbicides.
8. Mention any two pre emergence herbicides used in seed crop.
9. NAA spraying arrest flower drop justify.
10. What is the role of GA_3?

ANSWER KEYS

I. FILL UPS

1. Isolation
2. Off-types
3. Roguing
4. Isolation distance
5. 50 m
6. 3 m
7. Pearl millet
8. Potassium
9. Molybdenum
10. Potassium
11. Molybdenum
12. NAA
13. 2 % DAP
14. Planting ratio
15. GA_3

II. TRUE OR FALSE

1.	True	6.	True
2.	False	7.	True
3.	True	8.	False
4.	False	9.	True
5.	False	10.	False

III. MATCH THE FOLLOWING

(i)		(ii)		(iii)	
1.	D	1.	E	1.	C
2.	E	2.	D	2.	D
3.	A	3.	A	3.	E
4.	C	4.	C	4.	A
5.	B	5.	B	5.	B

IV. ONE WORD ANSWER

1. Presence of B line in A line rows in hybrid seed production field.
2. Rope pulling or rod driving
3. Rubbing or installation of bee hives

4. i. Staggered sowing
   ii. Withholding irrigation
   iii. Application of urea or DAP
5. i. Volunteer plants
   ii. Weeds/noxious weeds
6. In cotton, 2 % DAP spray at boll formation stage improves seed quality. In pulses, 2 % DAP spray at flowering stage produces bold seeds.
7. Glyphosate
   2, 4-D
8. Atrazine
   Butachlor
9. In tomato and chilli, 2 sprays of NAA @ 40 ppm at flowering will arrest the flower drop.
10. Spraying of GA_3 @ 70-75 g twice aids in complete panicle exertion in hybrid rice seed production, since, GA_3 is acts as elongation factor.

V. AT A GLANCE

1. Environmental induced disease symptoms

Disease symptom	Crop
Blonded seed	Peas
Dimpled seed	Peas, French bean, cluster bean
Off-coloured seed	Pulses

2. Nutrient deficiency symptoms

Nutrients	Deficiency	Crop
Potassium	Blossom end rot	Tomato
Calcium	Blotching	Tomato
Boron	Black rot	Cabbage and cauliflower
Molybdenum	Whip tail	Crucifers
Manganese	Marsh spot	Peas
Boron	Hollow heart	Garden pea
Boron	Darkened or blackened plumule	Groundnut

3. The physical contaminant rogues are

- Weeds / noxious weeds
- Objectionable weed plants
- Volunteer plants
- Designated diseased plants
- Other crop plants

4. Synchronized flowering

Uniformity of flowering between parental lines. To achieve uniformity, any one of techniques can be done :

1. Staggered sowing
2. Withholding irrigation
3. Application of urea or DAP

Staggered sowing: Adjusting the sowing time of parental lines in order to have synchronized flowering between parental line for proper seed set. The early flowering line should be sown later. *E.g.* Sunflower KBSH-1 hybrid seed production, the male parent is late flowered by 6 days than the female. So, sowing of male line 6-D-1, 6 days earlier than female line ensures synchronized flowering.

In the case of rice, exertion of panicle from boot leaf in female parent is a problem. To have complete exertion, spray GA_3 @ 70-75 g/ha twice during flowering time. Since, GA is cell elongation factor, it aids in exertion of panicle.

5. Special techniques for hybrid seed production

Detasseling: Removal of tassel from the female row in maize.

Emasculation and dusting: These techniques are to be done at proper time of flowering to have good yield and also to avoid contamination in cotton.

Supplementary pollination: It is followed in rice and sunflower to have good seed set.

Rice: Rope pulling or rod driving.

Sunflower: Rubbing or installation of bee hives.

6. Genetic contaminants

1. *Off types:* Deviant of seed plant. Common for varieties and hybrids
2. *Pollen shedders:* Presence of B line in A line in the case of hybrid seed production field.
3. *Shedding tassel:* Presence of tassel in the female row of maize hybrid seed production plot.
4. *Selfed bolls:* In the case of cotton hybrid seed production plot, selfed bolls without emasculation and dusting.
5. *Selfed fruits:* In the case of other vegetables.

12

Nutritional Disorders

I. FILL UPS

1. _____ is the necessary component for vitamins.
2. _____ is vital for seed formation.
3. _____ is essential for protein synthesis.
4. _____ is essential for nut development in peanuts.
5. _____ is the key element for chlorophyll production.
6. _____ is the integral part of amino acids.
7. _____ is essential for seed and cell wall formation.
8. _____ catalyzes several plant processes.
9. _____ acts as an oxygen carrier.
10. _____ increases the availability of P and CA.
11. _____ aids in the formation of legume nodules.
12. Die back symptom is caused by _____ deficiency.
13. Marginal chloroms or chlorotic blotches is caused by _____ deficiency.
14. Older leaves turn yellow is the symptom caused by _____ deficiency.
15. Mottling in the interveinal areas is caused by _____.

II. TRUE OR FALSE

1. Leaves become narrow and disorted due to molybdenum deficiency.
2. Split or cracked rough stem is deficiency symptom of zinc.
3. Internodes are shortened due to boron deficiency.
4. Chlorotic areas and upward curling of leaves are the deficiency symptoms of Mg.
5. Leaf margins become scorched and cup downward is caused due to potassium deficiency.

MATCH THE FOLLOWING

(i)

1.	Manganese	A	Shortened internodes
2.	Zinc	B	Chlorotic veins
3.	Iron	C	Mottling
4.	Boron	D	Marginal chlorosis
5.	Magnesium	E	Split or cracked stem

(ii)

1.	Nitrogen	A	Leaf margins scorched
2.	Phosphorus	B	Red-purple leaves
3.	Potassium	C	General chlorosis
4.	Calcium	D	Wilting and chlorosis
5.	Copper	E	Die back

(iii)

1.	Molybdenum	A	Chlorophyll synthesis
2.	Manganese	B	Legume nodule formation
3.	Iron	C	Catalyst
4.	Copper	D	Germination of pollen grain
5.	Boron	E	Oxygen carrier

IV. ONE WORD QUESTION

1. Mention the macronutrient which activates enzymes.
2. What is the important role of phosphorus?
3. What nutrient is directly related to grass tetany role of calcium?
4. What is the major function of sulphur?
5. Which nutrient is necessary for peanut seed formation?

ANSWER KEYS

FILL UPS

1. Nitrogen	2. Phosphorus	3. Potassium
4. Calcium	5. Magnesium	6. Sulphur
7. Boron	8. Copper	9. Iron
10. Manganese	11. Molybdenum	12. Calcium
13. Magnesium	14. Molybdenum	15. Manganese

II. TRUE OR FALSE

1.	True	2.	False
3.	False	4.	True
5.	True		

III. MATCH THE FOLLOWING

(i)		(ii)		(iii)	
1.	C	1.	C	1.	B
2.	A	2.	B	2.	A
3.	B	3.	A	3.	E
4.	E	4.	E	4.	C
5.	D	5.	D	5.	D

IV. ONE WORD ANSWER

1. Potassium
2. Vital for seed formation
3. Magnesium
4. Integral part of amino acid
5. Calcium

13

Method of Seed Production in Vegetables

I. FILL UPS

1. The beheaded portion of cabbage is called _____.
2. _____ method is followed for cauliflower seed production in India.
3. In carrot, _____ method is followed among seed companies for large commercial seed production.
4. Knob to seed method is followed in _____.
5. Bulb to seed method is followed in _____.

II. TRUE OR FALSE

1. In radish, root to seed method is commonly followed in India.
2. Bulb to seed production in onion can only be done in a location where the winter temperature do not drop below 15-20°F.
3. In bulb to seed method, seed yield obtained are more as compared to seed to seed method.
4. Seed to seed method is the most economical method.
5. Seed to seed method is the suitable for breeder and foundation seed production.

III. MATCH THE FOLLOWING

1.	Bulb to seed method	A Cauliflower
2.	Stump method	B Onion
3.	Root to seed method	C Knol khol
4.	Knob to seed method	D Cabbage
5.	Head to seed method	E Radish

IV. ONE WORD QUESTION

1. Mention the 3 methods of seed production in onion.
2. Mention the methods of seed production in cabbage.

3. Methods of seed production in cauliflower.
4. Methods of seed production in knol-khol.
5. Methods of seed production in carrot.

ANSWER KEYS

I. FILL UPS

1. Stump
2. Seed to seed
3. Seed to seed
4. Knol-khol
5. Onion

II. TRUE OR FALSE

1. True 2. False
3. False 4. True
5. False

III. MATCH THE FOLLOWING

1. B
2. D
3. E
4. C
5. A

IV. ONE WORD ANSWER

1. i) Seed to seed method
   ii) Bulb to seed method
   iii) Spring replanted bulb to seed method
2. i) Stump method
   ii) Stump with central core intact
   iii) Head intact
3. i) Seed to seed method
   ii) Head intact method
4. i) Seed to seed method
   ii) Knob to seed method
5. i) Seed to seed method
   ii) Root to seed method

V. AT A GLANCE

1. Seed production methods in vegetables

S.No.	Method	Examples
1.	Seed to seed	Tomato, brinjal, chilli, okra, cucurbits, garden peas, onion, cauliflower, knol khol, radish, carrot, turnip, beet root
2.	Bulb to seed	Onion
3.	Head to seed method	Cabbage, cauliflower
4.	Stump method / Head intact method	Cabbage
5.	Stump with central core intact method	Cabbage
6.	Root to seed method	Turnip, carrot, beet root, radish
7.	Knob to seed method	Knol khol

14

Rice Seed Production

I. FILL UPS

1. The inflorescence of rice is _____.
2. The rice flower is called _____.
3. The stigma receptivity of rice crop is_____ period.
4. The pollen viability of rice is for _____.
5. The grain stem of rice is called_____.
6. Rice is _____ pollinated crop.
7. Seed rate for short duration variety is _____.
8. Seed rate for long duration variety is _____.
9. Rice seeds are soaked in _____ to break dormancy.
10. _____ disease is common in nursery for rice.
11. The most common pest in nursery is _____.
12. The objectionable weed found in rice is _____.
13. The optimum seed moisture content of rice during storage is _____.
14. The isolation distance of rice is _____.
15. Recommended planting ratio for rice hybrid seed production is _____.
16. _____ has a defined role in exertion of the panicle.
17. The seed yield of normal rice hybrid is _____.
18. Pericarp consists of 3 fibrous layers of _____, _____ and _____.
19. Pericarp is modified and restricted into small fleshy portion is called _____.
20. The number of stamens present in rice is _____.

II. TRUE OR FALSE

1. Flag leaf cutting is one of the supplementary pollination technique followed in hybrid rice.

2. Three line method (or) CGMS system is used for rice hybrid seed production.
3. The seed moisture content during threshing should be less than 13%.
4. The recommended spacing for short duration variety is 20 cm x 20 cm.
5. The recommended age of seedlings for transplantation in medium duration variety is 13-22 days.
6. India is the second largest country in rice cultivation area and production.
7. Seed yield of rice will be affected if the temperature is below 20°C and above 35°C.
8. Harvesting should be done 28 days after anthesis in short duration varieties.
9. To adjust the flowering date, the late parent should be sprayed with quick releasing nitrogen spray like urea.
10. The seed rate of A line for hybrid seed production is 10 kg/ha.

III. MATCH THE FOLLOWING

1.	2% DAP	A	Upgradation technique
2.	2% Urea	B	Supplementary pollination
3.	GA_3	C	For delaying flowering
4.	Flag leaf cutting	D	For quick flowering
5.	Egg floatation technique	E	Panicle exertion

IV. ONE WORD QUESTION

1. What is the upgradation technique used for rice?
2. Mention the seed treatment technique to break dormancy during dry storage?
3. What is the mid-storage treatment followed in rice?
4. How is the flowering date adjusted in rice crop?
5. Mention any two advantages of GA_3 application.
6. Mention the supplementary pollination techniques followed in hybrid seed production of rice?
7. How harvesting is done in rice hybrid seed production plot?
8. What is the isolation distance for varietal and hybrid seed production in rice?
9. What is the seed storage treatment followed in rice to prevent insect attack?
10. Mention any two barrier isolation for rice seed production?

ANSWER KEYS

I. FILL UPS

1. Panicle
2. Spikelet
3. 3 days
4. 10 minutes
5. Rachilla
6. Self
7. 60 kg/ha
8. 30 kg/ha
9. 0.5 % KNO_3
10. Blast
11. Thrips
12. *Oryza sativa* var. *fatua*
13. 10-12%
14. 3 m
15. 8:2
16. GA_3
17. 100 kg/ha
18. Protein, cellulose & hemicellulose
19. Lodicules
20. 6

II. TRUE OR FALSE

1. True
2. True
3. False
4. False
5. False
6. True
7. True
8. True
9. False
10. False

III. MATCH THE FOLLOWING

1. D
2. C
3. E
4. B
5. A

IV. ONE WORD QUESTION

1. Egg floatation technique.
2. Seeds are soaked in KNO_3 @ 0.5% for 16 hours.
3. Alternate wetting and drying method using disodium hydrogen phosphate @ 3.6g/100 ml of water.
4. Late flowering parent should be sprayed with 2 % DAP and early flowering parent should be sprayed with quick releasing nitrogen fertilizer.
5. i) Enhances panicle & stigma exertion.

   ii) Flag leaf angle is increased.

6. i) Rope pulling.
   ii) Rod driving.
   iii) Flag leaf cutting.
7. Male parent is harvested first.
8. 3 m and 100 m.
9. Celphos (Aluminium phosphide) tablets can be used at tablet/m^3.
10. Hills, woodlot or vegetative barrier like maize, sesbania.

15

Wheat Seed Production

I. FILL UPS

1. Green revolution in wheat was started by _____ in Mexico.
2. Wheat revolution in India was started by_____.
3. Isolation distance for wheat seed production is _____.
4. Seed rate for wheat seed production is _____.
5. Wheat is a _____ pollinated crop
6. Seed multiplication ratio for wheat is ranged from _____.
7. Spacing adopted in wheat seed production plot is _____.
8. Average seed yield in wheat is _____.
9. _____ is the critical moisture content for wheat seed storage
10. The minimum pure seed percentage for wheat foundation seed is_____.

II. TRUE OR FALSE

1. India is the first largest producer of wheat in the world for last 10 years.
2. Wheat inflorescence borne singly at the nodes on alternate sides of zigzag rachis.
3. Pollen viability of wheat is five hours.
4. Critical moisture content for wheat seed storage is 45%.
5. Wheat seed reaches physiological maturity between 10-12%.

III. MATCH THE FOLLOWING

1.	Norin 10	A	Mexico
2.	Triticale	B	Dwarfing gene
3.	Long duration variety	C	M.S.Swaminathan
4.	Norman Borlaug	D	Manmade cereal
5.	Wheat revolution in India	E	C306

IV. ONE WORD QUESTION

1. What is the best period of rogueing in wheat crop?
2. What is the manmade cereal?
3. From which variety dwarf wheat was developed?

ANSWER KEYS

I. FILL UPS

1. Norman Borlaug 2. Dr. M.S. Swaminathan 3. 3 m
4. 85-100 kg/ha 5. Self 6. 45-160
7. 20-22.5 cm 8. 3-4 tonnes/ha 9. 12 %
10. 98 %

II. TRUE OR FALSE

1. False 2. True
3. True 4. False
5. False

III. MATCH THE FOLLOWING

1. B
2. D
3. E
4. A
5. C

IV. ONE WORD ANSWER

1. Heading stage and maturity stage.
2. Rye crossed with wheat and resulted in offspring known as Triticale otherwise known as manmade cereal.
3. Norin 10.

16

Maize Seed Production

I. FILL UPS

1. _____ crop is known as the Queen of cereals.
2. Maize is a _____ pollinated crop.
3. Male inflorescence of maize is known as_____.
4. Female inflorescence of maize is known as_____.
5. Pollen viability in maize crop is_____.
6. Silk receptivity in maize crop is _____.
7. Isolation distance for maize certified seed production is_____.
8. Spacing adopted for maize seed production is _____.
9. Moisture content of cob during harvesting should be around_____.
10. The effect of foreign pollen on endosperm character is called _____.
11. The effect of foreign pollen on stomatic lying outside the endosperm is known as _____.
12. The seed yield of maize hybrid seed production is _____.
13. An example for three way cross hybrid is _____.
14. Isolation distance requirement for maize hybrid seed production for foundation stage is _____.
15. Planting ratio for maize single cross hybrid seed production is _____.

II. TRUE OR FALSE

1. Maize is a monoecious crop.
2. Tassel is produced in the lateral branch of one of the longest foliage.
3. Moisture content for cobs during shelling should be 15%.
4. The minimum germination percentage for maize seed crop is 80%.
5. In maize hybrid seed production, female lines should be harvested first and then male lines.

III. MATCH THE FOLLOWING

1.	Ganga 2	A Endosperm character
2.	Ganga 5	B Stomatic lying
3.	Xenia	C Queen of cereals
4.	Metaxenia	D Double cross
5.	Maize	E Three way cross

IV. ONE WORD QUESTION

1. How many border rows should be present for maize hybrid seed production?
2. Isolation distance for maize hybrid seed production of foundation and certified seeds.
3. What is the seed treatment given for maize during storage?
4. Mention the types of maize.
5. Mention the types of hybrids in maize with example.

ANSWER KEYS

I. FILL UPS

1. Maize	2. Cross	3. Tassel
4. Cob	5. 12-18 h	6. 8 to 10 days
7. 200 m	8. 60 x 20 cm	9. 25 %
10. Xenia	11. Metaxenia	12. 2500 kg/ha
13. Ganga 5	14. 400 m	15. 4:2

II. TRUE OR FALSE

1. True	2. False
3. False	4. True
5. False	

III. MATCH THE FOLLOWING

1. D
2. E
3. A
4. B
5. C

IV. ONE WORD ANSWER

1. 4
2. a) FS: 400 m
   b) CS: 200 m
3. Halogen mixture @ 3 g / kg
4. Flint, dent, floury, pop and sweet corns
5. Single cross hybrid : COH(M)1; Double cross hybrid: Gang 2; Three way cross hybrid: Ganga 5.

17

Sorghum Seed Production

I. FILL UPS

1. The inflorescence of sorghum is _____.
2. The pollen viability in sorghum is_____.
3. Spacing adopted in sorghum seed production is _____.
4. Seed rate recommended for sorghum seed production is_____.
5. Seed yield of sorghum is _____.
6. The moisture content of sorghum seed should be _____ during storage.
7. Isolation distance for hybrid sorghum seed production is_____.
8. Sorghum is a_____ pollinated crop.
9. _____ crop is used as a feedstock for production of ethanol.
10. _____ hybridization technique is followed for sorghum.

II. TRUE OR FALSE

1. Maximum germination percentage for sorghum is 75%.
2. For sorghum seed production, the moisture content of seeds should be 10-12% during harvesting.
3. In sorghum, sterility occurs when night temperature is above 12-15°C during flowering period.
4. Sessile spikelet in a sorghum seed is smaller than staminate spikelet.
5. Sorghum is the fifth most important cereal crop grown in the world.

III. ONE WORD QUESTION

1. What is the seed treatment given to sorghum before storage?
2. What are the methods followed to achieve synchronization of flowering?
3. What is the pre-sowing treatment done in sorghum?

ANSWER KEY

I. FILL UPS

1. Panicle
2. 10-20 min
3. 45x15 cm
4. 7.5-10 kg/ha
5. 2000 kg/ha
6. 12 %
7. 200 m
8. Self
9. Sorghum
10. CMS

II. TRUE OR FALSE

1. True
2. False
3. False
4. False
5. True

III. ONE WORD ANSWER

1. Seeds are treated with bavistin @ 2-4 g / kg of seeds.
2. Advance parent - 500 mg of maleic hydrazide in 1litre of water.
   Late parent - 1 % urea solution.
3. Seed hardening in 2 % potassium dihydrogen phosphate for 10 h.

18

Pearl Millet Seed Production

I. FILL UPS

1. Pearl millet is a_____ pollinated crop.
2. An example for protogyny is______.
3. The isolation distance for foundation seed production of pearl millet is ______.
4. The spacing adopted for pearl millet is ______.
5. Seed yield of pearl millet is______.
6. The moisture content of pearl millet seed during storage should be______.
7. The planting ratio for pearl millet hybrid seed production is ______.
8. Presence of fertile counter part of female plants in the female rows is called ______.
9. In some female plants, fertile anthers may be hanging out only from a portion of the panicle. Such plants are called ______.
10. ______ technique is used for hybrid seed production of pearl millet.

II. TRUE OR FALSE

1. Pearl millet is an example for protoandry.
2. Two line breeding is followed in pearl millet.
3. The development of a small dark layer at the bottom of the seed is the index for physiological maturity of pearl millet.
4. During threshing of pearl millet, the moisture content should be around 25 to 35%.
5. The temperature favourable for seed setting is 37°C.

III. ONE WORD QUESTION

1. What is the seed rate of pearl millet for A & R line during hybrid seed production?
2. What is the mid-storage seed treatment done for pearl millet?

3. What is the temperature favourable for seed setting in pearl millet?
4. What is the isolation distance for pearl millet foundation and certified seed?
5. What are the critical stages of irrigation for pearl millet seed production?

ANSWER KEY

I. FILL UPS

1. Cross
2. Pearl millet
3. 400 m
4. 45x20 cm
5. 3500-4000 kg / ha
6. 12 %
7. 6:1
8. Pollen shedders
9. Partials
10. CMS

II. TRUE OR FALSE

1. False
2. False
3. True
4. False
5. True

III. ONE WORD ANSWER

1. A- 3.5 kg, R line: 0.75 kg / ha.
2. Seeds are treated with disodium phosphate (36 g / lit. of water) solution at 1:2 ratio for 6 h.
3. 37ºC.
4. FS: 400 m, CS: 200 m.
5. Panicle initiation, flowering and maturation.

19

Redgram Seed Production

I. FILL UPS

1. Redgram is commonly is known as _____.
2. _____ is the second most important pulse crop after chick pea.
3. Redgram, being a _____ capable of fixing atmospheric nitrogen.
4. Pigeon pea contains_____% protein.
5. Isolation distance of redgram must be_____.
6. The spacing adopted for short duration red gram is_____.
7. The moisture content for redgram seed during storage should be _____.
8. The minimum isolation distance for hybrid seed production of redgram should be _____.
9. Planting ratio for redgram hybrid seed production should be _____.
10. _____technique is used for hybrid seed production of redgram.

II. TRUE OR FALSE

1. Yellow anther plants in the female rows are removed during hybrid seed production of redgram.
2. The border rows of redgram should be of male parent to give more pollen during hybrid seed production.
3. The female parent is to be sown one week after sowing of male parent.
4. The variety in redgram is identified based on the back of standard petal colour.
5. In GMS technique followed in redgram, 50% of sterile pollens should be removed and remaining 50% is allowed to grow.

III. ONE WORD QUESTION

1. What is the seed treatment done in red gram before storage?
2. What is the presowing treatment done in red gram for seed production?

ANSWER KEYS

I. FILL UPS

1. Arhar
2. Redgram
3. Legume crop
4. 22
5. 100 m
6. 45x30 cm
7. 10 %
8. 200 m
9. 4:2
10. Genetic male sterility

II. TRUE OR FALSE

1. True
2. True
3. False
4. True
5. False

III. ONE WORD ANSWER

1. Bavistin @ 2 g / kg of seeds.
2. Seeds possessing hard seeds are treated with commercial sulphuric acid @ 100 ml / kg of seeds.

20

Blackgram Seed Production

I. FILL UPS

1. Blackgram is commonly known as _____.
2. Adopted spacing for blackgram is _____.
3. Seed rate for blackgram is _____.
4. Moisture content must be reduced to _____ for short term storage of blackgram seeds
5. Isolation distance for blackgram seed crop is _____.

II. TRUE OR FALSE

1. For long term storage of blackgram seeds, the moisture content must be reduced to 9%.
2. Flowers of blackgram is determinate.
3. India is the primary origin of blackgram.
4. The offtypes permitted for blackgram is 0.2% for certified seeds.

III. ONE WORD QUESTION

1. What is the pre sowing treatment given to blackgram?
2. What is the seed treatment followed in blackgram during storage?

ANSWER KEYS

I. FILL UPS

1. Urad 2. 30x10 cm 3. 20-25 kg / ha
4. 9 % 5. 5 m

II. TRUE OR FALSE

1. False 2. False
3. True 4. True

III. ONE WORD ANSWER

1. Seeds are soaked in succinic acid, ascorbic acid @ 8 g/ 4 lit. of water for 1 acre.
2. Bavistin @ 4 g / kg of seeds.

21

Greengram Seed Production

I. FILL UPS

1. The isolation distance for seed crop of greengram must be _____.
2. Spacing adopted for greengram seed production is _____.
3. Seed rate of greengram is_____.

II. TRUE OR FALSE

1. Greengram seeds are free from heaviness and tendency to flatulence
2. The occurrence of offtypes in greengram seed production is permitted upto 0.5% for CS.

III. ONE WORD QUESTION

1. What is the seed treatment adopted for greengram during storage?

ANSWER KEYS

I. FILL UPS

1. 5 m   2. 30x10 cm   3. 8-10 kg / acre

II. TRUE OR FALSE

1. True
2. False

III. ONE WORD ANSWER

1. Activated clay is used to treat the seeds @ 100 g / kg of seeds.

22

Cowpea Seed Production

I. FILL UPS

1. Cowpea is a _____ crop.
2. Isolation distance for cowpea foundation seed production is _____.
3. Spacing adopted for cowpea is _____.
4. Seed rate for cowpea seed production is _____.
5. The maximum permitted limit of offtypes for CS is _____.

II. TRUE OR FALSE

1. Germination of cowpea is rapid at temperature above 65°F.
2. Cowpea is not affected by soil crusting under certain soil and environmental conditions.
3. Tendril growth reduces seed yield in cowpea.

III. ONE WORD QUESTION

1. Why is the tendril clipping done in cowpea?
2. What is the presowing seed treatment done for seed storage?
3. What is the seed treatment done for storage of cowpea?

ANSWER KEYS

I. FILL UPS

1. Self pollinated 2. 10 m 3. 45x20 cm
4. 20-25 kg / ha 5. 0.2 %

II. TRUE OR FALSE

1. True 2. False
3. True

III. ONE WORD ANSWER

1. Tendril growth generally delays flowering, thus leading to reduced seed yield and to avoid this, the tendrils are removed.
2. Seed possessing hard seeds are treated with commercial sulphuric acid.
3. Seeds are treated with vegetable oil / neem oil @ 3 ml / kg of seeds.

23

Field Lablab Seed Production

I. FILL UPS

1. Lab lab is a _____ crop.
2. Spacing adopted for lablab seed production is _____.
3. The isolation distance for lab lab crop is _____.
4. The offtypes permitted for CS in lab lab crop is _____.
5. Seed rate for field lab lab is _____.

II. ONE WORD QUESTION

1. What is the seed treatment given for lab lab during storage?
2. What is the presowing treatment followed in lab lab?

ANSWER KEYS

I. FILL UPS

1. Self pollinated
2. 45x15 cm
3. 5 m
4. 0.2 %
5. 20-25 kg / ha

II. ONE WORD ANSWER

1. Lablab seeds are treated with bavistin @ 4 g / kg of seeds.
2. Seeds are treated with bavistin @ 2 g / kg of seeds.

24

Soybean Seed Production

I. FILL UPS

1. Soybean is also known as_____.
2. _____ is the largest oil seed crop in the world.
3. Soybean is a_____ crop.
4. The isolation distance for soybean is _____.
5. Spacing adopted for soybean is _____.
6. Seed rate for soybean is _____.
7. _____ extracted from soybean oil used as emulsifier and lubricant.

II. TRUE OR FALSE

1. The processed soybean is the largest source of protein feed.
2. Soybean is the first largest source of vegetable oil in the world.
3. The maximum permitted limit of offtypes is 0.10% for CS.
4. In soybean, long term low temperature treatment before the flowering stage reduces pod set.
5. If the soybean seeds are to be stored for longer period, thick polythene bags can be used.

III. ONE WORD QUESTION

1. What is the pre-sowing treatment adopted for soybean crop?

ANSWER KEYS

I. FILL UPS

1. Golden bean	2. Soybean	3. Self pollinated
4. 3 m	5. 30x10 cm	6. 40 kg / ha
7. Lecithin		

II. TRUE OR FALSE

1. True 2. False
3. False 4. True
5. True

III. ONE WORD ANSWER

1. Seeds are treated with carbendazim @ 4 g / kg of seeds.

25

Cotton Seed Production

I. FILL UPS

1. _____ is called as 'king of fibres' and 'white gold'.
2. _____in the cotton meal is toxic to monogastric animals.
3. A purple spot is found in the claw of the petals is called _____
4. The isolation distance adopted for cotton is _____ for foundation seed.
5. Spacing adopted for cotton is _____.
6. The off types permitted for cotton certified seed production is_____.
7. The minimum isolation distance for certified seed class of cotton is _____.
8. The method of emasculation done in cotton is_____.
9. The minimum temperature requirement for cotton seed germination is _____.
10. _____ and _____ represent the outgrowth of epidermal cells on the seeds.
11. Cotton is _____ pollinated crop.
12. Seed rate of fuzzy seeds is _____.
13. Planting ratio adopted for cotton hybrid seed production is_____.
14. Seed rate recommended for female rows in cotton hybrid seed production is_____.
15. Seed rate recommended for male rows in cotton hybrid seed production is_____.

II. TRUE OR FALSE

1. Ginning should be done only that cotton with moisture content of 6 to 8.5%
2. Pinching of terminal bud arrests the horizontal growth of the plant.
3. The lint hair is multicellular.

4. Cotton is the natural vegetable fibre of great economic importance.
5. Vegetative branches in the cotton crop is called sympodial branches.

III. MATCH THE FOLLOWING

1.	Sympodial branch	A Cotton
2.	Monopodial branch	B Toxic
3.	White gold	C 4.5 to 5.5 kg
4	Gossypol	D Vegetative
5.	Ginning	E Reproductive

IV. ONE WORD QUESTION

1. What are the foliar sprays given to cotton?
2. What is the technique followed to arrest terminal growth?
3. What is the rate of ginning?
4. What is the mid-storage treatment followed in cotton?
5. What is kapas sorting?

ANSWER KEYS

I. FILL UPS

1. Cotton	2. Gossypol	3. Petal spot
4. 50 m	5. 75x30 cm	6. 0.20 %
7. 30 m	8. Doak's method	9. 16ºC
10. Lint and fuzz	11. Often cross	12. 15-20 kg / ha
13. 8:2	14. 3.0 - 3.5 kg / ha	15. 8-10 kg / ha

II. TRUE OR FALSE

1. True	2. False
3. False	4. True
5. False	

III. MATCH THE FOLLOWING

1. E
2. D
3. A
4. B
5. C

IV. ONE WORD ANSWER

1. 1% DAP at 70, 80 and 90 DAS for more seed recovery.
2. Pinching of terminal bud.
3. 4.5 to 5.5 kg
4. Seed soaking in double the volume of disodium phosphate for 2 h in case of fuzzy seeds and 1 h for delinted seeds.
5. Stained, discolored, hard locks, unopened, pest and disease infected kapas removal is called kapas sorting.

26

Jute Seed Production

I. FILL UPS

1. The isolation distance is _____ for foundation seed production of jute.
2. The maximum permitted limit of off types for foundation seed is _____.
3. The water requirement of jute crop is _____.
4. Seed rate recommended for olitorius type of jute is _____.
5. Seed rate recommended for capsularis type of jute is _____.

II. TRUE OR FALSE

1. The fruit of jute is a cylindrical capsule ribbed with a short beak.
2. The isolation distance for certified seed production of jute is 50 m.
3. The number of stamens present in the jute inflorescence is 5.
4. The woody central core of the jute crop after removal of bast can be processed into paper, board and cellulose.

III. ONE WORD QUESTION

1. What is the seed treatment followed for jute seed production?
2. How many field inspections are done in jute and when?

ANSWER KEYS

I. FILL UPS

1. 50 m 2. 0.50 % 3. 500 mm
4. 5 kg / ha 5. 7 kg / ha

II. TRUE OR FALSE

1. True 2. False
3. False 4. True

III. ONE WORD ANSWER

1. Hot water soaking and bavistin @ 4 g / kg of seed.
2. 3 inspections.
   i) Prior to flowering
   ii) Bud stage to peak flowering
   iii) Prior to harvesting

27

Groundnut Seed Production

I. FILL UPS

1. Groundnut contains _____ oil.
2. Groundnut contains _____ protein.
3. Groundnut is a _____ crop.
4. Stigma receptivity is for _____ after anthesis.
5. Fertilization occurs about _____ after pollination.
6. Hypogea means _____.
7. A peg is otherwise known as _____.
8. Isolation distance adopted for groundnut is _____.
9. Seed rate recommended for bunchy type of groundnut is _____.
10. The pod moisture at harvest will be around _____.
11. Earthing up is to be done during _____ days after sowing.
12. A stalk like structure becomes visible within 4-6 days after fertilization is called _____.
13. The maximum permitted offtypes in foundation seed production of groundnut is _____.
14. Earthing up after sowing facilitates _____.
15. The seed coat of groundnut will be _____.

II. TRUE OR FALSE

1. Earthing up helps for the penetration of pegs.
2. In fastigata, inflorescence are compound.
3. Groundnut pod is dehiscent in nature.
4. For easy harvesting, the field can be irrigated.

III. MATCH THE FOLLOWING

1.	Vulgaris	A	Simple inflorescence
2.	Fastigata	B	Compound inflorescence
3.	Carpophore	C	Gypsum application
4.	Earthing up	D	Peg

IV. ONE WORD QUESTION

1. What is the purpose of doing earthing up operation in groundnut field?
2. What is the maturity indice of groundnut seed crop?

ANSWER KEYS

I. FILL UPS

1. 48-50 %	2. 26-28 %	3. Self pollinated
4. 12 hours	5. 6 hours	6. Under the earth
7. Carpophores	8. 3 m	9. 100-130 kg / ha
10. 35-40%	11. 40-45	12. Peg
13. 0.10 %	14. Increased pod development	15. Papery

II. TRUE OR FALSE

1. True	2. False
3. False	4. True

III. MATCH THE FOLLOWING

1. B
2. A
3. D
4. C

IV. ONE WORD ANSWER

1. Earthing up is to be done within 40-45 days after sowing as it helps for penetration of pegs in the soil and also facilitates for increased pod development.
2. Rattling sound.

28

Sunflower Seed Production

I. FILL UPS

1. _____ is the fastest growing oilseed crop in India.
2. The inflorescence of sunflower is _____.
3. The tiny flowers (or) florets are attached on a platform called _____.
4. Sunflowers in bud stage exhibit _____.
5. _____ is a tuft of hairs on the fruit.
6. Composite flower consisting only of disc florets are called _____.
7. Stigma receptivity of sunflower for certified seed production is _____.
8. Sunflower is a highly _____ plant.
9. Fruit of sunflower is called _____.
10. Isolation distance for sunflower certified seed production is _____.
11. Seed rate for sunflower is _____.
12. The technique followed for hybrid seed production of sunflower is _____.
13. Isolation distance adopted for hybrid sunflower seed production is _____.
14. Planting ratio of sunflower is _____.
15. Disc flowers are _____ in nature.

II. TRUE OR FALSE

1. The sunflower oil contains low level of linoleic acid.
2. Sunflower is a self pollinated crop.
3. The moisture content of sunflower seed at physiological maturity stage is 35%.
4. Ray florets are actinomorphic in nature.
5. Disc florets are zygomorphic in nature.

III. MATCH THE FOLLOWING

1.	Ray florets	A Actinomorphic
2.	Disc florets	B Heliotrophism
3.	Agni	C Face to face rubbing
4.	Sunflower	D Zygomorphic
5.	Supplementary pollination	E Bird damage

IV. ONE WORD QUESTION

1. What is the supplementary pollination technique followed in sunflower for seed production?
2. What is the maturity indice of sunflower?

ANSWER KEYS

I. FILL UPS

1. Sunflower	2. Capitulum	3. Receptacle
4. Heliotrophism	5. Pappus	6. Discoid
7. 3-5 days	8. Cross pollinated	9. Achene
10. 200 m	11. 15 kg / ha	12. CMS
13. 600 m	14. 3:1	15. Protoandrous

II. TRUE OR FALSE

1. False	2. False
3. True	4. False
5. False	

III. MATCH THE FOLLOWING

1. D
2. A
3. E
4. B
5. C

IV. ONE WORD ANSWER

1. Face to face rubbing, rubbing palm covered with muslin cloth on male capitulum and then female capitulum.
2. The back of the head has turned from green to yellow and bracts are turning brown.

29

Gingelly Seed Production

I. FILL UPS

1. _____ seed is one of the oldest condiments the human race has ever known.
2. Sesame seed contains _____ oil and _____ protein.
3. Sesame oil contains about _____ % oleic acid.
4. Isolation distance for gingelly certified seed production is _____.
5. Seed rate of gingelly adopted for seed production is _____.
6. The seed moisture content during harvesting of sesame will be_____.
7. Isolation distance for gingelly foundation seed production is _____.
8. Gingelly is an _____ pollinated crop.
9. The maximum limit of offtype to be present in foundation seed plot is _____.
10. The germination percentage of gingelly is _____.

II. TRUE OR FALSE

1. Sesame seeds contain 39% oleic acid.
2. Sesame seed contains calcium, potassium, phosphorus, vitamin B and iron.
3. Temperature of 40°C seriously affect pollination.
4. Sesame is a long day plant.
5. Ideal optimum temperature for growth of sesame is 10°C.

III. ONE WORD QUESTION

1. What is the seed treatment done in gingelly during storage?
2. What is the isolation distance adopted for gingelly?

ANSWER KEYS

I. FILL UPS

1. Sesame
2. 50 % & 25 %
3. 47 %
4. 50 m
5. 2-4 kg / ha
6. 25-30 %
7. 100 m
8. Often cross
9. 0.1 %
10. 80 %

II. TRUE OR FALSE

1. False
2. True
3. True
4. False
5. False

III. ONE WORD ANSWER

1. Seeds are treated with bavistin @ 2 g / kg of seeds and stored in gada cloth.
2. FS:100 m, CS: 50 m.

30

Castor Seed Production

I. FILL UPS

1. Castor seeds contain _____ % oil.
2. The castor is rich in which triglycerides _____.
3. _____is a toxin present in castor seed.
4. Castor is a _____ crop.
5. Castor flower is _____ in nature.
6. The fruit has spinous outgrowths which is called _____.
7. The isolation distance for castor foundation seed is_____.
8. The isolation distance for castor certified seed is _____.
9. Seed rate of castor is _____.
10. Planting ratio for castor hybrid seed production is _____.

II. TRUE OR FALSE

1. At temperature less than 32°C, the plant tends to be male.
2. Castor seeds contain fleshy structures which is called as caruncle.
3. Castor is a dioecious crop.
4. Male flowers are seen on the apex and female flowers are seen below.
5. India is the worlds largest producer of castor seed.

III. MATCH THE FOLLOWING

1.	Ricinolein	A	Cross pollinated
2.	Ricin	B	Triglycerides
3.	Regma	C	Toxic
4.	Castor	D	Fleshy structures
5.	Caruncle	E	Spinous outgrowth

IV. ONE WORD QUESTION

1. What is the sex expression in the castor?
2. What is the arrangement of male and female flowers in castor?

ANSWER KEYS

I. FILL UPS

1. 40 to 60
2. Ricinolein
3. Ricin
4. Cross pollinated
5. Protogyny
6. Regma
7. 600 m
8. 300 m
9. 10 kg / ha
10. 3:1

II. TRUE OR FALSE

1. False
2. True
3. False
4. False
5. True

III. Match the following

1. B
2. C
3. E
4. A
5. D

IV. ONE WORD ANSWER

1. Less than 32°C the plant tends to be female, more than 32°C plants tends towards male.
2. Male flowers are seen below and female flowers are found near the apex.

31

Safflower Seed Production

I. FILL UPS

1. _____ is a multipurpose crop that has been grown for orange red dye.
2. Safflower oil contains _____ % linoleic acid.
3. Orange red dye extracted from safflower flowers is called _____.
4. The fruit of safflower is _____.
5. The seed oil content of safflower ranges from _____.
6. Isolation distance of safflower for foundation seeds is _____.
7. Seed rate of safflower is _____.
8. Spacing adopted for safflower is _____.
9. Yield of safflower is _____.
10. In safflower, _____ florets are absent.

II. TRUE OR FALSE

1. Safflower oil is rich in saturated fatty acid.
2. Disc florets are absent in safflower.
3. Safflower seed produces edible oil.
4. It takes nearly 150-180 days for harvesting safflower.
5. Excessive and frequent irrigation are recommended for safflower.

III. ONE WORD QUESTION

1. Give any one important use of safflower?
2. What is the seed treatment followed for safflower during storage?

ANSWER KEYS

I. FILL UPS

1. Safflower
2. 78
3. Carthamin
4. Cypsela
5. 30 to 45 %
6. 400 m
7. 10-15 kg / ha
8. 40-50x20-25 cm
9. 1.5-2.0 t / ha
10. Ray

II. TRUE OR FALSE

1. False
2. False
3. True
4. True
5. False

III. ONE WORD ANSWER

1. Orange red dye extracted from its brilliantly coloured flowers.
2. Seeds are treated with halogen @ 3 g / kg of seeds.

32

Tomato Seed Production

I. FILL UPS

1. Tomato is a _____ pollinated crop.
2. _____ pigment is responsible for red colour of tomato.
3. Seed rate recommended for tomato is _____.
4. Isolation distance recommended for foundation seeds of tomato is _____.
5. Spacing adopted for tomato is _____.
6. Yield of tomato seed crop is_____.
7. Seed recovery of tomato is _____.
8. Planting ratio recommended for tomato is _____.
9. Fruit of tomato is a _____.
10. Fruits of tomato are borne on _____.

II. TRUE OR FALSE

1. Tomato fruit supplies vitamin C and variety of colours and flavours.
2. Half ripe tomatoes offer an excellent remedy in all sorts of liver troubles.
3. The flower cluster of tomato is called a truss.
4. Lycopene pigment is responsible for yellow colour of tomato.
5. The viability of tomato seeds can be maintained upto 25 to 30 months in cloth bags.

III. MATCH THE FOLLOWING

1.	Lycopene	A	Flower cluster
2.	Carotene	B	Red colour
3.	Truss	C	Yellow colour
4.	Berry	D	Emasculation & pollination
5.	Staking	E	Fruit

IV. ONE WORD QUESTION

1. What is the isolation distance recommended for tomato hybrid seed production?
2. What are the seed extraction methods in tomato?
3. What is the pre-sowing seed treatment done in tomato?
4. What is the purpose of staking?

ANSWER KEYS

I. FILL UPS

1. Self	2. Lycopene	3. 350 g / ha
4. 50 m	5. 45x45 cm	6. 100 to 150 kg / ha
7. 0.8-1.0 %	8. 5:1	9. Berry
10. Persistent calyx		

II. TRUE OR FALSE

1. True	2. True
3. True	4. False
5. False	

III. MATCH THE FOLLOWING

1. B
2. C
3. A
4. E
5. D

IV. ONE WORD ANSWER

1. FS: 200 m
   CS: 100 m
2. i) Acid method
   ii) Alkali method
   iii) Fermentation method
   iv) Mechanical seed extraction
   v) Citric acid method
3. Seeds are treated with IAA @ 100 ppm for 16 h
4. Staking prevents rotting of fruits.

33

Brinjal Seed Production

I. FILL UPS

1. Brinjal is rich in _____ and _____.
2. In brinjal, _____ is the common feature in case of style.
3. Stigma receptivity of brinjal is _____.
4. Pollen viability in brinjal is _____.
5. The isolation distance recommended for brinjal certified seed production is _____.
6. The recommended seed rate for brinjal seed production is _____.
7. Spacing adopted for brinjal is _____.
8. The planting ratio of brinjal is _____.
9. Seed recovery for brinjal is_____.
10. Seed yield obtained from brinjal is _____.

II. TRUE OR FALSE

1. The objectionable weed of brinjal is *Argemone mexicana.*
2. The brinjal crop after full ripening turn to purple colour.
3. Pseudo-short styled and short styled flowers produce fruits in brinjal.
4. Chances of cross pollination are more in long styled flowers.
5. Brinjal seeds are borne in fleshy placenta having round embryos.

III. ONE WORD QUESTION

1. What are the four types of flowers in brinjal?
2. What is the pre-sowing seed treatment given to brinjal?
3. What are the seed extraction methods in brinjal?

ANSWER KEYS

I. FILL UPS

1. Vitamin A & B
2. Heterostyle
3. 2 days
4. 10 days
5. 100 m
6. 300-400 g / ha
7. 75x60 cm
8. 10:1
9. 2 %
10. 300-350 kg / ha

II. TRUE OR FALSE

1. True
2. False
3. False
4. True
5. False

III. ONE WORD ANSWER

1. i) Long styled with large ovary
   ii) Medium-styled with medium size ovary
   iii) Pseudo short styled with medium size ovary
   iv) True short styled with rudimentary ovary
2. Soaking of seeds in GA_3 @ 200 ppm for 12 hours
3. i) Fermentation method
   ii) Acid method
   iii) Mechanical extraction

34

Chilli Seed Production

I. FILL UPS

1. Dehydrated green chilli is a good source of _____.
2. Isolation distance adopted for chilli for foundation seed production is _____.
3. Seed rate of chilli is _____.
4. Spacing generally adopted for chillies are _____.
5. Seed yield of chilli seed production of large fruited type_____.
6. The planting ratio of chilli seedlings should be _____.
7. Isolation distance recommended for certified seed production of chilli are _____.
8. Seed yield of hybrid chilli seeds is _____.
9. Maximum offtypes permitted for chilli foundation seed production is_____.
10. Seed rate for female parent for chilli hybrid seed production is _____.

II. TRUE OR FALSE

1. In chilli, high temperature and low RH at the time of flowering decrease the transpiration rate and causes abscission of flowers.
2. Both self and cross pollination occur in chilli.
3. Oleoresin in capsicum is used in pain palms and vaporubs.
4. The oleoresin and capsaicin contents are present in tomato.
5. Hydrated green chilli is a good source of Vitamin C.

III. ONE WORD QUESTION

1. What is the seed storage treatments followed in chilli?
2. What are the pre-sowing treatments done in chilli?
3. What is the foliar application followed for improved fruit set in chilli?

ANSWER KEYS

I. FILL UPS

1. Vitamin C
2. 400 m
3. 1 kg / ha
4. 30x30 cm
5. 350-400 kg / ha
6. 2:1
7. 200 m
8. 50-60 kg / ha
9. 0.10 %
10. 1 kg

II. TRUE OR FALSE

1. False
2. True
3. True
4. False
5. False

III. ONE WORD ANSWER

1. Seed treatment with bavistin @ 2-4 g / kg of seed
2. Treat the seeds with *Trichoderma viride* @ 4 g / kg and *Pseudomonas* @ 5 g / kg
3. NAA @ 50 ppm at full bloom or ethrel @ 400 ppm at full bloom.

35

Capsicum Seed Production

I. FILL UPS

1. Capsicum belongs to _____ family.
2. _____ active ingredient is present in capsicum.
3. Ideal day temperature for flowering is _____
4. A minimum isolation distance for foundation seeds of capsicum is_____.
5. A minimum isolation distance for certified seeds of capsicum is _____.
6. Seed rate of capsicum is _____.
7. A spacing adopted for capsicum seed production is _____.
8. Planting ratio adopted for capsicum is _____.
9. Seed rate of capsicum for female parent is _____.
10. 1 kg of capsicum fruit yields _____ seeds.

II. TRUE OR FALSE

1. Capsicum is used in self defense pepper spray.
2. Chilies are used to help people who have difficulty in swallowing.
3. Relatively high temperature (>12°C) during night affects the fruit size, shape and seed.

III. ONE WORD QUESTION

1. What foliar application is given for capsicum to increase flowering?

ANSWER KEYS

I. FILL UPS

1. Solanaceae
2. Capsaicin
3. 26-28°C
4. 400 m
5. 200 m
6. 1 kg / ha
7. 90x45 cm
8. 4:1
9. 100 kg / ha
10. 5-7 g

II. TRUE OR FALSE

1. True
2. False
3. False

III. ONE WORD ANSWER

1. **Spraying of 2,4-D @ 2 ppm at fortnight interval during flowering stage increases flowering.**

36

Okra Seed Production

I. FILL UPS

1. _____ crop stabilizes the blood sugar by curbing the rate at which sugar is absorbed from the intestinal tract.
2. Okra is _____ crop.
3. The isolation distance adopted for okra for foundation seeds is _____.
4. Seed rate of okra is _____.
5. Spacing adopted for okra seed production is _____.
6. Seed yield obtained from okra is _____.
7. _____ helps in lubricating the large intestine due to its laxative qualities.
8. Increased fruit yield in okra can be obtained by spraying of _____.
9. The origin of okra is _____.
10. Seed recovery of okra is _____ of dry weight of pods.

II. TRUE OR FALSE

1. The normal grey colour seeds of okra will have better storage potential.
2. The seeds of okra is so curved that the micropyle and funiculus are very close to each other.
3. Domesticated type of okra unless wild has higher number of carpel.
4. Okra is good for asthma and preenting diabetes.
5. Okra helps in lubricating small intestine.

III. ONE WORD QUESTION

1. What is the seed treatment given to okra during storage?
2. What seed up gradation technique is done in okra?
3. What foliar application can be given to okra?
4. What is the presowing treatment done in okra?

ANSWER KEYS

I. FILL UPS

1. Okra	2. Often cross pollinated	3. 400 m
4. 10-12 kg / ha	5. 45x30 cm	6. 1000-4000 kg / ha
7. Okra	8. Vipul	9. Africa
10. 50-55 %		

II. TRUE OR FALSE

1. False	2. True
3. True	4. True
5. False	

III. ONE WORD ANSWER

1. Seeds can be slurry treated with bavistin @ 2 g / kg to maintain vigour and viability beyond 30 months of age.
2. By water floatation techniques seeds immersed in the column of water (1:10) by volume.
3. Fruit yield and weight can be increased by spraying NAA @ 75 mg / l (or) ethrel @ 150 mg / l.

37

Onion Seed Production

I. FILL UPS

1. Onion is a bulbous _____ herb.
2. Onion is a _____ pollinated crop.
3. Thin white mass within the seed coat is called _____.
4. _____ method is commonly followed for onion seed production.
5. The minimum isolation distance for foundation seed is _____.
6. Seed rate of onion is _____.
7. Spacing adopted for onion seed production is _____.
8. The minimum isolation distance for certified seed production should be_____.
9. _____ temperature range is quite suitable for good bolting.
10. The temperature suitable for flowering and seed setting of onion is _____.

II. TRUE OR FALSE

1. Onion is a annual crop.
2. The pungency of onion can be considered as condiments.
3. The flower of onion is protoandrous in nature.
4. Onion is self pollinated in nature.
5. The method commonly used for seed production of onion is seed to bulb method.

III. ONE WORD QUESTION

1. What is the seed storage treatment done in onion?
2. What is the seed extraction method followed in onion?
3. What is the presowing seed treatment given to onion?

ANSWER KEYS

I. FILL UPS

1. Biennial (or) perennial
2. Cross
3. Endosperm
4. Bulb to seed production
5. 1000 m
6. 8-10 kg / ha
7. 20x20 cm
8. 500 m
9. 10 to 15°C
10. 4-5° to 14°C

II. TRUE OR FALSE

1. False
2. True
3. True
4. False
5. False

III. ONE WORD ANSWER

1. Seeds are treated with bavistin @ 4 g / kg of seeds.
2. Seeds can be separated by hand rubbing (or) by manual winnowing.
3. Soaking of seeds in GA_3 @ 100 ppm for 3 hours increases germination and vigour.

38

Pumpkin Seed Production

I. FILL UPS

1. _____ vegetable is botanically called as a fruit.
2. Fruit of pumpkin is called _____.
3. The isolation distance for pumpkin foundation seed production is _____.
4. The isolation distance for pumpkin certified seed production is _____.
5. Seed rate of pumpkin is _____.
6. The maximum permitted offtype for foundation seed production is _____.
7. The average seed yield in pumpkin is _____.
8. The planting ratio of pumpkin is _____.
9. The seed rate of female line is _____.
10. The seed rate of male line is _____.

II. TRUE OR FALSE

1. Pumpkin is one of the vegetables which is very high in calories.
2. Pumpkin is normally dioecious in nature.
3. Pumpkin seeds are good source of saturated fatty acid.
4. Seeds of pumpkin after removing seed coat are also used in confectionary.
5. Pumpkin is the store house of many anti-oxidants.

III. ONE WORD QUESTION

1. What is the seed treatment given to pumpkin seeds ?
2. How is seed extraction done in pumpkin?
3. What is the seed treatment done during seed storage?
4. What spray must be given to increase the femaleness?

ANSWER KEYS

I. FILL UPS

1. Pumpkin
2. Pepo
3. 1000 m
4. 500 m
5. 6-8 kg / ha
6. 0.10 %
7. 250-300 kg / ha
8. 4:1
9. 6 kg / ha
10. 2 kg / ha

II. TRUE OR FALSE

1. False
2. False
3. False
4. True
5. True

III. ONE WORD ANSWER

1. Seeds need to be treated with vitavax @ 2 g / kg of seeds to avoid seed borne diseases.
2. Scooping out seeds and by continuous rolling and raking.
3. Seeds should be treated with bavistin @ 4g / kg of seeds.
4. Spraying of ethrel @ 200-250 ppm at two leaf stage.

39

Ashgourd Seed Production

I. FILL UPS

1. Ashgourd is a _____ crop.
2. Stigma receptivity is for _____.
3. Ashgourd is a _____ pollinated crop.
4. Ashgourd fruit is a _____.
5. The isolation distance for ashgourd certified seed production is_____.
6. Seed rate of ashgourd is _____.
7. Seed yield of ashgourd is _____.
8. In ashgourd, spraying of _____ increases production of female flowers.
9. Maximum permitted off types for pumpkin foundation seed production is _____.
10. Maximum permitted off types for pumpkin certified seed production is _____.

II. TRUE OR FALSE

1. Ash gourd is dioecious crop.
2. Sex ratio of ash gourd varies from 20:1 to 33:1.
3. The waxy coat of fruit ensures storage of ash gourd.
4. Soaking the seeds in conc.HNO_3 for half an hour facilitates easy removal of seeds.
5. Storing half matured fruits over sand bed at ambient condition followed by seed extraction ensures quality seed.

III. ONE WORD QUESTION

1. What is the sex expression in ash gourd?
2. How is seed extracted from ash gourd?
3. What is the pre-sowing seed treatment done in ash gourd?

ANSWER KEYS

I. FILL UPS

1. Monoecious
2. 18-36 hours
3. Cross pollinated
4. Berry
5. 500 m
6. 2.5 kg / ha
7. 80-100 kg / ha
8. Ethephon 250 ppm
9. 0.10 %
10. 0.20 %

II. TRUE OR FALSE

1. False
2. True
3. True
4. False
5. True

III. ONE WORD ANSWER

1. Spraying of ethephon @ 250 ppm at 4 times increases production of female flowers.
2. Scooping along with pulp and washing with water.
3. Soaking of seeds in KNO_3 (1%) improves field emergence.

40

Bittergourd Seed Production

I. FILL UPS

1. _____ vegetable contain anti-diabetic properties.
2. Bittergourd has _____ similar to bovine insulin.
3. Bittergourd is popularly seen as a _____.
4. Bittergourd is a _____ plant.
5. The seed rate for bittergourd is _____.
6. The isolation distance for bittergourd foundation seed production is _____.
7. The isolation distance for bittergourd certified seed production is _____.
8. The off-type permitted limit for certified seed is _____.
9. The planting ratio recommended for bittergourd is _____.
10. The seed rate for female parent in bittergourd is _____.
11. The seed rate for male parent in bittergourd is _____.
12. The isolation distance for hybrid bittergourd foundation seed production is _____.
13. The isolation distance for hybrid bittergourd certified seed production is _____.

II. TRUE OR FALSE

1. Bittergourd have hypoglycaemic properties.
2. The trellis needs to be provided for bittergourd crop.
3. Low nitrogen and low temperature conditions promotes maleness in flowering.

III. ONE WORD QUESTION

1. How gynoecious sex expression in bittergourd is promoted?
2. What is the seed storage treatment done in bittergourd?
3. What are the seed extraction methods of bittergourd?

ANSWER KEYS

I. FILL UPS

1. Bittergourd
2. P-insulin (or) polypeptide –p
3. Plant insulin
4. Monoecious
5. 1.8 kg / ha
6. 1000 m
7. 500 m
8. 0.2 %
9. 4 : 1
10. 4 kg / ha
11. 1 kg / ha
12. 1500 m
13. 1000 m

II. TRUE OR FALSE

1. True
2. True
3. False

III. ONE WORD ANSWER

1. Spraying of ethephon to monoecious cucurbits is followed to promote the development of gynoecious sex expression in female parent.
2. Seeds are treated with carbendazim @ 4 g / kg
3. i) Wet method
   ii) Mechanical extraction
   iii) Natural fermentation
   iv) Chemical extraction

41

Ribbedgourd Seed Production

I. FILL UPS

1. The stigma receptivity of ribbedgourd is_____.
2. Ribbedgourd is a _____ pollinated crop.
3. Isolation distance for foundation seed production of ribbedgourd is _____.
4. Isolation distance for certified seed production of ribbedgourd is _____.
5. Seed rate for ribbedgourd is _____.
6. Maximum off types permitted in ribbedgourd seed production is _____.
7. The planting ratio for ribbedgourd hybrid seed production is _____.
8. The seed rate of male parent in ribbedgourd hybrid seed production is _____.
9. The seed rate of female parent in ribbedgourd hybrid seed production is_____.
10. The seed yield of ribbedgourd is _____.

II. TRUE OR FALSE

1. In ridgegourd, a variety called 'satputia' bears a hermaphrodite sex condition.
2. Ethrel (250 ppm) is used for initiating staminate flowers and suppressing pistillate flowers at flowering time.
3. The germination of ribbedgourd is when the day temperature is below 25ºC.
4. Pollen fertility is upto 1 to 5 days in rainy season.
5. Oil of ribbedgourd seeds are effective in skin diseases.

III. ONE WORD QUESTION

1. How is sex expression being promoted in ribbedgourd?
2. What is the chemical expression technique in ribbedgourd?

3. What is the use of gynoecious lines in ribbedgourd?
4. What is the purpose of pinching of male flowers?
5. What is the foliar application given to ribbedgourd?

ANSWER KEYS

I. FILL UPS

1. 84 hours	2. Cross	3. 1000 m
4. 500 m	5. 1.5 kg / ha	6. 300 kg / ha
7. 4 : 1	8. 0.75 kg / ha	9. 3.25 kg / ha
10. 250-300 kg / ha		

II. TRUE OR FALSE

1. True	2. False
3. False	4. True
5. True	

III. ONE WORD ANSWER

1. The seedlings should be sprayed with ethrel @ 250 ppm for 4 times to encourage production of female flowers.
2. Ethrel is used for suppressing staminate flowers and initiating pistillate flowers at flowering time.
3. Gynoecious lines are crossed with monoecious male parents to produce F1 hybrids.
4. Pinching of male flower before the opening of female flower is followed to allow natural cross pollination.
5. Spraying of MH @ 400 ppm enhances the female flower production.

42

Snakegourd Seed Production

I. FILL UPS

1. The viability of pollen grains in snakegourd is for _____.
2. Stigma receptivity is for _____hours after opening.
3. The isolation distance for snakegourd foundation seed production is_____.
4. The wild species of snakegourd is _____.
5. The isolation distance for snakegourd certified seed production is_____.
6. Seed rate for snakegourd is _____.
7. Foliar application of _____ increased the female flower production in snakegourd
8. The seed yield of snakegourd is _____.
9. The planting ratio of snakegourd is_____.
10. The isolation distance for snakegourd hybrid foundation seed production is_____.
11. The isolation distance for snakegourd hybrid certified seed production is_____.
12. Seed rate of female parent in snakegourd hybrid is _____.
13. Seed rate of male parent seed production is _____.
14. Most of cucurbits germinate well when the day temperature is above _____.
15. The mature fruit of snakegourd has been reported as _____.

II. TRUE OR FALSE

1. The bitterness of fruit in snakegourd increases with maturity.
2. Young fruits in cucurbits bitterness increases with cooking.

III. ONE WORD QUESTION

1. What is the intercultivation practice done in snakegourd?
2. What is the foliar application given to snakegourd?

3. What is the seed treatment given to snakegourd crop?
4. How seeds are extracted in snakegourd?

ANSWER KEYS

I. FILL UPS

1. 10 hours	2. 51	3. 1000 m
4. *Trichosanthus palmate*	5. 500 m	6. 1.5 kg / ha
7. MH @ 400 ppm	8. 200 kg / ha	9. 4:1
10. 1500 m	11. 1000 m	12. 1.5 kg / ha
13. 0.5 kg / ha	14. 25ºC	15. Purgative

II. TRUE OR FALSE

1. True
2. False

III. ONE WORD ANSWER

1. Hoeing and weeding. Stacks are provided to make the plants to reach pandal height.
2. Foliar application of maleic hydrazide @ 400 ppm at 2nd and 5th leaf stage
3. Seeds are treated with *T. viride* @ 4 g / kg
4. Seeds are extracted by scooping the pulp out and rubbed and then washed.

43

Cole Crops Seed Production

I. FILL UPS

1. The botanical name of radish is _____.
2. The botanical name of knol-khol is _____.
3. The botanical name of cauliflower is _____.
4. The botanical name of cabbage is _____.
5. The botanical name of carrot is _____.
6. The botanical name of beetroot is _____.
7. The botanical name of turnip is_____.
8. The pod of cabbage is called _____.
9. Stigma receptivity of radish is for _____.
10. Radish is a_____ pollinated crop.
11. The inflorescence of carrot is called _____.
12. The inflorescence of beetroot is called _____.
13. Turnip is a _____ pollinated crop.
14. The isolation distance for cole crops certified seed production is _____.
15. The isolation distance for cole crops foundation seed production is _____.
16. Spacing adopted for seed production of cabbage is _____.
17. Spacing adopted for seed production of radish is _____.
18. Spacing adopted for seed production of knol khol is _____.
19. Spacing adopted for seed production of carrot is _____.
20. Spacing adopted for seed production of beetroot is _____.

II. TRUE OR FALSE

1. Radish contains cancer protective properties.
2. Cauliflower is used to prevent stomach and breast cancer.

3. The pod of cauliflower & cabbage is called siliqua.
4. The inflorescence of radish is umbel.
5. Seed rate of cauliflower is 3-4 kg / ha.
6. Seed rate of cabbage is 600 g / ha.
7. Seed rate of carrot is 5 to 6 kg / ha for European varieties.
8. Seed rate of beetroot is 7-10 kg / ha multigerm varieties.
9. Seed yield of knol-khol is 500-600 kg / ha.
10. Seed yield of carrot is 1500 kg / ha.

III. MATCH THE FOLLOWING

1.	Turnip	A	Umbel inflorescence
2.	Black leg	B	Parchment colour
3.	Beet root	C	Head to seed method
4.	Cabbage	D	Beet root
5.	Carrot	E	Steckling method

IV. ONE WORD QUESTION

1. What is the foliar application given to cole crops like cabbage?
2. What is the presowing seed treatment done in radish?
3. What is the presowing seed treatment done in carrot?
4. What is the presowing seed treatment done in cauliflower?
5. What is the presowing seed treatment done in cabbage?
6. What is the presowing seed treatment done in beet root?

ANSWER KEYS

I. FILL UPS

1. *Raphanus sativus*	2. *Brassica oleraceae* var *gonglyodes*
3. *Brassica oleraceae* var *cauloriapa*	4. *Brassica oleraceae* var *capitata*
5. *Daucus carota*	6. *Beta vulgaris*
7. *Brassica campestris* var *rapa*	8. Siliqua
9. 4 days	10. Cross
11. Umbel	12. Spike
13. Cross	14. 1000 m
15. 1600 m	16. 45x45 cm
17. 45x45 cm	18. 60x45 cm
19. 40x30 cm	20. 30x20 cm

II. TRUE OR FALSE

1.	True	6.	True
2.	False	7.	True
3.	True	8.	True
4.	False	9.	True
5.	False	10.	False

III. MATCH THE FOLLOWING

1. B
2. D
3. E
4. C
5. A

IV. ONE WORD ANSWER

1. Foliar spraying of NAA @ 10 ppm at vegetative stage to increase curd yield.
2. Treating the seeds with GA_3 to increase the germination percentage.
3. Seed soaking in water @ 20°C for 24 hours and drying.
4. Hot water treatment @ 50°C for half an hour.
5. Pre-drying of seeds @ 40°C.
6. A. Seed to seed method

   B. Steckling method
7. 3 sprays of 200 ppm GA_3 may be adopted for getting more yield.

44

Potato Seed Production

I. FILL UPS

1. The potato is made up of _____ and _____.
2. Potato is a _____ pollinated crop
3. Potato fruit is called as_____.
4. An example of stem tuber is a _____.
5. Isolation distance of potato is _____ to prevent the spread of diseases
6. The seed rate of potato tuber is _____.
7. The seed yield of potato is_____.
8. TPS refers to_____.
9. The average seed yield of true potato seeds is _____.
10. _____ tuber crop is used for the processing of alcohol such as vodka.

II. TRUE OR FALSE

1. Potato is a self pollinated crop.
2. The tubers of potato varieties with white flowers have white skin.
3. The tubers of potato varieties with coloured flowers tend to have pinkish skin.
4. Maximum high temperature is of great significance for potato tuberization and yield.
5. An isolation distance of 5m between two plots of seed potato to prevent the spread of diseases.

III. ONE WORD QUESTION

1. What is the seed storage treatment done in potato?
2. What are the production methods of TPS?

ANSWER KEYS

I. FILL UPS

1. Water & starch
2. Cross
3. Seed apple (or) apple (or) berry
4. Potato
5. 30m
6. 2.5-3t/ha
7. 12-15t
8. True potato seeds
9. 100kg/ha
10. Potato

II. TRUE OR FALSE

1. False
2. True
3. True
4. False
5. False

III. ONE WORD ANSWER

1. The seeds are stored in moisture proof containers with a sufficient number of silica gel bags.
2. i) Direct field sowing
   ii) Transplanting from nursery bed to field
   iii) Planting of tubers (or) tuberlets derived from TPS.

45

Seed Production in Forage Legumes and Grasses

I. FILL UPS

1. The isolation distance of fodder cowpea for certified seed production is _____.
2. The isolation distance of lucerne for foundation seed production is _____
3. The isolation distance of lucerne for certified seed production is _____.
4. The isolation distance of berseem for certified seed production is _____.
5. The isolation distance of berseem for foundation seed production is _____.
6. The isolation distance of cluster bean for foundation seed production is _____.
7. The isolation distance of cluster bean for certified seed production is _____.
8. The isolation distance of stylo for foundation seed production is _____.
9. The isolation distance of stylo for certified seeds production is _____.
10. Seed rate of fodder cowpea is _____.
11. The seed rate of lucerne is _____.
12. The seed rate of stylo is _____.
13. The seed rate of clitoria is_____.
14. The seed rate of desmanthus is _____.
15. The spacing adopted for desmanthus is _____.
16. The spacing adopted for stylo is _____.
17. The spacing adopted for cluster bean is _____.
18. The spacing adopted for berseem is_____.
19. The spacing adopted for fodder cowpea is_____.
20. The isolation distance of napier – bajra (Pearl millet) hybrid for certified seed production is_____.

21. The isolation distance of napier – bajra (Pearl millet) hybrid for foundation seed production is_____.
22. The isolation distance of guinea for foundation seed production is_____.
23. The isolation distance of guinea for certified seed production is_____.
24. The seed rate of napier – bajra (Pearl millet) hybrid is _____.
25. The seed rate of guinea is _____.
26. The spacing adopted for napier – bajra (Pearl millet) hybrid is _____.
27. Spacing adopted for guinea is _____.
28. Spacing adopted for deenanath is _____.
29. Seed rate recommended for anjan is _____.
30. The maximum permitted % of offtypes for napier-bajra hybrid for foundation seed is_____.

II. TRUE OR FALSE

1. The optimum temperature requirement of napier-bajra hybris is 31°C
2. The optimum temperature requirement of berseem is 21°C.

III. MATCH THE FOLLOWING

1.	Desmanthus	A 25 cm
2.	Guinea	B 30x15 cm
3.	Lucerne	C 50x50 cm
4.	Fodder cowpea	D 50 cm
5.	Napier-bajra	E 50x30 cm

ANSWER KEYS

I. FILL UPS

1. 25 m	2. 400 m	3. 100 m
4. 100 m	5. 400 m	6. 10 m
7. 5 m	8. 50 m	9. 25 m
10. 25 kg/ha	11. 20 kg/ha	12. 10 kg/ha
13. 20 kg/ha	14. 20-25 kg/ha	15. 50 cm
16. 30x15 cm	17. 60x30 cm	18. 20-25 kg/ha
19. 30x15 cm	20. 10 m	21. 10 m
22. 20 m	23. 10 m	24. 40,000 rooted slips/ha

25. 2.5 kg/ha or 60000 rooted slips
26. 50x50 cm
27. 50x30 cm or 90x45 cm
28. 35x10 cm or solid sowing in 30 cm rows
29. 5-7.5 kg/ha
30. 0.01 %

II. TRUE OR FALSE

1. True
2. False

III. MATCH THE FOLLOWING

1. D
2. E
3. A
4. B
5. C

46

Fruit Seed Production

I. FILL UPS

1. The botanical name of mango is ______.
2. The family name of mango is ______.
3. The botanical name of banana is ______.
4. The family name of banana is ______.
5. The botanical name of sapota is ______.
6. The family name of sapota is______.
7. The botanical name of guava is ______.
8. The family of guava is ______.
9. The botanical name of papaya is______.
10. The family of papaya is______.
11. The botanical name of citrus is______.
12. The family of citrus is______.
13. The botanical name of jack fruit is______.
14. The family of jack fruit is______.
15. The inflorescence of mango is ______.
16. The inflorescence of banana is ______.
17. The inflorescence of sapota and guava is ______.
18. The inflorescence of jack fruit is ______.
19. The inflorescence of papaya is ______.
20. The fruit of jack fruit is ______.
21. The fruit of papaya is ______.
22. The fruit of citrus is ______.
23. The fruit of mango is ______.

24. Mango is a _____ pollinated crop.
25. Banana is a _____ pollinated crop.
26. Sapota is a _____ pollinated crop.
27. Citrus is a _____pollinated crop.
28. Papaya is a_____ pollinated crop.
29. Jack fruit is a _____ pollinated crop.
30. The period of dormancy in papaya is _____.
31. The period of dormancy in banana is _____.
32. The botanical name of pomegranate is _____.
33. The family of pomegranate is _____.
34. The inflorescence of fig is _____.
35. The type of dormancy in pine apple is _____.
36. The period of dormancy in pineapple is _____.
37. The botanical name of strawberry is _____.
38. The method of propagation of walnut is _____.
39. The type of dormancy present in apple is _____.
40. Apple is a _____ pollinated crop.

II. TRUE OR FALSE

1. The seed storage behavior of strawberry is orthodox
2. The seed storage behavior of almond is recalcitrant
3. The method of propagation of apple is through rootstock
4. The method of propagation of walnut is through seed
5. The method of propagation of litchi is through rootstock

III. MATCH THE FOLLOWING

(i)

1. Apple	A Secondary dormancy
2. Apricot	B Embryo dormancy
3. Plum	C Seed coat dormancy
4. Pineapple	D Endogenous dormancy
5. Cherry	E Phyiological dormancy

(ii)

1.	Jack fruit	A Synconium
2.	Apple	B Panicle
3.	Mango	C Terminal cyme
4.	West Indian cherry	D Cauliflorous
5.	Fig	E Solitary

IV. ONE WORD QUESTION

1. Mention any two examples for orthodox seeds in fruits
2. Mention any two examples for recalcitrant seeds in fruits
3. Mention the pre-treatment done in apple
4. What is the pretreatment done in banana?
5. What is the period of seed storage for sapota?
6. What is the pretreatment done in papaya?

ANSWER KEYS

I. FILL UPS

1. *Mangifera indica*	2. Anacardiaceae	3. *Musa* spp
4. Musaceae	5. *Achras sapota*	6. Sapotaceae
7. *Psidium gujava*	8. Myrtaceae	9. *Carica papaya*
10. Caricaceae	11. *Citrus reticulata*	12. Rutaceae
13. *Artocarpus heterophyllus*	14. Moraceae	15. Panicle
16. Spathe	17. Solitary	18. Cauliflorous
19. Branched inflorescence	20. Compound (or) aggregate fruit	21. Berry
22. Hesperidum	23. Drupe	24. Cross
25. Cross	26. Cross	27. Self
28. Self	29. Cross	30. 35 days
31. 2 to 3 months	32. *Punica granatum*	33. Punicaceae
34. Synconium	35. Seed coat	36. 10 days
37. *Fragaria ananassa*	38. Seed	39. Embryo dormancy
40. Cross		

II. TRUE OR FALSE

1.	True	2.	False
3.	True	4.	True
5.	False		

III. MATCH THE FOLLOWING

(i)		(ii)	
1.	B	1.	D
2.	E	2.	E
3.	D	3.	B
4.	C	4.	C
5.	A	5.	A

IV. ONE WORD ANSWER

1. Apple, strawberry
2. Pineapple, litchi
3. Ethephon treatment, removal of seed inner and outer coats
4. Scarification with sulphuric acid, chipping of testa, softening of testa by soaking and use of alternating temperatures.
5. 24 months in air dry storage at 5ºC
6. Matric conditioning at 25ºC for 4 days and GA for 4 days.

47

Flower Seed Production

I. FILL UPS

1. The botanical name of carnation is _____.
2. The family of carnation is _____.
3. The botanical name of chrysanthemum is _____.
4. The family of chrysanthemum is _____.
5. The botanical name of gerbera is _____.
6. The family of gerbera is _____.
7. The botanical name of marigold is _____.
8. The botanical name of orchid is_____.
9. The botanical name of rose is _____.
10. The botanical name of anthurium is _____.
11. The inflorescence of anthurium is _____.
12. The flower of anthurium is _____.
13. Anthurium is a _____pollinated crop.
14. Carnation is a_____ pollinated crop.
15. Anthurium is _____ in nature.
16. An example of protoandry flower crop is _____.
17. The method of propagation of petunia is only through _____.
18. The type of dormancy found in orchid is _____.
19. The botanical name of crossandra is _____.
20. The family of jasmine is _____.
21. The botanical name of jasmine is _____.
22. The botanical name of nerium is _____.
23. The botanical name of lotus is _____.

24. The inflorescence of bougainvillea is _____.
25. The inflorescence of crossandra is _____.
26. Crossandra is a _____ pollinated crop
27. Heliconia is propagated only through_____.
28. The isolation distance of annual carnation for foundation seed production is _____.
29. The isolation distance of marigold for certified seed production is _____.
30. The isolation distance of marigold for foundation seed production is _____.

II. TRUE OR FALSE

1. The period of storage of lotus seeds is 100 years.
2. Zinnia is recalcitrant seed.
3. The pod of heliconia is called as drupe.
4. The pod of bougainvillea is called as achene
5. The inflorescence of lilium is a simple spike.
6. The fruit of petunia is called as hip.
7. The propagation of marigold is through seed.
8. The propagation of china aster is through vegetative propagation.
9. Anthurium is protogyny in nature.
10. Cactus is a orthodox seed.

III. MATCH THE FOLLOWING

1.	Lotus	A Protogyny
2.	Bougainvillea	B Orthodox
3.	Rose	C Achene
4.	Gladiolus	D Hip
5.	Anthurium	E Protogyny

IV. ONE WORD QUESTION

1. Mention any two example for orthodox seeds in flower crops
2. Mention any two flowers propagated only through seeds
3. Mention any two flower crops with seed coat dormancy?
4. Which flower crop flower is known as candle?
5. What pretreatment is done in petunia?
6. What is the germination improvement treatment done in zinnia?
7. What is the germination improvement treatment done in celosia?

ANSWERS KEYS

I. FILL UPS

1. *Dianthus caryophyllus*
2. Caryophyllaceae
3. *Chrysanthemum indicum*
4. Asteraceae
5. Gerbera jamesonii
6. Asteraceae
7. *Tagetes erecta*
8. *Phalaenopsis* sp.
9. *Rosa hybrida*
10. *Anthurium andreanum*
11. Spathe
12. Spadix
13. Cross
14. Self
15. Protogyny
16. Gladiolus
17. Seed
18. Morphological
19. *Crossandra infundibuliformis*
20. Oleaceae
21. *Jasminum officinale*
22. *Nerium oleander*
23. *Nelumbo nucifera*
24. Cluster
25. Compact spike
26. Cross
27. Seed
28. 600m
29. 300m
30. 600m

II. TRUE OR FALSE

1. True
2. False
3. True
4. True
5. False
6. False
7. True
8. False
9. True
10. True

III. MATCH THE FOLLOWING

1. B
2. C
3. D
4. E
5. A

IV. ONE WORD ANSWER

1. Lotus, zinnia
2. Marigold, petunia
3. Chrysanthemum, lilium
4. Anthurium
5. Colchicine
6. Treatment with H_2O_2
7. Continuous light (or) alternating light and dark.

48

Seed Production in Plantation Crops

I. FILL UPS

1. The fruit of coffee is called _____.
2. Coffee is a_____ pollinated crop
3. The fruit of tea is called _____.
4. Tea is a _____ pollinated crop.
5. The fruit of cardamom is called _____.
6. The fruit of pepper is called _____.
7. The seed rate of coffee is_____.
8. The seed rate of cardamom is_____.
9. The seed rate of rubber is_____.
10. The spacing adopted for rubber is_____.
11. The spacing adopted for cocoa is _____.
12. The spacing adopted for pepper is _____.
13. Rubber is a _____ pollinated crop.
14. Cardamom is a_____ pollinated crop.
15. Cocoa is a _____ pollinated crop.
16. Pepper is a _____ pollinated crop.
17. The nature of dormancy in coffee is _____.
18. The nature of dormancy in tea is _____.
19. The spacing adopted for tea for single hedge system is_____.
20. The spacing adopted for tea for double hedge system is _____.

II. TRUE OR FALSE

1. The fruit of cardamom is called berry.
2. The optimum temperature of rubber is 21° to 35°C.

3. The seed rate of cocoa is 1111 plants/ha.
4. The spacing adopted for coffee for dwarf varieties is 1x1 m.
5. Cocoa seed is orthodox.

III. MATCH THE FOLLOWING

1.	Coffee	A 2.7x2.7 m
2.	Tea	B 1x1 m
3.	Rubber	C 1.2x0.75 m
4.	Cardamom	D 3x2 m
5.	Pepper	E 2.0x1.5 m

IV. ONE WORD QUESTION

1. Give two examples for orthodox seeds in plantation crops
2. Give two examples for recalcitrant seeds
3. Name any two plantation crops with mechanical dormancy
4. What is the maturity indice for cocoa?

ANSWER KEYS

I. FILL UPS

1. Berry	2. Self	3. Capsule
4. Cross	5. Capsule	6. Small drupe
7. 1.5 kg/ha	8. 600 g/ha	9. 1667 plants
10. 5x5 m or 3x2 m	11. 3x3 m	12. 2.7x2.7 m
13. Self	14. Self	15. Cross
16. Self	17. Hard endocarp	18. Mechanical
19. 1.20x0.75m	20. 1.35x0.75m	

II. TRUE OR FALSE

1. False	2. False
3. True	4. True
5 False	

III. MATCH THE FOLLOWING

1. B
2. C
3. D
4. E
5. A

IV. ONE WORD ANSWER

1. Cardamom and pepper
2. Tea and rubber
3. Cardamom and pepper
4. The pod turns light yellow when ripe.

49

Nursery Management

I. FILL UPS

1. _____ number of beds measuring 8 m, 0.6 m are sufficient for raising sufficient seedling for one hectare.
2. Seeds are sown singly at _____distance apart in the furrow.

II. TRUE OR FALSE

1. At 4 to 6 leaf stage, irrigation should be cut down .
2. The furrow to furrow distance for seed sowing should be 0.50 cm.

III. ONE WORD QUESTION

1. Mention any two seedling selection strategies for transplanting
2. What is the optimum age of seedlings used for transplanting for different crops?

ANSWER KEYS

I. FILL UPS

1. 20 2. 2.0-2.5cm

II. TRUE OR FALSE

1. True
2. False

III. ONE WORD ANSWER

1. i) Stocky and sturdy
   ii) Should have good root system
2. 25-40 days

50

Micropropagation

I. FILL UPS

1. _____ is the growing of plants from meristematic tissue (or) somatic cells of superior plants on nutrient media under controlled conditions.
2. _____ is a group of undifferentiated palnt cells.
3. Explants used is _____ in shape.
4. Meristem forms _____ at its cut end on which a large number of shoot primordia develop.
5. _____ is absent in meristem.
6. _____ has prime importance in the travelling of viruses through the body.
7. _____ cells are actively dividing and high metabolic activity
8. _____ is a mass of unorganized cells
9. The callus by induced re-differentiation can give rise to_____.
10. _____ are plant cells with the cell wall removed.
11. The stage '0' of micropropagation was proposed by_____.
12. An example for disinfectant is _____.
13. _____ is the most frequently used basal medium.
14. _____ number of shoots can be produced from a single explants in a year.
15. _____ refers to the preparation of the plants for a normal growth environment.
16. Explant used for micropropagation in anthurium is _____.
17. The explants used for micropropagation of banana is_____.
18. The medium used for micropropagation of rhododendron is _____.
19. The medium used for micropropagation of eucalyptus is _____.
20. _____ propagation can be used to produce disease-free plants.

21. _____ is the only viable method of regenerating genetically modified cells (or) cells.
22. The medium used for micopropagation of rose is______.
23. Micropropagation techniques are not available for _____.
24. The explants used for micropropagation of rose is _____.
25. The explants used for micropropagation of carnation is _____.

II. TRUE OR FALSE

1. Labor cost of micropropagation is more than 70%.
2. The medium used for micropropagation of bottle brush is WPM.
3. Micropropagation techniques is available for mango.
4. Vegetative buds are the explants of gerbera for micropropagation.
5. Meristem culture is used in the propagation of haploid plants.

III. ONE WORD QUESTION

1. Mention one advantage of micropropagation
2. Mention one disadvantage of micropropagation
3. Mention any two objectives of micropropagation
4. Mention any two application of meristem culture

ANSWERS KEYS

I. FILL UPS

1. Micropropagation	2. Meristem	3. Dome
4. Callus	5. Vascular system	6. Vascular system
7. Meristematic cells	8. Callus	9. Embryoids
10. Protoplasts	11. Debergh and Maene	12. Sodium hypochlorite
13. Murashige and Skoog medium	14. 4.3x107	15. Hardening
16. Vegetative buds	17. Suckers	18. Anderson formula
19. WPM medium	20. Micropropagation	21. Micropropagation
22. MS Medium	23. Mango	24. Shoot tip
25. Meristem tip		

II. TRUE OR FALSE

1. True 2. False
3. False 4. False
5. True

III. ONE WORD ANSWER

1. Micropropagation can be used to produce disease-free plants.
2. Micropropagation is very expensive
3. i) Production of virus free stock

   ii) germplasm exchange
4. i) Used in propagation of haploid plants

   ii) Storing genetic resources of seed producing plants of heterozygous nature.

V. AT A GLANCE

1. Steps in micropropagation

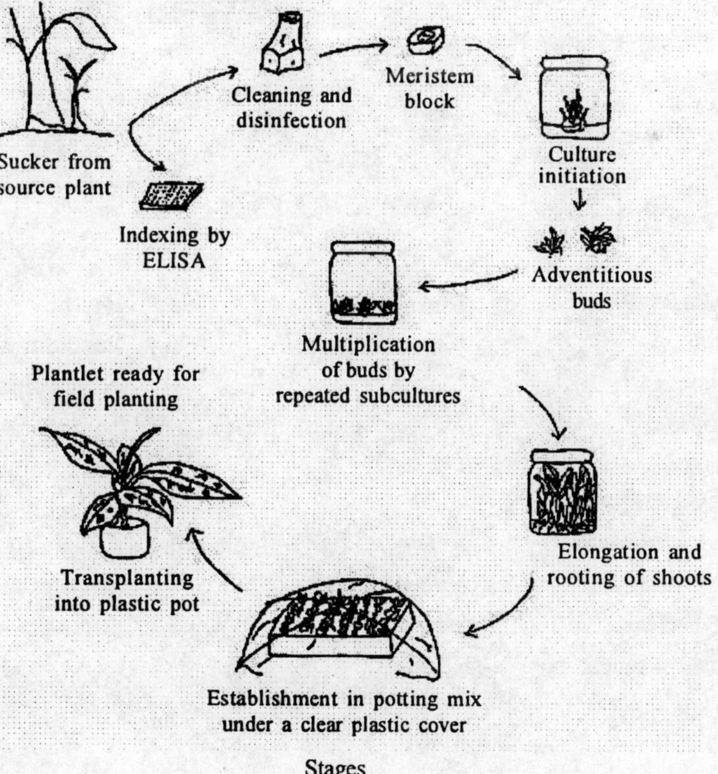

Stages

2. Micropropogation of Selected Plants

Species	Explant	Medium
Gerbera	Shoot-tip	MS
Rose	Shoot-tip	MS
Carnation	Meristem tip	MS
Rhododendron	Shoot-tip	Anderson formula
Anthurium	Vegetative buds	MS
Rosemary	Shoot-tip	MS
Banana	Suckers	MS
Eucalyptus	Shoot-tip	WPM
Melaluca (Bottle brush)	Shoot-tip	WPM

51

Varietal Seed Production Technology At a Glance

Chapter start from next page

Crop	Isolation (m)	Season	Seed rate (kg/ha)/ Seed treatment	Spacing (cm)/ Seedling age	Fertilizer (NPK kg/ha)	Foliar spray/ Seed treatment	Harvesting	Grading (Sieve size)	Seed yield (kg/ha)
Rice (*Oryza sativa*)			Seed soaking in 0.5% KNO_3 for 16h			2%DAP 1[st]spray-60 days 2[nd]spray-80 days		7/64"	3000-6000
Short duration (105-110 days)		November-December	60	20 x 30 13-22 days old seedlings	120:40:540 $ZnSO_4$ at 25		28 DAA		
Medium duration (110-125 days)	3	November	40	20 x 15 25-30 days old seedlings	150:50:60		35 DAA		
Long duration (125-145 days)		August	30	20 x 20 30-35 days old seedlings	150:50:80		35 DAA		
Maize (*Zea mays*)	200	November–December June-July Sep-Oct	10 Seed soaking in 2% KH_2PO_4 for 8h	60 x 20 45 x 15	150:75:75	-	Sheath turns yellow and dry (Moisture 25%)	18/64"	2500
Wheat *(Triticum aestivum)*	150	November	85-100	20-22.5 (row spacing)	120:60:40	-	At 30-35% Moisture	6mm (TS) 1.8/2.1mm (BS)	3000-4000
Sorghum (*Sorghum bicolor)*	FS: 200 CS: 100	June-July October–November	7.5–10 Seed soaking in 2% KH_2PO_4 for 10h	45 x 15	50:50:50		40-45days after 50% flowering, 20-22% moisture, black layer at base of seed	9/64"	2000
Pearl millet (*Pennesitum glaucum*)	FS: 400 CS: 200	November–December	3.75 Seed hardening with 2% KCl for 16 h	45 x 20 18 days old seedling	100:50:50		20 to 25 DAF, small dark layer at seed bottom	4/64"	2000

Redgram (***Cajanus cajan***)	100	June – September February–March	20-25 Seed soaking in 100 ppm $ZnSO_4$ for 3h	45 x 30 (Short duration) 90 x 30 (Long duration)	25:50:25	2% DAP at first flowering and 15 days after	75-80 DAS	3.35 mm (larger seed) 2.8 mm (medium seed)	2000-2500
Blackgram (***Vigna mungo***)	5	June– September February–March	20-25 Seed soaking in 100 ppm $ZnSO_4$ for 3h	30 x 10	25:50:25	1% DAP at first flowering and 15 days after	55-65 DAS/ 30 days after 50% flowering	2.36 mm	1200-1300
Greengram (***Vigna radiata***)	5	June- September February- March	8-10 Seed soaking in 100 ppm $ZnSO_4$ for 3h	30 x 10	25:50:25	1% DAP at first flowering and 15 days later	55-65 DAS/ 30 days after 50% flowering	2.36 mm	1000-1200
Cowpea (***Vigna unguiculata***)	FS: 10 CS : 5	February–March	20-25	45 x 20	25:50:25	2% DAP on 25-35 DAS	70-80 DAS/ 30 days after 50% flowering	3.50 mm (small seed) 4.00 mm (bold seed)	1300-1400
Field lablab (***Lablab purpureus*** **var. *lignosus***)	5	March-April September-October	20-25	45×15	25:25:25	2% DAP on 45 DAS	90-140 DAS/ 70% pods turn straw colour	18/64"	700
Soybean (***Glycine max***)	3	June-July September-October	40	30 x10	25:50:25	2% DAP on 25-35 DAS	30 days after 50% flowering / 70% pods turn yellow	14/64" – 12/64"	1800-2100
Bengalgram	3	November	75-90 Seed soaking in 1% KH_2 PO_4 or 3-4 h	30 x10	25:50:25		30-40 DAA	13/64" or 18/64"	2000 - 2500
Cotton (*Gossypium sp*)	FS: 50 CS: 30	July- August	FS: 15-20 DS: 7.5-10	75 × 30 / 90×45 / 120×60	120:60:60 / 80:40:40 / 60:30:30	1% DAP on 70,80 and 90 DAS	45-55 DAA	18/64" (FS) / 10/64" (DS)	
Acid delinting: Conc. H_2SO_4 at 100 ml/kg of seed									

Jute (*Corchorus spp*)	50	Late February to May	Line sowing: 5 -7 Broadcasting: 7 -10	30×10-15	20:20:20		-	-	1300
Groundnut (*Arachis hypogea*)	5-10	June – July Sep – Oct	BT: 100-130 ST: 80-100	30×15	40:40:60 +10kg borax Gypsum @ 400 kg/ha on 40-45 DAS	1% FeSO4 and 50 DAS	Drying and falling down of lower leaves, inner side of the pod turns black	9/64”	1200-1400 (pod yield of ST) 800-1000 (pod yield of BT)
Soaking in 0.5% $CaCl_2$ for 6h, incubate soaked seed in between two moist gunny bag for 12h, separate radicle sprouted seeds at 2h interval, shade dry and sow									
Sunflower (*Helianthus annus*)	CS: 200 FS:400	April-August	15 Soaking in 0.5% KH_2PO_4 for 16h/2% $ZnSO_4$ for 12h	45×30	60:45:45	-	Back of head turns to yellow, bracts turn brown	9/64”	1500
Gingelly (*Sesamum indicum*)	CS: 50 FS:100	Jan-Feb May-June	2-4	30×30	20:10:10 2kg $MnSo_4$	-	Seeds turn chocolate brown, stem turns brown, most pods turn yellow	4/64”	300-350
Castor (*Ricinus communis*)	FS:200 Cs:150	Jun-Sep Feb-May	10	90-120x 45-60	40:40:20		90-120 DAS	8/64”	3000
Safflower (*Carthamus tinctorius*)	FS:400 CS:200	Sep-Oct	10-15	40-50×20-25	20:30:20		150-180 DAS	BSS 6×6	1500-2000
Tomato (*Lycopersicon esculentum*)	25	May-June December	350g/ha	75×60 80×75 45×45 25-30 days old seedling	150:60:60 120:60:60 100:100:100	NAA 20-40ppm Borax spray:2.5kg/ha	40 DAA	BSS 10×10	100 -150
Seed soaking in 100ppm IAA for 16 or 2% KNO_3 for 48 h; Seed extraction sing HCl at 25ml/kg of pulp for 30 minutes									
Brinjal (*Solanum melongena*)	FS:200 CS:100	May – June	300-400g/ha	75×60 60×45 30-35 days old seedling	100:100:60	NAA 20ppm,	50 DAA	5/64”	300-350
Seed soaking in GA_3 at 200ppm for 12h; Seed extraction using HCl at 10ml/kg of pulp for 45 minutes									

Chilli (*Capsicum annuum*)	FS:400 CS:200	Round the year June- July February-March	1kg/ha	30×30 45×45 4-6 weeks old seedling	140:70:35	NAA 50ppm Ethrel 400ppm	35-41 DAA	8/64"	400-600
Seed treatment with *Trichoderma viridi* at 4g and *Pseudomonas fluorescens* at 10g/kg of seed									
Sweet pepper/bell pepper (*Capsicum* sp.)	FS: 400 CS:200	June – July Nov-Feb Sep-Oct	1	90×45	140:75:35	2ppm 2,4-D spray	50 DAF Reddening of fruit	-	80-90
Bhendi (*Abelmoschus esculentus*)	FS:400 CS:200	Jun-July Nov-Dec	10-12	45×30 60×20 60×30	20:50:30	DAP 0.5% NAA 75mg/l Ethrel 150 mg/l 2,4-D 10mg/l.	35 DAA Dry fruits with hair line cracks	10/64"	1000-1400
Onion (*Allium cepa*) Bulb production	FS: 1000 CS:500	June-September	8-10 100ppm GA_3 soaking for 3h	20×20	60:60:30	-	110-115 DAT	-	1200-1500
Seed production	FS: 1000 CS:500	October-March	3000-3500kg bulb/ha Select 40-50g bulb and cut 1/3rd portion of top	50×10	60:60:30	-	A week after 75% plants show neck fall 3-4 pickings	10×10mm sieve	800
Pumpkin (*Cucurbita moschata*)	FS:800 CS:400	July-August February-March	2	2-2.5× 1-1.5m	100g of NPK 6:12:12 mixture as basal+ 10g of N (Top dressing) per pit	Ethrel 250ppm four times from 10-15 DAS	Fruits turn orange or yellow and drying of stalk	16/64"	500-1000
Ashgourd (*Benincasa hispida*)	FS:800 CS:400	June-July Jan- Feb	2.5 Seed soaking in 0.5% KH_2PO_4	2.5×2 m	Urea 30g SSP 72g Potash 19 g per pit	Ethephon 250 ppm four times starting from four leaves stage	Seeds have complete ash coating	16/64"	80-100
Seed extraction using HCl at 1:1 ratio for 30 mins (Diluted 6 times with water)									

Bittergourd (*Momordica charantia*)	FS:800 CS:400	Late October June-July	1.8-2	2.5×2m	Urea 30g SSP 72g MP 19g per pit		Fruits turn to bright yellow	16/64"	100-150
Ribbedgourd (*Luffa acutangula*)	FS:1000 CS:500	June- July January-February	2.5-3.0	2.5×2m	Urea 20g SSP 90g MP 15g (basal) Urea 22g (top dressing) per pit	Ethrel 100-200 ppm from first flowering at weekly intervals	60 DAA Fruits dry and turn straw yellow	16/64"	300
Snakegourd (*Trichosanthes cucumerina*)	FS:1000 CS:500	June- July January-February	1.5	2.5×2m	100g 6:12:12 NPK mixture + 10g N (top dressing) per pit	Ethrel 100-200 ppm from first flowering at weekly intervals	Skin colour changes from yellow to orange	16/64"	200

ST: Spreading type; BT: Bunch type; FS: Fuzzy seed; DS: Delinted seed; DAS: Days after sowing; DAT: Days after transplanting; DAA: Days after anthesis; DAF: Days after flowering; SSP: Single super phosphate; MP: Muriate of potash; PS: Potassium sulphate; TS: Top screen; BS: Bottom screen; BSS: British Standard Sieve

52

Hybrid Seed Production Technology At a Glance

Chapter start from next page

Crop	Isolation (m)	Season	Seed rate (kg/ha)		Planting ratio	Border rows	Spacing (cm)	Fertilizer (kg/ ha)	Method of hybrid seed production/Special technique	Seed yield (kg/ ha)
			M	F						
Rice	100	Kharif: May-June Rabi: December – January	10	20	8:2	4	F×F-10×15 F×M-20 M×M-30×15	150:60:60	CMS Rod driving/Rope pulling for supplemental pollination	100
For synchronous flowering: Spray 2% DAP for late flowering parent; spray 2% urea for early flowering parent; spray 75g/ha GA_3, first on 15-20% ear head emergence and second on next day to enhance seed set Time isolation: 25 days; Barrier isolation: Vegetative barrier: Sesbania, maize, sugarcane -30m distance, Artificial barrier: Plastic sheet at 2m height										
Maize	FS:400 CS:200		10	15	Single cross-4:2 Double cross 6:2 3 way cross 6:2	4	60 x 20	200: 100: 100	Detasseling in female parent	1500
Sorghum	FS: 200 CS:200	October-December	5	7.5	-5:2	4	F: 45x30 M: 45x10	100: 50:50	CMS	1500
Synchronisation of flowering: Staggered sowing: Late flowering parent should be sown early and late sowing of early flowering parent; Spray 500ppm of malic hydrazide /300 ppm CCC/skip one irrigation to advancing parent for delay flowering; 1% urea spray to late parent.										
Pearl millet	FS: 1000 CS: 200	November - December	0.75	3.5	6:1 or 4:2	4	45 x 20	100: 60: 40	CMS	1500
Redgram	200	June – September February - March	5	30	4:2	4	45 x 30	25: 50: 25	GMS	
Cotton	FS:50 CS:30	June – July September - October	3-3.5	8-10	8:2 (Block system)	4	Male: 60×45 (or) 90×60 Female: 120×60	100: 50: 25	Emasculation and hand pollination	
Sunflower	600	April – August	1-1.5	4-4.5	3:1	4	45x30	60: 45: 45	CMS, Rubbing with muslin cloth for pollination	
Castor	FS: 200 CS: 150	June – September February – May	4	6	3:1 4-6:1	4	90-120 x 45-60	40: 40: 20	Temperature based sex expression < 32°C-Female expression >32°C-Male expression	1000-1200
Tomato	FS: 200 CS: 100	May-June	25g	100g	5:1	4	60x60 60 x 45	150: 60: 60	Emasculation and pollination Stalking of female parent	100-150

Brinjal	FS:200 CS:100	May – June	50g	200g	5:1	4	75 x60 60 x 45	100: 100: 60	Emasculation and pollination	600-800
Chilli	FS:400 CS:200	Jan-Feb, June-July Sep-Oct, Oct-Nov	0.25	1.00	5:1	4	90 x45	120:60:30	Emasculation and pollination	100-150
Bhendi	FS:400 CS:200	January-March June-August	1	4	5:1	4	75 x30 60 x45	100:60:50	Emasculation and pollination	1000-1200
Pumpkin	FS:1500 CS:1000	August-October	2	6	3:1	4	2mx1.5m	100:75:50	Emasculation and pollination	500
Bittergourd	FS:1500 CS:1000	August-October	1	4	4:1	4	2.5x2m	100:75:75	Emasculation and pollination	500
Ribbedgourd	FS:1500 CS:1000	June-July February-March	0.75	3.25	4:1	4	2.5x2m	50:40:30	Pinching of male flowers/ Chemical sex expression/ Use of gynoecious lines/ Male sterility	250-300
Snakegourd	FS:1500 CS:1000	June-July Dec-Jan	0.5	1.5	4:1		2.5x2m	60:50:40	Emasculation and pollination	220-250

F: Female parent; M: Male parent; CMS: Cytoplasmic male sterility; GMS: Genetic male sterility; FS: Foundation seed; CS Certified seed; CCC: Cycocel; DAP: Diammonium phosphate

Genetic contaminants:

Pollen shedders and partials: Rice, sorghum, pearl millet

Shedding tassel: Maize

Fertile plants: Redgram

Selfed bolls: Cotton

Selfed fruits: Tomato, brinjal, chilli

UNIT - 3

SEED PROCESSING

1

Harvesting and Threshing

I. FILL UPS

1. The type of harvest in paddy is _____.
2. The type of harvest in cumbu is _____.
3. The type of harvest in bhendi is _____.
4. The type of harvest in brinjal is _____.
5. _____consists of separation of grains from the plant stalk.
6. Rubbing and squeezing method of threshing is done in_____.
7. Beating practice is followed in seed extraction of _____.
8. Stripping is done in_____ crop.
9. _____ method involves spreading the stalk on a hard surface and applying impact friction to the panicles by trampling.
10. The average rate of manual treading is_____.
11. _____ is necessary after threshing to remove the trash and the debris from the grain.
12. Flailing and pounding is done in_____.
13. The pedal drum thresher must be operated from _____ per hectare of rice
14. _____ number of sieves are present in multicrop thresher
15. Types of maize threshers are_____ and _____.
16. The thresher used for decortication of groundnut is called_____.
17. Drum thresher is used for threshing_____.
18. Animal threshing is done in _____ crop.
19. Manual harvesting is done in_____ and _____.
20. Mechanical harvesting is done in _____ and _____.

II. TRUE OR FALSE

1. Six to eight harvests are done in gourds.
2. Two to three harvests are done in pulses.

3. Manual harvesting can be done in case of pulses.
4. Seed germination is higher with mechanically extracted seeds as compared to manual method
5. Introduction of animal drawn olpad thresher, the drudgery of the operator increased.

III. MATCH THE FOLLOWING

(i)

1.	Paddy	A	4-5 pickings
2.	Pulses	B	Once over harvest
3.	Bhendi	C	2-3 harvests
4.	Cotton	D	2 harvests
5.	Cumbu	E	5-6 pickings

(ii)

1.	Manual harvest	A	Sunflower
2.	Flailing and pounding	B	Groundnut
3.	Stripping	C	Rice
4.	Corn picker	D	Pulses
5.	Sunflower thresher	E	Maize

IV. ONE WORD QUESTION

1. Mention any two traditional threshing practices with examples
2. Mention any two threshers with examples
3. What are the types of maize threshers ?
4. What are the different power threshers?
5. Mention any two functions of threshing

ANSWER KEYS

I. FILL UPS

1. Once over harvest
2. Two harvests
3. 4-5 pickings
4. 6-8 pickings
5. Threshing
6. Rice
7. Pulses
8. Ground nut
9. Treading method
10. 30 to 40 kg/ha
11. Cleaning
12. Rice
13. 8-12 hour
14. 6

15. Spring and cylinder type sheller
16. Axial flow groundnut thresher
17. Cereals and pulses
18. Sorghum, ragi, pulses
19. Pulses and vegetables
20. Cereals and millets

II. TRUE OR FALSE

1.	False	2.	True
3.	True	4.	True
5.	False		

III. MATCH THE FOLLOWING

(i)		(ii)	
1.	B	1.	D
2.	C	2.	C
3.	A	3.	B
4.	E	4.	E
5.	D	5.	A

IV. ONE WORD ANSWER

1. i) Flailing and pounding - Rice
   ii) Stripping - Groundnut
2. Pedal thresher for rice
   Decorticator for groundnut
3. Spring and cylindrical type
4. To thresh the seed out of the head
   To clean the seed and delivered it to the outlet

V. AT A GLANCE

1. Type of harvest

Types of harvest	Crops
Once over harvest	Paddy, sorghum, maize, bajra, sunflower, groundnut, gingelly
2-3 harvests	All pulses
4-5 harvests	Bhendi, gourds
6-8 harvests	Tomato, brinjal

2. Harvest methods

Crops

Manual (pulses, vegetables)

Mechanical using reaper, binder, thresher, combine, corn picker (All cereals and millets)

3. Traditional methods

1. Rubbing and squeezing (Rice, bajra, ragi, pulses)
2. Beating (Pulses)
3. Stripping (Groundnut)
4. Treading by animals and tractor (Cereals, pulses)
5. Flailing and pounding (Rice)
6. Animal threshing (Sorghum, bajra, ragi, pulses)
7. Tractor/power tiller threshing (Cereals, pulses)

Threshers

1. Pedal thresher (Rice)
2. Drum thresher (Cereals, pulses)
3. Multicrop thresher (Cereals, pulses)
4. Maize sheller
5. Paddy thresher
6. Sunflower thresher
7. Groundnut decorticator
8. Vegetable seed extractor

2

Seed Extraction

I. FILL UPS

1. The seed removal in wet fruits is known as _____.
2. The seed removal in dry fruits is known as _____.
3. _____ is used for mechanical extraction.
4. Dry method of extraction is done in _____ crops.
5. Wet method of extraction is done in _____.
6. The tomato seeds extracted by _____ method will be dull in colour
7. In tomato, seed extraction is done by _____ (or) _____ method.
8. The acid used for extraction of tomato is _____.
9. The seed recovery from acid extraction is _____.
10. The seed recovery from scooping method in ashgourd is _____.

II. TRUE OR FALSE

1. Extraction of vegetable seed using NaOH showed high germination percentage.
2. In alkali extraction of brinjal, washing soda is used.
3. Citric acid method is a widely practiced method of tomato seed extraction.
4. Dry extraction is done in fleshy fruits of vegetables.
5. In ashgourd, seed is extracted by scooping method.

III. MATCH THE FOLLOWING

1.	Dry extraction	A	Tomato
2.	Ashgourd seed extraction	B	Field crops
3.	Alkali method of seed extraction	C	Washing soda
4.	Acid extraction	D	Dry extraction using curry leaf powder machine
5.	Chilli	E	Scooping

IV. ONE WORD QUESTION

1. Mention the methods of wet extraction in brinjal.
2. How is ashgourd seed extraction done.

ANSWER KEYS

I. FILL UPS

1. Extraction	2. Threshing	3. Threshers
4. Agricultural	5. Brinjal	6. Fermentation method
7. Fermentation (or) acid	8. HCl	9. 0.5 to 1%
10. 0.5 to 0.75 %		

II. TRUE OR FALSE

1. False	2. True
3. False	4. False
5. True	

III. MATCH THE FOLLOWING

1. B
2. E
3. C
4. A
5. D

IV. ONE WORD ANSWER

1. i) Fermentation
   ii) Acid method
   iii) Alkali method
2. Fruits are cut open and the seeds are scooped out and wased with water.

V. AT A GLANCE

Threshing : Seed removal from dry fruits

Extraction: Seed removal from wet fruits

Seed extraction method	Separation of seeds
1. Dry extraction	Beating and separation (All field crops)
2. Wet extraction	Pulping /soaking/fermenting and seed separation (Tomato, brinjal, gourds)

Fermentation: Ferment well mature and sliced fruits for 24-48 h and separate seed (Tomato and brinjal)

Acid method: Add HCl @ 25-30 ml/kg of pulp and kept for 30 min. Wash 3-4 times and separate seeds. Seed recovery is 0.5-1%. Seeds are bright coloured and stored longer than fermentation method.

3

Seed Drying

I. FILL UPS

1. The process of eliminating moisture from the seed is called_____.
2. _____ is the common conventional method, in which drying of harvested crop is carried out in the field.
3. In _____ method the outside air is heated with the help of burner heater and circulated into the godown.
4. _____ is a continuous column heated air drier largely used for paddy.
5. During _____ moisture concentration equalizes in the kernel and then evaporation of surface moisture is nearly as rapid as the start of drying.

II. TRUE OR FALSE

1. Non-mixing column dryer consists of a tall vertical column through which paddy flows by gravity.
2. LSU dryers is for paddy.
3. Greater the seed moisture content, greater should be the drying temperature.
4. Drying between 12 noon and 2 pm should be avoided.
5. When the rate of moisture loss from the seed to the surrounding atmosphere is not equal to the rate of moisture gained by the seed from the atmosphere.

III. MATCH THE FOLLOWING

1.	LSU dryers	A	Burner heater
2.	Forced heated air drying	B	90ºF
3.	Physical drying	C	Paddy
4.	10 %	D	Radiant energy of the sun
5.	18-30 %	E	110ºF

IV. ONE WORD QUESTION

1. Mention any two factors affecting drying
2. What are the different methods of drying?
3. What are the different metal bin dryers?
4. What are the different continuous flow dryers?

ANSWER KEYS

I. FILL UPS

1. Drying
2. Physical drying
3. Forced heated air –drying
4. Louisiana State University dryer
5. Tempering

II. TRUE OR FALSE

1. True
2. True
3. False
4. True
5. False

III. MATCH THE FOLLOWING

1. C
2. A
3. D
4. E
5. B

IV. ONE WORD ANSWER

1. i) Size of the bin and capacity
   ii) Depth of the spread of seed
2. i) Physical drying
   ii) Mechanical drying
3. i) Circular metal bin dryers
   ii) Rectangular metal bin dryers
4. i) LSU dryers
   ii) Non-mixing column dryer

V. AT A GLANCE

Seed drying	Removal of surface moisture which caused imbalance between moisture of surface and inner portion of seed leading to integration of outer layer
Equilibrium moisture	Rate of loss is equal to rate of gain
Factors	Initial moisture, Size and capacity of bin, Rate of air blow, Temperature and RH of atmosphere, Static pressure, Drying temperature
Methods	1. Natural drying – Avoid drying between 12 noon to 2 pm
	2. Mechanical drying- forced natural air drying /forced heated air drying. Temperature should not exceed 42°C
Metal bin driers	Rectangular bin drier; Continuous flow drier (LSU drier, non mixing column drier)

4

Seed Processing

I. FILL UPS

1. The _____ is used in modern seed handling and storage systems for preliminary cleaning.
2. _____ removes large inert matter from the seeds.
3. _____ is a machine that do the rubbing action and debeard the seeds and polish the seed.
4. _____ is the basic cleaner in most seed processing plants.
5. _____ is done to remove light matter from the seed mass.
6. _____separator method makes use of a combination of weight and surface characteristics of the seed to be separated.
7. In_____ separator seeds are separated according to the length.
8. _____separator separates the seed according to its surface texture (or) related seed characteristics.
9. _____ is used to separate discoloured seed, greatly of lower quality.
10. If the debris has a different surface texture, it may be possible to remove by _____.
11. _____ separator classifies seed according to its shape and rolling ability
12. _____ is the removal of undesirable materials, weed seed and other crop seeds to improve physical and physiological qualities
13. _____ removes husk and scratching of seed coat
14. _____ is a method that separates / upgrades based on weight, shape, length, texture, affinity to liquid, colour etc.
15. _____ separates the seed based on seed size.

II. TRUE OR FALSE

1. Pre-cleaning is required for hand harvested and winnowed seeds.
2. A huller removes beards and polishes the seed.

3. A scalper removes lighter inert matter from the seeds.
4. The magnetic separator separates seed according to its surface texture.
5. Different surface textured debris can be removed by friction cleaning.

III. MATCH THE FOLLOWING

1.	Air screen cleaner	A	Seed length
2.	Magnetic separator	B	Seed size
3.	Spiral separator	C	Surface texture
4.	Indented cylinder separator	D	Seed weight
5.	Specific gravity separator	E	Seed shape

IV. ONE WORD QUESTION

1. Mention any two seed separator based on physical properties
2. Mention any two pre-cleaning machines?

ANSWER KEYS

I. FILL UPS

1. Pre-cleaner
2. Scalper
3. Debearder
4. Air-screen cleaner cum grader
5. Aspiration
6. Specific gravity separator
7. Indented cylinder seperator
8. Magnetic separator
9. Colour separator
10. Friction cleaning
11. Spiral separator
12. Seed processing
13. Huller-scarifier
14. Upgrading
15. Air screen cleaner

II. TRUE OR FALSE

1. False
2. False
3. False
4. True
5. True

III. MATCH THE FOLLOWING

1. B
2. C
3. E
4. A
5. D

IV. ONE WORD ANSWER

1. Magnetic separator – surface texture, spiral separator- seed shape
2. Debearder, scalper

V. AT A GLANCE

1. Flow chart depicting processing sequence in different crops

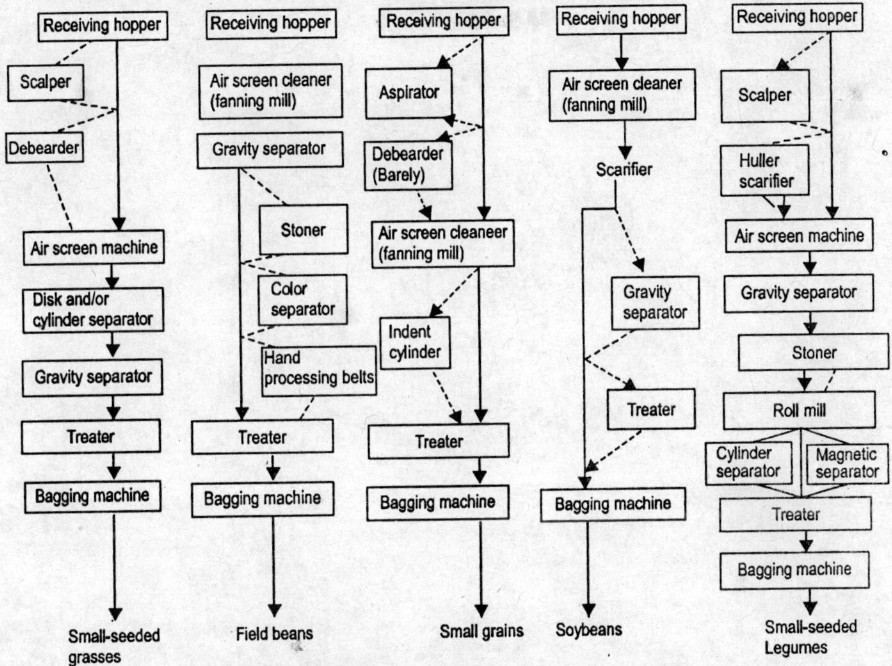

Flow chart for processing sequence

2. Seed processing principles

Seed processing	Removal of undesirable materials, weed seed, other crop seeds, illfilled immature and damaged seed to improve physical and physiological qualities.
Physical properties	*Seed size:* Air screen cleaner, *Seed weight:* Specific gravity separator, *Seed length:* Indented cylinder separator, *Surface texture:* Magnetic separator, *Seed colour:* Electronic Colour separator, *Seed shape:* Spiral separator.
Precleaning	*Precleaner* – Removes trash, stones, clods, plants reminants, chaff, other inert material which are larger or lighter than seeds, *Scalper* – Removes large materials and allow seed to pass through, *Debeader* – Remove awns, beads, dehull, polish, *Huller – Scarifier* – Removal of husk and scratching of seed coat.
Cleaning – grading	2 and 4 screen models used very common, but larger one upto 8 screens.
Upgrading	Separates / upgrades based on weight, shape, length, texture, affinity to liquid, colour etc.

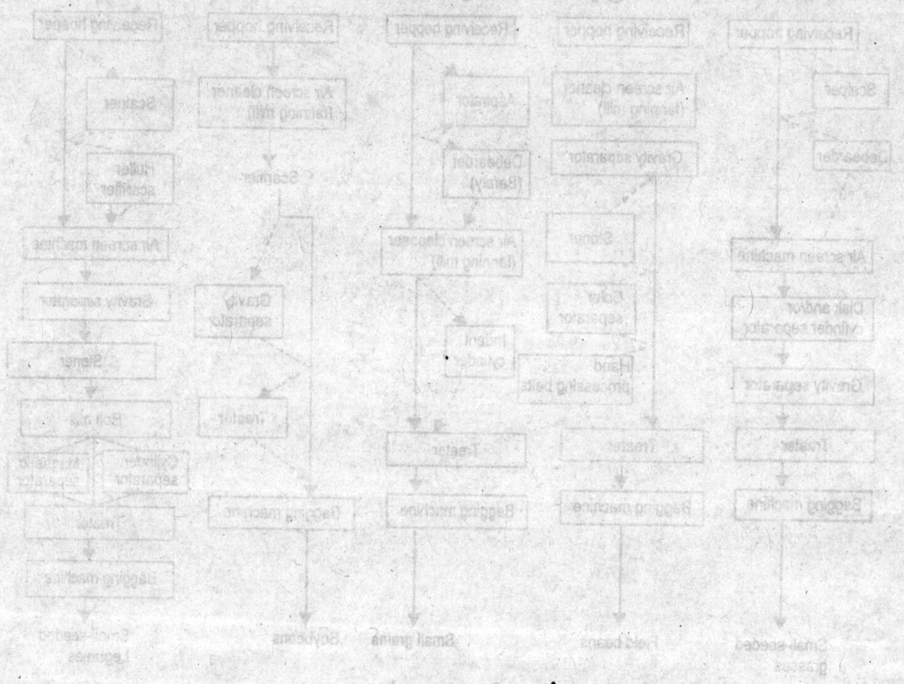

5

Special Techniques in Seed Upgradation

I. FILL UPS

1. _____ is the step in which the seeds are allowed to attain enough water holding capacity facilitating separation.
2. _____ process helps to draw the precise difference between filled live and filled dead seeds in IDS method.
3. PREVAC stands for_____.
4. NIR stands for_____.
5. IDS stands for_____.
6. _____works on the principle of interaction of electromagnetic radiation with matter, which takes several forms.
7. _____ helps in detection of internal insect infestation in *Cordia arficana.*
8. _____ technique is based on the principle density, the seeds are floated using salt solution and quality seeds are separated.
9. _____ process separates dead and damaged seeds.
10. The final step in IDS method is _____.

II. TRUE OR FALSE

1. The duration of separation in IDS method.
2. IDS will increase the seed value due to faster germination.
3. The upgradation technique used for paddy is water floatation technique.
4. Winged seeds will be dewinged in IDS method.
5. The sound seeds absorbs and desorbs water at a different rate than dead filled seed and damaged seeds which is the principle of IDS technique.

III. MATCH THE FOLLOWING

1.	NIR technique	A. Density principle
2.	Water floatation technique	B. Monochromatic radiation
3.	PREVAC	C. Incubation
4.	IDS	D. Evacuate air bubbles

IV. ONE WORD QUESTION

1. Mention any two special techniques employed for upgradation of seed lot
2. What are the three steps of IDS technique?
3. Mention any two uses of NIR technique
4. Mention any two advantages of water floatation technique
5. Mention any one disadvantage of IDS method

ANSWER KEYS

I. FILL UPS

1. Incubation
2. Drying
3. Pressure vacuum method
4. Near infrared
5. Incubation-drying -separation
6. NIR spectroscopy
7. NIR spectroscopy
8. Water floatation technique
9. PREVAC method
10. Separation

II. TRUE OR FALSE

1. False
2. True
3. True
4. False
5. True

III. MATCH THE FOLLOWING

1. B
2. A
3. D
4. C

IV. ONE WORD ANSWER

1. i) Near Infrared Technique

   ii) Pressure vacuum method
2. i) Incubation

   ii) Drying and separation
3. Rapid analysis of seed vigour of *Pinus patula*

   Identification of seed source and parents of *Pinus sylvestris*

4. i) Separate immature and ill filled seeds
   ii) Check on pathogen infection
5. i) Winged seeds need to be dewinged before applying IDS treatment

V. AT A GLANCE

IDS (Incubation, Drying and Separation): To separate dead or deteriorated seeds from live seeds

PREVAC method: Separate dead, insect and mechanically damaged seed from live and good seeds.

Water floation technique: Using sat solution (2kg common salt/10 litres of water) and floating fresh egg, floated seeds are separated from sinkers. Ten kilograms of seeds are separated by using above salt solution.

6

Seed Quality Enhancement

I. FILL UPS

1. _____ means the application of physical, biological, chemical agents to the seed in order to enhance the physical, genetical, biochemical and health qualities of seed.
2. _____ coined the term seed priming.
3. _____ is the impregnation of the needy substance into seed through imbibition phase.
4. In paddy, seed fortification is done with _____ chemical.
5. In groundnut, seed fortification is done with _____ chemical.
6. In green gram, seed fortification is done with _____ vitamins.
7. The organic acid used for seed fortification in greengram is _____.
8. _____ is the process of hydrating the seed followed by dehydration.
9. _____ and _____ are vitamins used for seed hardening.
10. _____ is the process of controlled hydration of seeds to a level that permits pre-germinative metabolic activity.
11. _____ is commonly used as a priming osmoticum.
12. _____ involves soaking of seeds in salt solutions.
13. _____ priming method consists of mixing seeds with an organic (or) inorganic carrier and water for a period of time.
14. In _____ priming method, seeds are coated with biological agents like bacteria and soaking in warm water.
15. _____ is the misting of seed with water and redrying before they complete germination.
16. _____ is the series of molecular events that allows cells to duplicate and segregate their chromosomes to new cells.
17. In _____ seeds are first either pregerminated in water (or) an osmoticum.

18. An example for fungicide additive is _____.
19. An example for additives in microorganisms _____.
20. _____ is the process of enclosing a seed with a small quality of inert material to form a globular unit.
21. _____ is normally used to apply a thin, uniform layer of polymer over seeds without increasing size.
22. _____ is the application of precise amount of dyes (or) pigments directly on to the seed to improve its brand identity.
23. _____ ingredient used for hydrophilic coating.
24. Pelleting with biocontrol agents like *Pseudomonas* is known as_____.
25. Gum arabic is commonly used as_____.

II. TRUE OR FALSE

1. Seed colouring acts as insect and bird repellant.
2. Radicle mergence is stimulated by fluid drilling.
3. Soaking in osmotic solution is called hydropriming.
4. Leguminous seeds are responsive for seed hardening.
5. Leaves of hardened plants have more of starch.

III. MATCH THE FOLLOWING

(i)

1.	Seed fortification	A Hydration and dehydration
2.	Seed hardening	B Controlled hydration
3.	Seed priming	C Enrichment
4.	Fluid drilling	D Inert material enclosing
5.	Pelleting	E Laponite in water

(ii)

1.	Osmopriming	A Water
2.	Halopriming	B Polyethylene glycol
3.	Hydropriming	C Salt solution
4.	Biopriming	D Misting water and redrying
5.	Drum priming	E Bacteria

(iii)

1.	PEG	A	Filler
2.	Methyl cellulose	B	Botanical dyes
3.	Pungam	C	Encapsulation media
4.	Marigold	D	Adhesive
5.	Carrageenan	E	Osmotic solution

IV. ONE WORD QUESTION

1. Mention any two advantages of seed colouring
2. Mention one benefit of seed polymer coating
3. Mention any one disadvantage of seed pelleting
4. Mention any one advantage of seed pelleting
5. Mention any two characters of filler
6. Give any two examples of filler
7. Mention any two characteristics of adhesive
8. Give any two examples of adhesive
9. Mention any three different types of priming
10. Give any two examples of botanical dyes
11. Mention any one disadvantage of seed hardening
12. Mention any two benefits of seed fortification
13. Give any two examples for botanical dyes
14. Give any two factors affecting priming
15. Mention one benefit of fluid drilling

ANSWER KEYS

I. FILL UPS

1. Seed quality enhancement
2. Malnassy
3. Seed fortification
4. Potassium di hydrogen chloride and KCl
5. $CaCl_2$
6. Ascorbic acid
7. Succinic acid
8. Seed hardening
9. Vitamin K3, Adenine
10. Seed priming
11. Polyethylene glycol
12. Halopriming
13. Solid matric priming
14. Biopriming
15. Drum priming
16. Cell cycle
17. Fluid drilling
18. Bavistin

19. *Bacillus subtilis*
20. Seed pelleting
21. Seed polymer coating
22. Seed colouring
23. Magnesium carbonate
24. Protective pelleting
25. Adhesive

II. TRUE OR FALSE

1.	True	2.	False
3.	False	4.	True
5.	True		

III. MATCH THE FOLLOWING

(i)		(ii)		(iii)	
1.	C	1.	B	1.	E
2.	A	2.	C	2.	D
3.	B	3.	A	3.	A
4.	E	4.	E	4.	B
5.	D	5.	D	5.	C

IV. ONE WORD ANSWER

1. i) Gives protection to seed
   ii) Seal the cracks on seed coat
2. Polymer coating results in more even seeding rate due to the smooth flow of the seeds.
3. Delayed field emergence at low moisture level
4. Small and irregular shaped seeds can be handled easily by pelleting which changes the shape of seed
5. i) It should be non-toxic
   ii) Friendly to both seed, adhesive and environment
6. Lime, gypsum, arappu leaf powder
7. i) The coating must be porous to allow movement of air to the seed
   ii) Should have appropriate viscosity for each application
8. Gum arabic, methyl cellulose, gelatin
9. i) Osmopriming
   ii) Halo priming
   iii) Solid matrix priming

10. i) Flowering is slightly accelerated
    ii) Induces resistance to drought and salinity
11. Prolonged soaking may show adverse effects because of anaerobic respiration leading to accumulation of toxic metabolites.
12. i) The low and medium quality seeds can be upgraded
    ii) Seed fortification is a low cost technology compared to soil and foliar application
13. i) Beet root
    ii) Jamun
14. i) Aeration
    ii) Temperature
15. To control radicle emergence of pregerminated hydrated seed and also to protect from damage and emerged radicles.

V. AT A GLANCE

1. Terms

Malnassy (1971)	Coined the term "Seed Priming"
Heydecker (1975)	Acknowledged the term seed priming which is synonymous with seed invigouration; introduced the terms halopriming and osmopriming
Taylor *et al.* (1988)	Introduced the term "Solid Matric Priming" (SMP)
Khan *et al.* (1990)	Proposed "Matriconditioning" as an alternative for SMP
Callan *et al.* (1990)	Coined the word "Biopriming"

2. History

Middle Ages	Soaking of seeds in chlorine salts and manure
1600's	Soaking in salt water
1700's	Introduction of copper salts
1740	Introduction of arsenic chemicals
1765	Soaking in hot water
1808	Ban on arsenic chemicals in Germany
1915	Introduction of organo – mercurials
1960	Introduction of first systemic fungicide
1970	First systemic fungicide against air borne pathogens
1982	Ban on organo – mercurial compounds in western Europe
1990	Introduction of modern fungicides and insecticides

3. Seed fortification

In seed fortification, seeds are soaked in solutions of equal volume/in different seed to solution ratio for duration of 6–24h depending upon the crop to raise the moisture content of the seed to 20–25% just enough for endogenous impregnation of chemicals through exogenous application. Then, the seeds are sown after surface drying for easy handling or as such (not specified for drying back to original moisture content).

Crop	Chemical	Concentration	Duration
Wheat	Potassium dihydrogen phosphate	0.5%	12h
Groundnut	$CaCl_2$	1.0%	6h
Sunflower	Distilled water or KNO_3 or $FeSO_4$ or $ZnSO_4$	0.1%	12h
Sunflower	Ammonium acetate	400 mg l^{-1}	10h
Field bean	Ammonium molybdate	500 or 1000 ppm	24h
Sorghum and Cotton	KCl	2%	8h
Paddy	Potassium dihydrogen chloride and KCl	0.5% and 1.0%	12h
Cowpea	Zinc sulphate + Manganese sulphate + Na_2MO_4	Each 100 mg/kg of seed	3h
Mustard	Magnesium nitrate or $MgSO_4$	0.5 %	12h or 96h
Cluster bean	$FeSO_4$	1.0%	3h
Blackgram	$ZnSO_4$	100 ppm	3h

4. Seed hardening

It is the process of hydrating the seed to initiate the pre-germinative metabolism followed by dehydration which fixes the biochemical events.

Principle

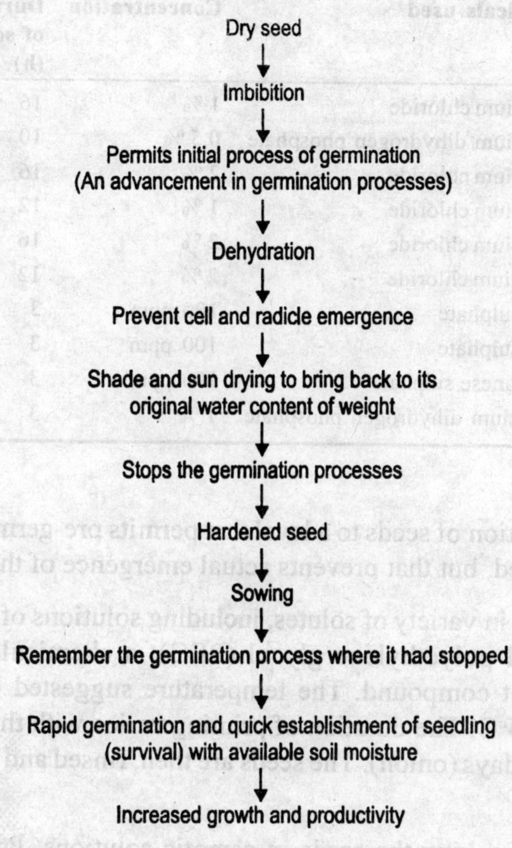

Method

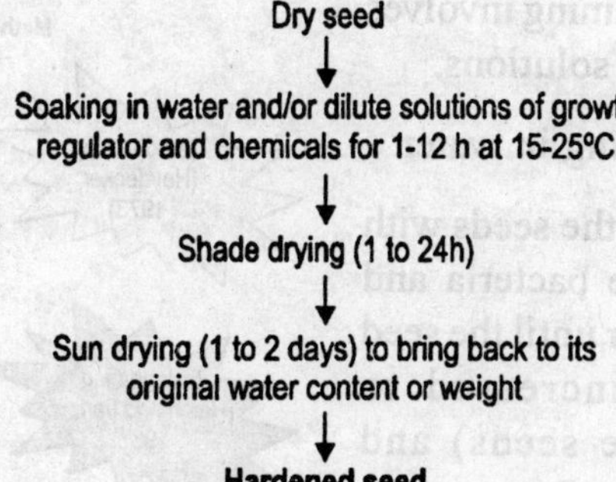

Techniques

Crop	Chemicals used	Concentration	Duration of soaking (h)	Seed to solution ratio
Paddy	Potassium chloride	1 %	16	1:0.6
Sorghum	Potassium dihydrogen phosphate	0.5 %	10	1:0.3
Cumbu	Potassium chloride	2 %	16	1:0.3
Ragi	Potassium chloride	1 %	12	1:0.7
Cotton	Potassium chloride	2 %	16	1:0.5
Sunflower	Potassium chloride	2 %	12	1:0.6
Redgram	Zinc sulphate	100 ppm	3	1:0.3
Blackgram	Zinc sulphate	100 ppm	3	1:0.3
Greengram	Manganese sulphate	100 ppm	3	1:0.3
Bengalgram	Potassium dihydrogen phosphate	1 %	3	1:0.3

5. Seed priming

Controlled hydration of seeds to a level that permits pre-germinative metabolic activity to proceed, but that prevents actual emergence of the radicle.

Seeds are soaked in variety of solutes, including solutions of various inorganic salts, sugars and polyethylene glycol (PEG), a chemically inert and high molecular weight compound. The temperature suggested during priming is between 10° – 15°C. The duration of priming varies with the crop from 1 day (sorghum) to 23 days (onion). The seeds are then, rinsed and redried to original water content.

Osmopriming: Soaking the seeds in osmotic solutions, Polyethylene glycol (PEG).

Halopriming: Halopriming involves soaking of seed in salt solutions.

Hydropriming: Soaking in water.

Biopriming: Coating the seeds with biological agents like bacteria and soaking in warm water until the seed moisture content increased to 35-40% (e.g. maize seeds) and redrying.

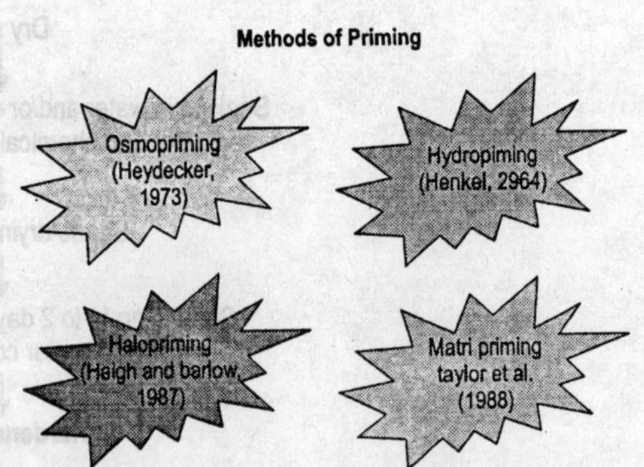

Drum priming: Misting of seed with water and redrying before they complete germination.

6. Seed pelleting

Enclosing a seed with a small quantity of inert material just large enough to produce a globular unit of standard size to facilitate precision planting.

Deposition of a layer of inert materials that may obscure the original shape and size of the seed, resulting in a substantial weight increase and improved plantability.

Steps

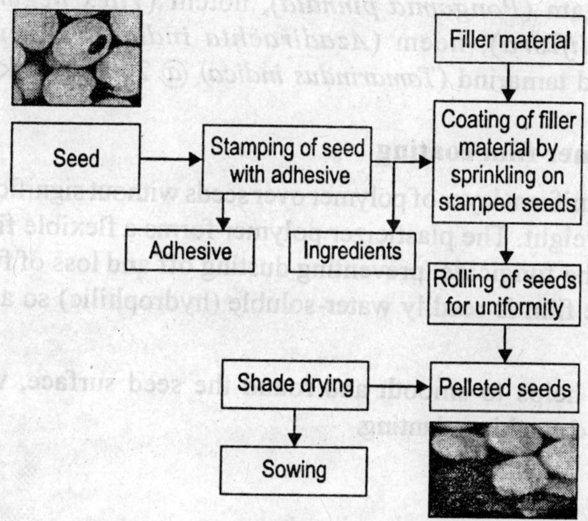

Types of pelleting

Types of pelleting	Ingredients for pelleting
Inoculant pelleting	Biofertilizer, viz., *Rhizobium*, *Phosphobacteria, Azospirillum, Azatobactor*, arbuscular mychorhizae, *Azophos*
Protective pelleting	Biocontrol agents like *Pseudomonas*, *Trichodermma, Rhizobacteria, Bacillus, Streptomyces,* and insecticides and fungicides
Herbicide pelleting	Filler antitode or absorbent coating. Herbicide antitode like 1,8 napthalic anhydride (NA)
Nutrient pelleting	Coating with micro and macronutrients namely ZnSO4, $FeSO_4$, $CuSO_4$, KCl, borax, diammonium phosphate (DAP) and other salts suitable for each crop.
Hydrophilic coating (Water stress condition)	Starch graft polymers, magnesium carbonate
Oxygen supplier coating (Flooded condition)	Peroxides of zinc and calcium
Organic pelleting	Leaf powders (arappu, pungam, acacias) and rhizome powders (turmeric, *Acorus*)

Adhesive

Gum arabic, methyl cellulose, gelatin, casein, plastic rexins, polyvinyl acetate, methyl ethyl cellulose, polyurethane polyvinyl alcohol, polyvinyl acetate, poly electrolyte or dextran and polyethylene oxide.

Filler

Lime, gypsum, dolomite, rock phosphate, montmorillonite, vermiculite, blood, peat, poultry manure, moss and mucilage. Leaf powders of arappu (*Albizia amara*), pungam (*Pongamia pinnata*), notchi (*Vitex negundo*), prosopis (*Prosopis juliflora*), neem (*Azadirachta indica*), moringa (*Moringa longifolia*) and tamarind (*Tamarindus indica*) @ 200-300 g kg^{-1} of seed.

7. Seed polymer film coating

Apply a thin, uniform layer of polymer over seeds without significantly increasing seed size or weight. The plasticizer polymer forms a flexible film that adheres and protects the fungicide, preventing dusting off and loss of fungicide during handling. The film is readily water-soluble (hydrophilic) so as not to impede germination.

Film coating helps to smooth and round the seed surface, which improves flowability and machine planting.

Steps

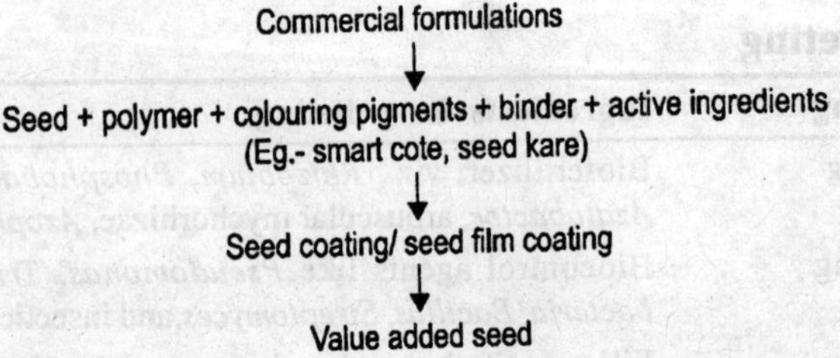

8. Seed colouring

Colouring of seeds with different naturally colouring dyes and artificial chemical dyes in order to enable brand identification and to give the seed a distinct and attractive look. Improve marketability, brand identity and enable the farmers for easy identification of the varieties based on colour. Acts as insect and bird repellant. Seed lots of different years could be easily identified and adulteration of seeds can be checked.

Natural dyes

Botanical dyes	Colour appearance	Active principle	pH after seed treatment
Henna	Sand stone	Not known	4.30
Beetroot	Teak	Betanin	6.20
Hibiscus	Sand stone	Syanidin diglycoside	5.49
Basella	Leaf brown	Not known	5.20
Anatto	Dawn glow	Bixin	4.35
Jamun (without seed)	Brandy	Jamboline	6.75
Jamun (with seed)	Sand stone	Jamboline	6.75
Marigold	Golden brown	α-terthienyl	4.35
Turmeric	Lemon yellow	Curcumin	2.88
Opuntia	Red	Not known	3.00

Chemical dyes

Dye	Chemical composition
Indigo caramine	$C_{16}HgN_2O_2(So_3Na)_2$
Tital yellow	Dehydrothio-P-toluidine
Methyl orange	$Me_2NC_6H_4N : NC_6H_4SO_2Na$
Methyl red	$Me_9NC_6H_4N : NC_6H_4COOH$
Nigrosine	$C_{38}H_{27}N_3$
Erichro black-T	$C_{20}H_{12}N_3O_7Sna$
Ammonium purpureate	(Mureoxide) $(NH_4)_4P_2O_7$
Boromocresol green	$C_{21}H_{14}Br_4O_5S$
Bromocresol purple	$C_{19}H_{10}Br_2Cl_2O_2S$
Crystal violet	$C_{25}H_{30}ClN_3$
Malachite green	$Me_2NC_6H_4C_6H_5C : NC_6H_4Me_2Cl$
Congo red	$C_{32}H_{22}O_6N_6S_2Na_2$
Phenol red	$C_{19}H_{14}O_5S$
Cotton blue	$C_{32}H_{25}N_3O_9S_3Na_2$
Gentian violet	$C_{25}H_{30}ClN_3$
Fuchsine	$C_{20}H_{17}N_3Na_2O_9S_3$
Methylene blue	$C_{19}H_{10}Br_2C_{12}O_25$
Rhodamine-B	$C_{28}H_{31}ClN_2O_3$
Neutral red	$Me_2NC_6H_3N : NC_6H_2MeNH_2HCl$
Fast green	$C_{37}H_{34}N_2Na_2O_{10}S_3$

9. Differentiate between polymer coating, colouring and pelleting

Particulars	Seed polymer coating	Seed colouring	Seed pelleting
Adhesive	It has a plasticizer and binding ability.	Natural /synthetic dye is needed.	Adhesives, nutrients, fillers, biofertilizers ar e required
Fungicide and insecticide	Can be combined	Can be combined	Can be combined
Shape of the seed	Not obscured	Not modified	Shape is modified as globular unit
Size of the seed	Not modified	Not modified	Modified due to addition of fillers
Filler materials	Not required	Not required	Gypsum (or) botanical leaf powders.
Nutrients and biofertilizers	Usualy combined	Not combined	Combined during pelleting
Process	Have coating process	Colouring process	Stamping, coating and rolling process
Safety and handling	More safe	More safe	No safety
Resistance to mechanical injury	More resistance	No resistance	More resistance
Stability	More stable	Varies according to dye used	Less stable
Prevention of dusting off fungicides	Prevents dusting off pesticide and fungicide	Not possible	Does not prevent
Wastage of pesti-cide and fungicide	Completely prevented	Not possible	Wastage is more during handling
Physical appearance	Improved	Improved	Improved but having no preference
Handling	Easy handling	Easy handling	Results in breakage
Identification	Brand identify	Brand identify	Not useful
Germination and vigour	Improved	Improved	Improved, but not preferred by consumers
Storability	Good storer	Good storer	Cannot be stored for more than 3 to 4 months
Applicability	Suitable for dry, garden and wet land situations	Suitable for dry and garden land situations	Suitable for only garden / wet land situation
Inter linking of technologies	Compatible	Compatible	Compatible

SEED COATING TECHNOLOGIES

Seed polymer coating

Sophisticated process of applying precise amount of active ingredients along with a liquid polymer directly on to the seed surface without obscuring its shape

Seed colouring

Application of precise amount of dyes or pigments directly on to the seed to improve its brand identify and marketability

Seed pelleting

Process of enclosing the seed with small quantity of ingredients along with filler material to produce a globular unit of standard size to facilitate precision planting.

Steps of various seed coating technologies

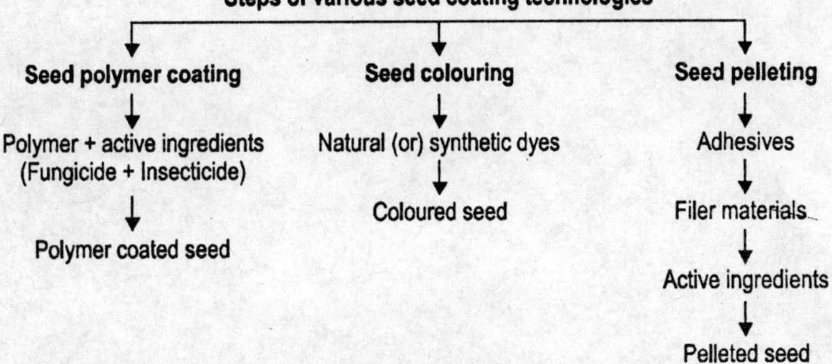

10. Pregermination technique for groundnut

Soak 1 kg of seeds in 650 ml of 0.5% $CaCl_2$ for 6 hours (For preparation of 0.5% $CaCl_2$ solution, dissovle 125gm of $CaCl_2$ in 25 litres of H_2O)

↓

Remove seeds after 6 hours, spread over moist gunny bag and covered with another moist gunny bag for 20-24 hours.

↓

After 24 hours separate the seeds with sprouted radicle (just visible expression of radicle).

↓

For every 2 hrs interval separate the germinated seeds for 2-3 times

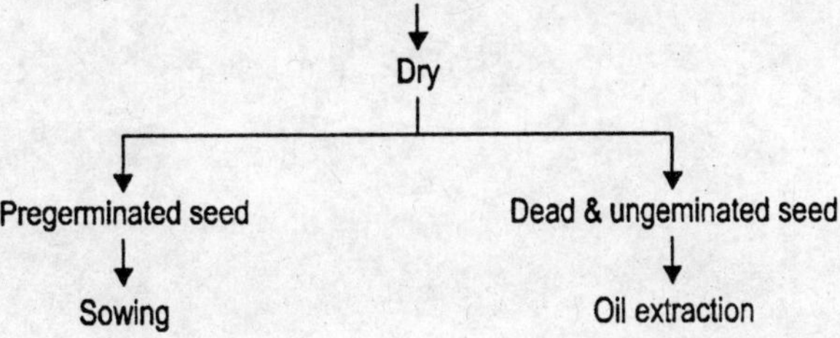

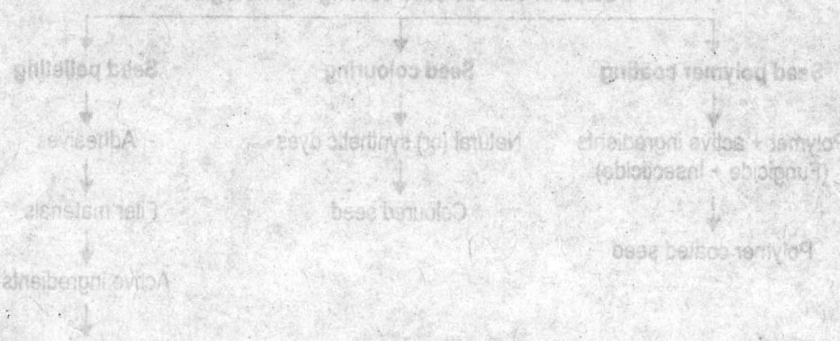

UNIT - 4

SEED CERTIFICATION

1

Seed Act and Rules

I. FILL UPS

1. The seed act was passed in the year_____.
2. _____ advise the central and state government regarding suitability of seed testing laboratories.
3. _____deals with all the problems related seed certification and to co-ordinate the work of state seed certification agencies.
4. _____ agencies take sample to inspect seed lot and certify seeds of any notified kind of varieties.
5. _____ initiate testing program and collaborate with state seed laboratory and designed to promote uniformity in test results between all seed laboratories in India.
6. _____ look into the grievances of certified seed producers against a seed certification officials.
7. _____ controls the quality of seeds sold in the market including suitable agencies for regulating seed quality.
8. _____ has power to examine records, register and document of seed dealer.
9. Seed control order was passed in the year_____.
10. The new seed policy was implemented in the year_____.
11. _____ laid a special emphasis of import of high quality seeds and to encourage the domestic industry.
12. Seed rules was enacted in the year _____.
13. Restriction on export and import of seeds is given in _____.
14. _____ is voluntary for notified kind / varieties.
15. _____ have the labelling, testing penalty, minimum standards etc like provisions.

II. TRUE OR FALSE

1. FS and CS only to be certified but not BS.
2. Seed act was enacted in the year 1968.
3. Renewal license of dealers is coming under gist of seed control order 1983.
4. Seeds of only those varieties which are notified under section 5 of seed act shall be eligible for certification.
5. Seed analyst can break open any container in which seed of any notified kind (or) variety is kept for sale.

III. MATCH THE FOLLOWING

1.	1966	A Essential commodity act
2.	1968	B New seed policy
3.	1955	C Seed control order
4.	1988	D Seed rules
5.	1983	E Seed act

IV. ONE WORD QUESTION

1. Mention any one function of state seed certification agencies
2. How many sections are present in seed act?
3. Mention one function of central seed committee
4. Mention one power of seed inspector
5. State any one duty of seed analyst
6. How many state seed testing laboratories in the country?

ANSWER KEYS

I. FILL UPS

1. 1966
2. Central seed committee
3. Central seed certification board
4. State seed certification
5. Central seed testing laboratory
6. Appellate authority
7. Regulatory legislation
8. Seed inspector
9. 1983
10. October 1, 1988
11. New seed policy
12. 1968
13. Seed control order
14. Seed certification
15. Regulatory legislation

II. TRUE OR FALSE

1. True 2. False
3. True 4. True
5. False

III. MATCH THE FOLLOWING

1. E
2. D
3. A
4. B
5. C

IV. ONE WORD ANSWER

1. Certified seeds of any notified kinds or varieties.
2. 25
3. To advise central and state governments on all matters related to seeds.
4. To take samples of seed of any notified kind/variety from any person selling such seed.
5. The seed analyst shall, from time to time, forward to state government the reports giving the result of analytical work done by them.
6. 130

IV. AT A GLANCE

1. Key to the Seeds Act, 1966 and the Seeds Rules, 1968

S. No.	Subject	Related Section(s)of the Seed Act	Related Rules of the Seed Rules	Related Forms of the Seed Rules
I.	**Minimum limits and labeling (Seed Quality control):**			
	A. General	1,2,23,25	Part I-1, 2 Part XI-38	
	B. Central Seed Committee	3	Part II-3, 4	
	C. Seed Testing Laboratory	4, 16(2), 16(3), 16(4)	Part III-5 Part X-36	
	D. Notification of kinds and varieties	5		
	E. Labeling provisions	6, 7, 17	Part V-7, 8, 9, 10, 11, 12 Part VI-13	
	F. Seed Analyst	12, 16(1)	Part IX-20, 21, 33, 35	VII
	G. Seed Inspector	13, 14, 15	Part IX-22,23 Part X-24, 25, 26, 27, 28, 29, 30, 31, 32, 34, 37, 39	III, IV, V, VI, VIII
	H. Penalty	19, 20, 21 22		
	I. Exemption	24		
II.	**Seed Certification:**			
	A. Certification Agency	8, 18	Part IV-6	
	B. Certification	9, 10	Part VI-14 Part VII-15, 16, 17	I, II
	C. Appeal	11	Part VIII-18, 19	

2

Seed Certification

I. FILL UPS

1. _____ is a legally sanctioned system for quality control on seed multiplication and production.
2. Certification consists of _____ phases.
3. In single application, the maximum area that can be offered for certification is _____.
4. AOSCA stands for_____.
5. _____ is the removal of unwanted plants
6. _____ is the presence of 'B' line in 'A' line
7. _____ is the shedding of pollen from female parent (i.e) A line
8. _____ is the male part/inflorescence left in the field without removal and are shedding pollen for outcrossing.
9. _____ are produced by self fertilization in female parent of cotton.
10. _____ number of counts to be taken for 11-15 acres of field.

II. TRUE OR FALSE

1. For 11-15 acres of area, 7 counts to be taken
2. Seeds are certified within 9 months from the date of harvest
3. FORM-1 for seed certification should be submitted within 30 days
4. During first inspection, source of the seed is not necessary to be verified
5. FORM-1 in duplicate to be submitted to the concerned assistant director of seed certification

III. MATCH THE FOLLOWING

(i)

1.	Pollen shedders	A. Redgram
2.	Pollen partials	B. Maize
3.	Shedding tassel	C. Rice
4.	Selfed bolls	D. Bajra
5.	Fertile plants	E. cotton

(ii)

1.	0-5 acres	A. 7
2.	6-10 acres	B. 9
3.	11-15 acres	C. 8
4.	16-20 acres	D. 6
5.	21-25 acres	E. 5

IV. ONE WORD QUESTION

1. Mention any two special types of rogues
2. What are the first two phases of seed certification?
3. Mention any two stages for rouging
4. What are the stages of field inspection?

ANSWER KEYS

I. FILL UPS

1. Seed certification 2. 6 3. 25 acres
4. Association of official seed certifying agencies
5. Roguing 6. Pollen shedders 7. Pollen partials
8. Shedding tassels 9. Selfed bolls 10. 7

II. TRUE OR FALSE

1. True 2. False
3. True 4. False
5. False

III. MATCH THE FOLLOWING

(i)		(ii)	
1.	C	1.	E
2.	D	2.	D
3.	B	3.	A
4.	E	4.	C
5.	A	5.	B

IV. ONE WORD ANSWER

1. Shedding tassels, pollen partials
2. i) Receipt and scrutiny of application
   ii) Verification of seed source, class and other requirements of the seed used for raising the seed crop

3. i) Vegetative
   ii) Seedling
4. i) Vegetative (or) pre-flowering stage
   ii) Flowering stage
   iii) Post-flowering and
   iv) Pre-harvest stage

V. AT A GLANCE

1. Phases of seed certification

Seed Certification is carried out in six broad phases listed as under:

- Receipt and scrutiny of application.
- Verification of seed source, class and other requirements of the seed used for raising the seed crop.
- Inspection of the seed crop in the field to verify its conformity to the prescribed field standards.
- Supervision at post-harvest stages including processing and packing.
- Drawing of samples and arranging for analysis to verify conformity to the seed standards
- Grant of certificate, issue of certification tags, labeling, sealing etc.

2. Roguing

Stages of crop	The plant characters based on which rogues / off types are to be identified and removed
Seedling	Other crop seedling (volunteers), diseased seedling, early types with rapid growth.
Vegetative	Plant stature (weak / healthy / bushy), leaf colour, stem colour, hairyness, early / late type.
Flowering	Early / late type, flower colour, anther colour, petal spot (cotton), pollen shedder, pollen partials, (cumbu, rice, sorghum – hybrids) and shedding tassel (maize–hybrid)
Maturation	Early / fruit shape (conical / cylindrical / oval)
	Fruit colour (mottled / pure)
	Shape and size of fruits
	Fruit characters (ridged / non-ridged)
	Selfed bolls (cotton hybrid)
Harvesting	- Early maturing plants
	- Late maturing plants
	- Re-checking of all above characters.

3. Special types of rogues in hybrid seed production

Bajra, sorghum, paddy, sunflower

- **Pollen shedders:** Presence of 'B' line in 'A' line.
- **Pollen partials:** A part of the earhead of the female parent (ie) 'A' line shedding pollen here and there.

Maize

- **Shedding tassels:** These are the male inflorescence / part of inflorescence left in the field without removal and are shedding pollen for outcrossing.

Cotton

- **Selfed bolls:** Bolls produced by self fertilization in female parent of cotton.

Redgram

- **Fertile plants:** In genic male sterility system, 50% of plants will be sterile and 50% will be fertile. On the basis of viable pollen (plumpy), the plants are to be removed at flowering.

4. Field count

Area of the field crops (acres)	No. of counts to be taken
0–5	5
6–10	6
11–15	7
16–20	8
21–25	9

5. Number of plants / head per count during field inspection

Crop	No. of plants/head per count
Bhendi, brinjal, bulb crops, capsicum, castor, root crops, chilli, cotton, cucurbits, groundnut, maize, redgram, tomato.	100
Beans, cowpea, gram, leaf crops, moong, sunflower, mustard, peas, sesame, sunhemp, safflower	500
Bajra, paddy, sorghum, wheat, millets, jute	1000

3

Field Inspection

I. FILL UPS

1. _____ is the observation of number of plants / earheads of seed crop which should be observed during field inspection as one unit depending upon cropping pattern and crop.
2. Number of plants / earheads to be observed in one count for paddy is ______.
3. Number of plants / earheads to be observed in one count for sesame is ______.
4. Number of plants per inspection for broadcasted seeds is______.
5. _____ is the maximum number of inspections.

II. TRUE OR FALSE

1. For verification of off-types in maize field inspection should be done before harvesting.
2. Maximum permitted limits for off-types in paddy for foundation seeds is 0.05%.
3. Minimum period gap required for seed production of rice is one season
4. Number of field inspections recommended for maize synthetic and composites are 3.
5. For narrow spaced non-tillering crops like sesame, chickpea, 100 plants to be observed in one count.

III. MATCH THE FOLLOWING

1.	Tillering plants	A 9 counts
2.	8.1-10 ha	B 1000 earheads
3.	Groundnut	C 3 inspections
4.	Rice	D 2 inspections
5.	Sorghum	E Two seasons

IV. ONE WORD QUESTION

1. If 1000 plants to be observed, how many steps should be covered

ANSWER KEYS

I. FILL UPS

1. Field inspection 2. 1000 earheads 3. 500 plants
4. 1000 plants 5. 4

II. TRUE OR FALSE

1. False 2. True
3. True 4. False
5. False

III. MATCH THE FOLLOWING

1. B
2. A
3. E
4. D
5. C

IV. ONE WORD ANSWER

1. For one step = 25 plants
   Therefore, for 1000 plants = 40 steps
   40 steps x 25 plants = 1000 plants.

V. AT A GLANCE

1. Cropping history of the field

Year/ season Last present	Crop	Variety
a.	Last year/season crop was different	
	Seed is separable	Permitted
	Seed is not separable	Not permitted
b.	Last year/season crop was the same	
	Variety was different	Not permitted
	Same variety but class was lower	Not permitted
c.	Last year/season crop was same with same variety and same or superior class	
	But, field /seed was rejected due to seed borne diseases	Not permitted
	But, field/seed was rejected due to objectionable weeds	Not permitted
	Passed during seed certification	Permitted

2. Minimum gap required for seed production programme of different varieties of the same crop in selected field

Gap	Crop
One season	Rice, wheat, pearl millet, sorghum, soybean, sesame, mustard
Two seasons	Groundnut, berseem

3. Minimum isolation distance to avoid transmission of loose smut

Crop	Field of crops infected with loose smut	Isolation distance (m)	
		F	C
Wheat	Wheat, triticale, rye	150	150
Barely	Barely	150	150
Triticale	Triticale, wheat, rye	150	150
Oat	Oat	150	150

4. Maximum permitted limits for off-types (%)

Crop	Foundation seed	Certified seed
Napier grass (*Pennisetum purpureum*)	0.01	0.3
Sorghum, pearlmillet, barely, linseed, niger, safflower, minor millets	0.05	0.1
Paddy, wheat, triticale, oat	0.05	0.1
Buffel, dharaf, dinanath, guinea grass, setaria and stylo	0.10	0.1
Urid, moong, chickpea, fieldpea, lentil, pigeonpea rajmash, lathyrus, cowpea, Indian bean, rice bean, cluster bean, kidney bean, horse gram, groundnut, sesame, cotton, castor	0.10	0.2
Sunflower *	0.10	0.2
Soybean, rape seed and mustard, taramira, teosinte	0.10	0.5
Berseem, senji (*Meliotus* sp.), marvel grass	0.20	1.0
Jute	0.50	1.0
Maize** (composite, synthetic and open pollinated varieties)	1.00	1.0
Vegetables		
Sweet potato	None	None
Lesser yam, potato	0.05	0.1
All cucurbits, brinjal, capsicum, chilli, okra, rat tail radish, tomato, amaranth, asparagus, fenugreek, lettuce, parsely, spinach, celery, cabbage, cauliflower, chinese cabbage, knol khol, garlic, mother bulb or root production of sugar beet, turnip, radish, onion, carrot	0.10	0.2

*** Sunflower: sterile plants of the variety under seed production programme are not considered as offtype.**

**** Maize: this is the MSCS for offtype pollen shedding plants when 5% or more of the plants in seed field have receptive silk.**

5. Field inspection stages for verification of off-types in field crops

Stage	Crop
Field and fodder crops	
During flowering	Maize (composite, synthetic and OPV)
At any one inspection at and after flowering	Sorghum, pearl millet, pigeonpea, castor, rape seed, mustard, niger, taramira, safflower, sesame, sunflower, cotton, berseem, lucerne, buffel grass, forage sorghum, guinea, marvel and setaria grass, stylo and teosinte
Final inspection before harvesting	Barely, wheat, paddy, triticale, minor millets, urid, moong, chickpea, cowpea, horsegram, lathyrus, lentil, kidney bean, field bean, Indian bean, rajmash, groundnut, linseed, soybean, jute, oat, rice bean, *Melilotus* sp,. cluster bean, buffel, dharaf grass, dinanath, napier grass
Vegetables	
At any one inspection	Sweet potato
I and II inspection	Potato
II inspection	Mother bulb/root production of onion, carrot, radish
At and after flowering	All cucurbits, brinjal, capsicum, chilli, okra, rat tail radish, amaranth, asparagus, celery, fenugreek, lettuce, parsley spinach, cabbage, cauliflower, Chinese cabbage, knol khol, mother bulb or root production of sugar beet, turnip, radish, onion, carrot
Final inspection	Tomato, fenugreek, garlic, colocasia, lesser yam

4. An overview

- Field inspection method
  If 1000 plants to be observed
  For one step = 25 plants
  So, for 1000 plants = 40 steps
  i.e., 40 (steps) x 25 plants = 1000 plants
- Number of inspections
  Minimum : 2
  Maximum : 4
  Compulsory : 1 inspection at flowering
- Number of plants per inspection
  Wide spaced non tillering : 100 plants
  Narrow spaced non tillering : 500 plants
  Broad casted : 1000 plants
  Tillering : 1000 heads

4

Objectionable Weeds

I. FILL UPS

1. The objectionable weed of paddy is _____.
2. The objectionable weed of sunflower is _____.
3. The objectionable weed of oat is _____.
4. The objectionable weed of napier grass _____
5. The objectionable weed of amaranthus is _____.
6. The objectionable weed of safflower is _____.
7. The objectionable weed of fenugreek is _____.
8. The objectionable weed of wheat is _____
9. The objectionable weed of rapeseed is _____.
10. The objectionable weed of bitter gourd is _____.

II. TRUE OR FALSE

1. The maximum permissible limit of objectionable weed in bitter gourd and snake gourd is 0.0.
2. The maximum permitted limit of objectionable weed in sunflower is 0.05% for foundation seed production.
3. Canada thistle is a objectionable weed in lucerne.
4. *Avena fatua* is the objectionable weed in oats.
5. *Amaranthus spinosus* is the objectionable weed in okra.

III. MATCH THE FOLLOWING

	Weeds		Crops
1.	*Lactuca scariola*	A	Watermelon
2.	*Citrullus colocynthis*	B	Cucumber
3.	*Cucumis prophetarum*	C	Berseem
4.	*Cucumis hardwickii*	D	Lettuce
5.	*Cichorium intybus*	E	Muskmelon

IV. ONE WORD QUESTION

1. Name the botanical name of the objectionable weeds in wheat and rice
2. Name the objectionable weeds in any two vegetable crops
3. Name any two objectionable weeds in napier grass

ANSWER KEYS

I. FILL UPS

1. *Oryza sativa* var *fatua*
2. Wild helianthus
3. *Avena fatua*
4. *Cirsium arvense* (Canada thistle)
5. *Amaranthus spinosus* (wild amaranthus)
6. *Catharanthus oxycantha*
7. Senji
8. *Convolvulus arvensis*
9. *Argemone mexicana*
10. *Momordica balsamina* [balsam apple (mocha)]

II. TRUE OR FALSE

1. True
2. False
3. False
4. True
5. False

III. MATCH THE FOLLOWING

1. D
2. A
3. E
4. B
5. C

IV. ONE WORD ANSWER

1. Rice - *Oryza sativa var.fatua*
   Wheat - *Convolvulus arvensis*
2. Okra - *Abelmoschus moschatus*
   Bitter gourd - Balsam apple (*Momordia balsamina)*
3. Canada thistle - (*Cirsium arvense)*
   Johnson grass - (*Sorghum halepense)*

V. AT A GLANCE

1. Stage of field inspection for verification of objectionable weeds

Stage of field inspection	Crop
Field and fodder crops	
At any one inspection at or after flowering	Safflower, sunflower, berseem, lucerne
Final inspection	Rice, napier grass, oat, rape seed, mustard
Vegetables	
At and after flowering	Bitter gourd, snake gourd, musk melon, water melon, okra, amaranthus
Final inspection	Fenugreek, lettuce

2. Maximum permitted limit (%) of objectionable weeds at field level

Crop	Weed	Foundation	Certified
Field crops			
Rice	Wild rice (*O. sativa var. fatua)*	0.01	0.02
Rapeseed, mustard, Taramira	Satyanashi (*Argemone mexicana*)	0.05	0.1
Safflower	Wild safflower (*Catharanthus oxyacantha*)	None	None
Sunflower	Wild *Helianthus*	None	None
Oat	Wild oat (*Avena fatua)*	0.01	0.02
Fodder crops			
Berseem	Chicory (Kasni) (*Cichorium intybus*)	None	0.05
Lucerne	Dodder (*Cuscuta* spp.)	None	0.05
Napier grass	Canada thistle (*Cirsium arvense),* dodder (*Cuscuta* spp.), Johnson grass (Saru) (*Sorghum halepense),* quack grass (Thitch grass, couch grass) (*Afropyron repens*), *C. arvensis*	None	None
Vegetables			
Bitter gourd	Balsam apple (mocha) (*Momordica balsamina*), jangli karela (*M. dioica*), bhat karela (*M. cochinchinensis)*	0.0	0.0
Cucumber	*Cucumis hardwickii*	0.0	0.0
Longmelon, muskmelon, snapmelon	*Cucumis prophetarum*, weed melon (Takmek) (*Cucumis melo var. argrestis)* and other non desert forms of *C. melo*	0.0	0.0
Snake gourd	*Trichosanthes palmate, T. lobata,* jangli chachinda (Rambek (*T. cucumerina))*	0.0	0.0

Watermelon	Wild water melon (indrayan) (*Citrullus colocynthis)*	0.0	0.0
Okra	Wild okra (*Abelmoschus fioulneus, A. manihot, A. moschatus*)	0.0	0.0
Amaranthus	Wild amaranthus (*Amaranthus spinosus)*	0.01	0.02
Fenugreek	Senji (*Melilotus* spp.)	0.01	0.02
Lettuce	Wild lettuce (*Lactuca scariola)*	0.01	0.02

5

Seed Standards

I. FILL UPS

1. Specific crop standard consists of _____and _____.
2. _____ and _____ standards constitute the minimum seed certification standards for seed certification.

II. TRUE OR FALSE

1. The maximum permissible limits for moisture content have been prescribed for the safe storage of seeds is given under seed standard.
2. The seed standard consists of the minimum isolation requirement that has been specified to minimize genetic contamination.

III. MATCH THE FOLLOWING

	Crop	Germination
1.	Paddy	A 65%
2.	Sorghum	B 70%
3.	Cowpea	C 75%
4.	Cotton	D 60%
5.	Bitter gourd	E 80%

IV. ONE WORD QUESTION

1. What are the two groups of minimum seed certification standard?
2. Mention any one of the field standard
3. Mention any one of the seed standard

ANSWER KEYS

I. FILL UPS

1. Field standard and seed standard
2. General seed certification standard and specific crop standard.

II. TRUE OR FALSE

1. True
2. False

III. MATCH THE FOLLOWING

1. E
2. C
3. B
4. A
5. D

IV. ONE WORD ANSWER

1. i) General seed certification standard

   ii) Specific crop standards
2. The minimum isolation requirement has been specified to minimize genetic contamination
3. The minimize percentage of pure seeds and maximum permissible limits for inert matter, other crop seeds etc., have been prescribed.

V. AT A GLANCE

1. Seed standards

Particulars	Germination (min) (%)		Moisture (min) (%)		Pure seed (min) (%)		Inert matter (max) (%)		O.C.S. (No./kg) (max)		O.D.V. (No./kg) (max)		O.W.S. (No./kg) (max)	
	F	C	F	C	F	C	F	C	F	C	F	C	F	C
Paddy	80	80	13	13	98	98	2	2	10	20	10	20	10	20
Ragi	75	75	12	12	97	97	3	3	10	20	-	-	10	20
Sorghum	75	75	12	12	97	97	3	3	10	20	10	20	5	10
Wheat	85	85	12	12	98	98	2	2	10	20	-	-	10	20
Maize														None
Hybrids	-	90	-	12	-	98	-	2	-	10	-	10	-	
Inbreds and single crosses	80	-	12	-	98	-	2	-	5	-	5	-	None	
Composites and synthetics	90	90	12	12	98	98	2	2	10	20	-	None		
Bajra (Pearl millet)	75	75	12	12	98	98	2	2	10	20	-	None		None
Redgram	75**	75**	9	9	98	98	2	2	5	10	10	20	5	10
Greengram and Blackgram	75**	75**	9	9	98	98	2	2	5	10	10	20	5	10
Horsegram	80	80	9	9	98	98	2	2	None	10	5	20	None	None
Bengalgram	85**	85**	9	9	98	98	2	2	Non	10	5	20	None	None
Cowpea	75**	75**	9	9	98	98	2	2	None	10	5	20	None	10
Castor	70	70	8	9	98	98	2	2	None	10	5	20	None	None
Groundnut	70	70	8	9	98	98	4	4	None	-	-	10	None	None
Sunflower	70	70	9	9	98	98	2	2	None	None	None	None	5	10
Safflower	80	80	9	9	98	98	2	2	None	None	None	None	5	10
Sesamum	80	80	9	9	97	97	3	3	10	20	10	20	10	20
Niger	80	80	9	9	98	98	2	2	10	20	10	20	10	20
Soybean	70**	70**	12	12	98	98	2	2	None	10	5	10	5	10
Cotton hybrids	75	75	10	10	98	98	2	2	5	10	-	-	5	10

Cotton varieties	65	65	10	10	98	98	2	2	5	10	-		5	10
Jute	80	80	9	9	97	97	3	3	10	20	10	20	10	20
Bhendi	65**	65**	10	10	99.0	99.0	1	1	None	5	10	20	None	None
Brinjal	70	70	8	8	98	98	2	2	None	None	-	-	None	None
Tomato	70	70	8	8	98	98	2	2	5	10	-	-	None	None
Capsicum and chilli	60	60	8	8	98	98	2	2	5	10	0	0	5	10
Clusterbean	70	70	9	9	98	98	2	2	10	20	10	20	None	None
Peas	75	75	9	9	98	98	2	2	None	5	5	10	None	None
Bottle gourd and pumpkin	60	60	7	7	98	98	2	2	None	None	-	-	None	None
Watermelon and ridge/bitter gourd	60	60	7	7	98	98	2	2	None	None	5	10	None	None
French bean	75	75	9	9	98	98	2	2	None	None	5	10	None	10

1. F: Foundation seed,
2. C: Certified seed
3. O.C.S.: Other crop seeds
4 O.D.V.: Other distinguishable varieties
5. O.W.S.: Objectionable weed seeds
** - Including hard seeds.

6

Seed Sampling

I. FILL UPS

1. A specified quantity of seed which is physically identifiable to the types of which certificate may be issued is called _____.
2. Taking small portions of seed random from different position of the lot and combining them is _____ of a seed lot.
3. A small portion taken from representative part of the seed lot is called _____.
4. A mixture of all primary samples taken from the seed lot is called_____.
5. The sample submitted to the seed testing laboratory is_____.
6. A reduced quantity of sample taken from submitted sample in the laboratory is called_____.
7. When there is 6 to 30 containers, sample should be taken from _____ number of containers.
8. When there is 31 to 400 containers, sample should be taken from _____ number of containers.
9. When there is 401 or more containers, sample should be taken from _____ number of containers.
10. For upto 500 kg atleast _____ number of samples should be taken.
11. For 3001 to 20000 kg atleast_____ number of samples should be taken.
12. For cereals(except maize), a trier should _____ slots to take sample.
13. _____ trier is used horizontally (or) vertically.
14. _____ is suitable for sampling a seed lot in a bag
15. The intensity of sampling should be maintained in accordance to the rules described by_____.
16. Submitted sample is_____ times higher than working sample size.
17. The submitted sample size is restricted to_____.
18. The working sample size of paddy is _____.

19. The working sample size of black gram is _____.
20. The working sample size of ground nut is _____.

II. TRUE OR FALSE

1. A mixture of all primary samples taken from the seed lot is called submitted sample.
2. A small portion taken from different representative part of the seed lot is called primary sample.
3. A reduced quantity of sample take from submitted sample in the laboratory is called working sample.
4. For 31 to 400 containers, sample 5 containers (or) one in every 3 containers, whichever is greater.
5. For 20001 kg sample and above, one individual sample for each 300 kg but not less than 5 samples.

III. MATCH THE FOLLOWING

1.	Upto 5 containers	A. 1 individual sample for each 300 kg
2.	6 to 30 containers	B. 1 individual sample for each 700 kg
3.	31 to 400 containers	C. 5 primary samples
4.	3001 to 20000 kg	D. Sample 5 (or) 1 in every 3 containers
5.	20001 and above	E. Sample 10 container or atleast one in every 7 container

IV. ONE WORD QUESTION

1. What are the types of samples?
2. Name any two sampling devices
3. What are the different sampling procedures?

ANSWER KEYS

I. FILL UPS

1. Seed lot	2. Representative sample	3. Primary sample
4. Composite sample	5. Submitted sample	6. Working sample
7. 5	8. 10	9. 80
10. 5	11. 1 for each 500 kg but not less than 10	12. Six

13. Sleeve or stick trier 14. Nobbe trier 15. ISTA
16. 10 17. 1000g 18. 40g
19. 150g 20. 1000g

II. TRUE OR FALSE

1. False 2. True
3. True 4. False
5. False

III. MATCH THE FOLLOWING

1. C
2. D
3. E
4. A
5. B

IV. ONE WORD ANSWER

1. i) Primary sample ii) Composite sample
   iii) Submitted sample iv) Working sample
2. i) Nobbe trier ii) Bin sampler
3. i) Bag sampling ii) Bulk sampling
   iii) Hand sampling iv) Automatic sampling

V. AT A GLANCE

1. Types of sample

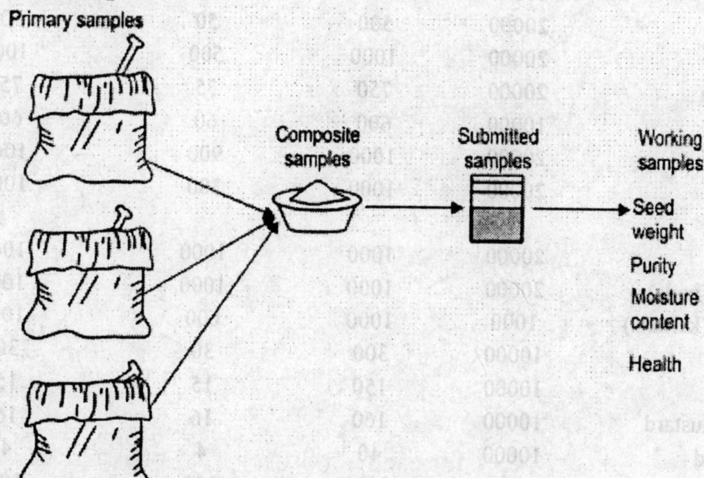

Types of samples

2. Size of seed lot and samples

Crop	Maximum weight of seed lot (kg)	Submitted sample (g)	Minimum weight of Working sample for purity analysis (g)	Working sample for count of other species seed (g)
Field crops				
Barley	20000	1000	120	1000
Paddy	20000	400	40	400
Triticale	20000	1000	120	1000
Wheat	20000	1000	120	1000
Millets				
Barnyard millet	10,000	80	8	80
Common millet	10,000	150	15	150
Finger millet	10,000	60	6	60
Italian millet	10,000	90	9	90
Kodo millet	10,000	80	8	80
Little millet	10,000	70	7	70
Maize	40,000	1000	900	1000
Pearl millet	10,000	150	15	150
Sorghum	10,000	900	90	900
Pulses				
Bengalgram	20000	1000	1000	1000
Blackgram	20000	1000	150	1000
Chickling vetch	20000	1000	450	1000
Cowpea	20000	1000	400	1000
French bean	20000	1000	700	1000
Greengram	20000	1000	120	1000
Horsegram	20000	500	50	500
Indian bean	20000	1000	500	1000
Kidney bean	20000	750	75	750
Lentil	10000	600	60	600
Pea	20000	1000	900	1000
Pigeon pea	20000	1000	300	1000
Oilseeds				
Castor	20000	1000	1000	1000
Groundnut (pods)	20000	1000	1000	1000
Groundnut (kernels)	1000	1000	600	1000
Linseed	10000	300	30	300
Niger	10000	150	15	150
Rape and mustard	10000	160	16	160
Rocket salad	10000	40	4	40
Safflower	10000	1000	180	1000
Sesame	10000	70	7	70

Soybean	20000	1000	500	1000
Sunflower	20000	250	125	250
Fibre crops				
Cotton varieties	20,000	350	35	350
Cotton hybrids	20,000	250	25	250
Jute	10000	100	10	100
Roselle	10000	700	70	700
Sunnhemp	10000	700	70	700
Forage crops				
Birdwood grass	20,000	25	3	25
Blue panic	10,000	25	2	20
Buffel grass	10,000	25	3	25
Cluster bean	10,000	1000	100	1000
Dharaf grass	10,000	-	-	-
Doob	10,000	25	1	10
Egyptian clover	10,000	60	6	60
Fenugreek	10,000	40	4	40
Guinea grass	10,000	25	2	20
Indian clover	10,000	100	10	100
Lucerne	10,000	50	5	50
Marvel grass	10,000	30	3	30
Napier grass	10,000	150	15	150
Oat	20,000	1000	120	1000
Para grass	10,000	30	3	30
Rice bean	10,000	-	-	-
Setaria grass	10,000	25	2	20
Shaflal	10,000	25	2	20
Stylo	10,000	70	7	70
Sudan grass	10,000	250	25	250
Teosinte	20,000	1000	90	1000
Velvet bean	20,000	500	50	500
Venezuela grass	10,000	25	5	25
Green manure and miscellaneous crops				
Dhaincha	20,000	900	90	900
Hemp	10,000	600	60	600
Indigo	20,000	600	60	600
Poppy	10,000	25	1	10
Sugar beet	20,000	500	50	500
Tobacco	10,000	25	0.5	5
Vegetablescucurbits				
Ashgourd	20,000	700	70	700
Bittergourd	20,000	1000	450	1000
Bottle gourd	20,000	700	70	700
Chow-chow	40,000	250	25	250

Cucumber	10,000	150	15	150
Indian squash	20,000	1000	250	1000
Musk melon	10,000	150	15	150
Pumpkin	10,000	350	180	350
Ridgegourd	20,000	1000	400	1000
Snakegourd	20,000	1000	250	1000
Spongegourd	20,000	1000	250	1000
Water melon	20,000	1000	250	1000
Winter squash	20,000	1000	700	1000
Fruit vegetables				
Brinjal	10,000	150	15	150
Chilli	10,000	150	15	150
Okra	20,000	1000	140	1000
Radish	10,000	300	30	300
Sweet pepper	10,000	150	15	150
Tomato varieties	10,000	70	7	70
Tomato hybrids	10,000	7	70	70
Bulb Crops				
Garlic	40,000	-	-	-
Onion	10,000	80	8	80
Green/leafy vegetables				
Amaranth	10,000	70	7	70
Asparagus	20,000	1000	100	1000
Celery	10,000	25	1	10
Coriander	10,000	400	40	400
Lettuce	10,000	30	3	30
Parsley	10,000	40	4	40
Spinach	10,000	250	25	250
Root crops				
Carrot	10,000	30	3	30
Radish	10,000	300	30	300
Sweet potato	40,000	250	25	250
Tapioca	40,000	250	25	250
Turnip	10,000	70	7	70
Legume vegetables				
Broad bean	20,000	1000	1000	1000
Field bean	20,000	1000	600	1000
Goa bean, jack bean	20,000	500	50	500
Lima bean	20,000	1000	1000	1000
Scarlet runner bean	20,000	1000	1000	1000
Sword bean	20,000	500	50	500
Cole crops				
Cabbage, Cauliflower, Broccoli, Knol-kohl, etc.	10,000	100	10	100
Chinese cabbage	10,000	40	4	40

3. Sampling intensity

Minimum required primary samples to be drawn from lots coming in one or more than one containers.

a. Upto 5 containers	Sample each container and always take atleast 5 primary samples
b. 6 to 30 containers	Sample 5 containers or one in every 3 containers, whichever is greater
c. 31 to 400 containers	Sample 10 containers or atleast one in every 5 containers, whichever is greater
d. 401 or more containers	Sample 80 containers or atleast one in every 7 containers, whichever is greater

When lots consist of more than 6 bags, samples should be taken from 5 bags plus 10% of the remaining bags, but not more than 30.

a. Upto 500 kg	Atleast 5 individual samples
b. 501 to 3000 kg	One individual sample for each 300 kg, but not less than 5 samples
c. 3001 to 20,000 kg	One individual sample for each 500 kg, but not less than 10 samples
d. 20001 and above	One individual sample for each 700 kg, but not less than 40 samples

4. Weight of working sample

Working sample (g)	Cereals and Millets	Pulses	Oilseeds	Fibres	Forages	Green manures & other crop	Vegetables
1					Doob	Poppy	Celery
2					Blue panic, guinea grass, setaria grass, shaflal		
3					Bird grass, buffel grass, marvel grass, paragrass		Lettuce, carrot
4			Raket salad			Fenugreek	Parsley, Chinese cabbage
5					Lucerne, Venezuela grass		
6	Finger millet				Egyptian clover		
7	Little millet		Sesame		Stylo		Tomato variety & hybrid, amaranth, turnip
8	Barnyard millet, Kodo millet						Onion
9	Italian millet						
10				Jute	Indian clover		Cabbage, cauliflower, broccoli, knol khol
15	Common millet, pearl millet		Niger		Napier grass		Brinjal, chilli, sweet pepper, muskmelon, cucumber
25				Cotton hybrid	Sudan grass		Chow-chow, spinach, sweet potato, tapioca
30			Linseed				Radish
35				Cotton variety			
40	Paddy						Coriander
50		Horsegram			Velvet bean	Sugar beet	
60		Lentil			Hemp, indigo		Goa bean, jack bean, sword bean

70				Roselle, sunnhemp			Ashgourd, bottlegourd
75		Kidney bean					
90	Sorghum				Teosinte	Daincha	
100							Asparagus cluster bean
120	Wheat, barley, triticale, oat	Greengram					
125			Sunflower				
140							Okra
150		Blackgram					
180			Safflower				Pumpkin
250							Snakegourd, Spongegourd, Indian squash, water melon
300		Pigeonpea					
400		Cowpea					Ridgegourd
450		Chickling vetch					Bittergourd
500		Indian bean	Soybean				
600			Groundnut				Field bean
700			French bean				Winter squash
900	Maize	Pea					
1000		Bengalgram	Castor, groundnut (pods)				Broad bean, lima bean, scarlet summer bean

Father of seed testing: Dr. Friedrich Nobbe, founder of seed testing 1869 in Tharandt Saxony, Germany.

Father of Indian Seed Industry: Dr. Badrinarayanan Ramulal Barwale, MAHYCO seeds.

7

Mixing and Dividing of Seed

I. FILL UPS

1. _____ works on the principle based on gravitational force
2. Gamet divider is otherwise known as_____.
3. Gamet divider works on the principle based on_____.
4. _____ method is suitable for seeds requiring working samples upto 10grams and seeds not chaffy and do not bounce and roll.
5. _____ method is suitable for single small seeded species.
6. _____ method is restricted to the chaffy seeds.
7. _____ divider is not suitable for chaffy seeds.
8. The main objective of mixing and dividing seeds is to obtain the representative _____ seed sample for analyzing.
9. The disadvantage of boerner divider is that it is difficult to check for _____.
10. _____ works on the principle as the boerner divider.

II. TRUE OR FALSE

1. The principle used in boerner divider is centrifugal force
2. Soil divider is suitable for large seeds and chaffy seeds
3. Mechanical method is suitable for chaffy and fuzzy seeds
4. Spoon method is suitable for single small seeded species
5. Hand halving method is restricted to non chaffy seeds

III. MATCH THE FOLLOWING

1.	Random cup method	A	Not suitable for chaffy seeds
2.	Hand halving method	B	Centrifugal force
3.	Mechanical divider	C	Only for chaffy seeds
4.	Gamet divider	D	Single small seeded species
5.	Spoon method	E	*Brassica* spp

IV. ONE WORD QUESTION

1. What is the objective of mixing and dividing?
2. What are the different types of divider?
3. What are the different methods of dividing?

ANSWER KEYS

I. FILL UPS

1. Boerner divider
2. Centrifugal divider
3. Gravitational force
4. Random cup method
5. Spoon method
6. Hand halving method
7. Mechanical divider
8. Homogenous
9. Cleanliness
10. Soil divider

II. TRUE OR FALSE

1. False
2. True
3. False
4. True
5. False

III. MATCH THE FOLLOWING

1. E
2. C
3. A
4. B
5. D

IV. ONE WORD ANSWER

1. To obtain homogenous representative working samples
2. i) Boerner divider
   ii) Soil divider
   iii) Gamet divider
3. i) Mechanical divider
   ii) Random cup method
   iii) Modified halving method
   iv) Spoon method
   v) Hand halving method

V. AT A GLANCE

- Mixing and dividing: To obtain homogenous representative working sample
- Dividers
    - Boerner divider: Works on gravitational force
    - Soil divider: Mix and divide large and chaffy seed based on gravitational force
    - Gamet divider: Based on centrifugal force
- Methods of dividing
    - Mechanical divider: Not suitable for chaffy seeds
    - Random cup method: Suitable for seeds that need working sample upto 10 g
    - Modified halving method: Alternate cups have no bottom
    - Spoon method: Suitable for single small seeded species
    - Hand halving method: Suitable for chaffy seeds.

8

Purity Analysis

I. FILL UPS

1. _____ and _____ seeds give highest grain yield.
2. Assessment of _____ is one of the basic requirement for quality control of seed under the seed act.
3. The minimum number of seeds for germination test of _____.
4. The purity analysis in groundnut is done with working sample size is _____.
5. _____ is done to estimate biotic and abiotic impurities.

II. TRUE OR FALSE

1. In ground nut, purity analysis is done on pods.
2. For > 1g <10g, the decimal upto which components must be weighed is 2.
3. Huskless seeds are to be determined as pure seed in groundnut.
4. Empty glumes are inert matter.
5. To separate the impurities and pure seeds purity working board is used.

III. ONE WORD QUESTION

1. How is huskless seeds are determined?
2. What is the objective of purity analysis?
3. How is the percentage of components is determined ?

ANSWER KEYS

I. FILL UPS

1. Nucleus and breeder seeds
2. Genetic purity
3. 400
4. 1000 g
5. Purity analysis

II. TRUE OR FALSE

1. True 2. False
3. False 4. True
5. True

III. ONE WORD ANSWER

1. $$\% \text{ of huskless seeds} = \frac{\text{Number of huskless seeds}}{400} \times 100$$

2. To estimate biotic and abiotic impurities

3. $$\% \text{ of components} = \frac{\text{Weight of individual component}}{\text{Total weight of all compounds}} \times 100$$

IV. AT A GLANCE

- Purity analysis: To estimate biotic and abiotic impurities
- Purity components:
  - Pure seed, inert matter, weed seed and other crop seed
  - Reported in percentage ; 4 decimals, if sample weight is 1 g.
  - If results is in border line, duplicate test can be done
- Groundnut: Purity analysis is done on pods
- Paddy and sunflower: Huskless seeds are counted

9

Seed Moisture Determination

I. FILL UPS

1. _____ is one of the most important deciding factors of seed viability and quality during storage.
2. Indirect method of moisture estimation is_____.
3. Karl fisher titration method is _____ method of moisture estimation
4. For volatile oil containing seeds moisture is estimated by_____.
5. _____ method is prescribed by ISTA for moisture estimation.
6. For large seeds with less than 12% moisture content, the tolerance limit is _____.
7. The temperature for high constant oven method is _____.
8. The temperature maintained in low constant oven method is _____.
9. The difference between two moisture tests should not exceed_____.
10. Lyophilization is otherwise known as_____.

II. TRUE OR FALSE

1. Moisture meter method is indirect method of moisture estimation.
2. Reversibility method is used for seeds containing volatile oils for moisture estimation.
3. Lyophilization is a indirect method of moisture estimation.
4. The temperature of high constant oven method is 103±2°C.
5. In moisture meter, the principle is moisture is directly proportionate to EC.

III. MATCH THE FOLLOWING

1.	Small seeds with <12% MC	A	Low constant oven
2.	130±3°C	B	Seeds with volatile oils
3.	103±2°C	C	Indirect method
4.	Toluene distillation method	D	High constant oven
5.	Moisture meter	E	0.3%

IV. ONE WORD QUESTION

1. State the principle of moisture meter
2. What are the different direct methods of moisture estimation?
3. Mention the formula for calculating moisture content in high constant oven method
4. What is the formula used for calculating moisture content in samples tested without pre-drying?

ANSWER KEYS

I. FILL UPS

1.	Seed moisture	2.	Moisture meter method	3.	Direct
4.	Toluene distillation method	5.	Air oven method	6.	0.4%
7.	130±3°C	8.	103±2°C	9.	0.2 %
10.	Freeze drying				

II. TRUE OR FALSE

1.	True	2.	False
3.	False	4.	False
5.	True		

III. MATCH THE FOLLOWING

1. E
2. D
3. A
4. B
5. C

IV. ONE WORD ANSWER

1. Moisture is directly proportional to EC
2. i) Toluene distillation method

   ii) Low constant oven

   iii) High constant oven
3. Moisture content% $= \frac{M_2 - M_3}{M_2 - M_1} \times 100$

$$= \frac{\text{Loss in weight}}{\text{Weight of seed}} \times 100$$

4. % Moisture content $= \frac{\text{Weight of fresh seeds} - \text{Weight of dry seeds}}{\text{Weight of fresh seeds}} \times 100$

V. AT A GLANCE

- **Seed moisture estimation**
  - Weight loss due to drying is calculated in percentage
  - Sample should be packed in vapour proof container
  - Estimate moisture in 2 minutes after repacking for species which need grinding; 30 minutes for seed that does not need grinding
- **Method**
  - Indirect method : Moisture meter and NMR
  - Moisture meter : Moisture is directly proportionate to EC
  - Direct method : Hot air oven method
- **Hot air oven**
  - Complete evaporation / removal of moisture
  - 4-5 g of sample for seeds having < 8 mm size
  - 10 g for seeds having >8 mm
  - Grind the larger seeds E.g. Paddy, wheat, oat, barley, sorghum, maize, blackgram, greengram, chickpea, pigeon pea, peas, beans, soybean, groundnut, castor, cotton
  - Low constant method : 103 ± 2^0C for 17 ± 1 h ; Oilseeds
  - High constant method : $130 + 3^0$C ; maize 4 h, cereals 2 h, others 1 h
- **Estimation**

  $$MC = \frac{\text{Loss of weight}}{\text{Original weight}} \times 100$$

- Report : Expressed in percentage in one decimal
  - Difference between two tests should not exceed 0.2 %
  - If, repeat the test

10

Germination Test

I. FILL UPS

1. ______ number of seeds are used for germination.
2. The seedlings which show the capacity for continued development into normal plant is called______.
3. The seedlings which do not show capacity for continued development into normal plant is called______.
4. Seeds which do not absorb moisture till the end of the test period is called ______.
5. ______ is suitable method for small seeds.
6. ______ is suitable method for medium sized seeds.
7. ______ is suitable method for larger sized seeds.
8. ______ seeds remain as such at final count.
9. ______ seeds undergoes imbibition but no germination.
10. ______ seeds on pressing yield white substances.

II. TRUE OR FALSE

1. Seeds which are neither hard nor have germinated is called hard seed.
2. Seeds which do not absorb moisture till the end of the test period is called dead seed
3. Seedling with any one of the essential structures missing (or) badly damaged so that the balanced growth is not expected is called damaged seedling
4. In sand method, the distance between holes should be atleast 2 times the seed diameter
5. Root and shoot development is geotrophic in between paper method.

III. MATCH THE FOLLOWING

1.	Small seeds	A	Sand method
2.	Medium sized seeds	B	Top of paper
3.	Large seeds	C	Between paper
4.	Dead seed	D	No absorption of water
5.	Hard seed	E	Milky paste

IV. ONE WORD QUESTION

1. What are the different methods of germination test?
2. What are the different types of abnormal seedling?
3. Mention any one character of normal seedlings?

ANSWER KEYS

I. FILL UPS

1. 400
2. Normal seedling
3. Abnormal seedling
4. Hard seeds
5. Top of paper method
6. Between paper method
7. Sand
8. Hard seed
9. Fresh ungerminated
10. Dead seed

II. TRUE OR FALSE

1. False
2. False
3. True
4. False
5. True

III. MATCH THE FOLLOWING

1. B
2. C
3. A
4. E
5. D

IV. ONE WORD ANSWER

1. i) Top of paper method
   ii) Between paper method
   iii) Sand

2. i) Damaged seedling
   ii) Decayed seedling
   ii) Hard seedling
   iv) Fresh ungerminated seeds
   v) Dead seeds
3. A well developed epicotyl in seedlings of hypogeal germination

V. AT A GLANCE

- **Method:** TP, BP
  - TP: Small seeds, light requiring seed
  - BP: Medium sized seeds, unwind the rolled paper for observation
  - Sand: Larger seeds, use river sand, holes distance should be 4 - 5 times the seed diameter
- **Seedling evaluation:**
- Normal seedling: Seedling with well developed root and shoot, cotyledon (one-monocot; two-dicot); limited damage to essential structures; diseased seedling source not from nearby seedling
  - Abnormal seedling: Seedling with loss of essential structures; diseased seedling source from nearby seedling; damaged, diseased and decayed seedling
  - Hard seed: Remain as such at final count
  - Fresh ungerminated: Imbibed seed, but no germination of seed
  - Dead seed: Seeds on pressing yield white substances

11

Quick Viability Test

I. FILL UPS

1. The quick viability test was developed by _____.
2. _____ is a biochemical test.
3. The indicator used for quick viability test is _____.
4. For maize seeds, the method followed for staining is _____.
5. _____ seeds need only conditioning for staining preparation.

II. TRUE OR FALSE

1. For small seeded species, seed coat should be removed for staining.
2. The optimum pH for staining is 7.
3. Completely stained seeds are non-viable.
4. Small seeded legumes need no conditioning or preparation.
5. To observe clean topography of the seeds, 2-3 drops of TZ solution can be added.

III. MATCH THE FOLLOWING

1.	Cut longitudinally	A	Conditioning only
2.	Remove seed coat	B	Small seeded grass
3.	Large seeded legumes	C	Maize
4.	Small seeded species	D	Dicots with hard coats
5.	Pierce with needle	E	No preparation

IV. ONE WORD QUESTION

1. Mention any two preparations for staining.

ANSWER KEYS

I. FILL UPS

1. Lakon
2. Quick viability test
3. 2,3,5 triphenyl tetrazolium chloride
4. Bisect longitudinally
5. Large seeded legumes

II. TRUE OR FALSE

1. False
2. True
3. False
4. True
5. False

III. MATCH THE FOLLOWING

1. C
2. D
3. A
4. E
5. B

IV. ONE WORD ANSWER

1. i) Bisect longitudinally – maize
   ii) No preparation (small seeded species)

V. AT A GLANCE

- Quick viability test: Developed by Lakon (1942) in Germany.
- Principle:

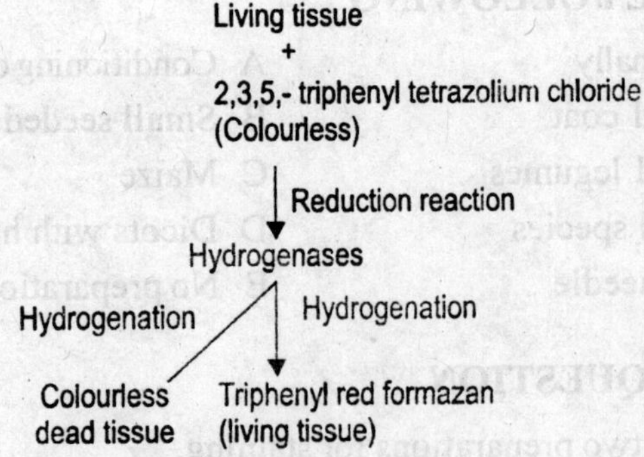

- **Method:**
  - **Preparation of TZ solution:**
    - 0.25 to 1.0% concentration
    - Optimum pH 7 for good staining.
    - Pre-conditioning of seed: Soak in water 3-4 h.
  - **Preparation of seed:**
    - Cut longitudinally (maize, sorghum etc).
    - Cut laterally (small seeded grass).
    - Pierce with needle (small seeded grass).
    - Remove seed coat (dicots with hard coats).
    - Conditioning only (large seeded legumes).
    - No preparation (small seeded species).
  - **Staining:** Immerse in TZ solution and kept in dark.
  - **Evaluation:** Categorise into germinable and non-germinable seed based on staining pattern.

12

Seed Viability Tests

I. FILL UPS

1. _____ is the measure of how many seeds are alive and could develop into plants which will reproduce themselves.
2. _____ method is useful for determining viability of forest tree seeds.
3. In _____ test, dead seeds turns black colour.
4. _____ gives quick assessment of germination than normal test.
5. _____ is an non-destructive method, that assess the empty ill filled and damaged seeds.

II. TRUE OR FALSE

1. In vital colouring method, live tissue remain unstained.
2. In catalyse (oxidation) method, catalyse content is higher in immature grains than that of ripe grains.
3. In selenium method, the colour disappears rapidly.
4. Excised embryo test gives quick assessment of germination than normal test.
5. Selenite method is very fast and useful test that provides a rapid estimation of abnormal seedlings.

III. MATCH THE FOLLOWING

1.	Vital colouring	A. Peroxidase
2.	Enzymes activity	B. Non-destructive
3.	X-ray analysis	C. Indigo carmine
4.	Indoxy acetate test	D. Aqueous $BaCl_2$ treatment
5.	Contrast method	E. Seed coat damage in soyabean

IV. ONE WORD QUESTION

1. Mention any two seed viability test
2. Which is the quick test method of assessment of viability than normal method?

ANSWER KEYS

I. FILL UPS

1. Seed viability
2. Vital colouring method
3. Ferric chloride test
4. Excised embryo test
5. X-ray analysis method

II. TRUE OR FALSE

1. False
2. True
3. False
4. True
5. False

III. MATCH THE FOLLOWING

1. C
2. A
3. B
4. E
5. D

IV. ONE WORD ANSWER

1. i) Vital colouring method
   ii) Indoxyl acetate test
2. Excised embryo test

V. AT A GLANCE

1. **Vital colouring:**

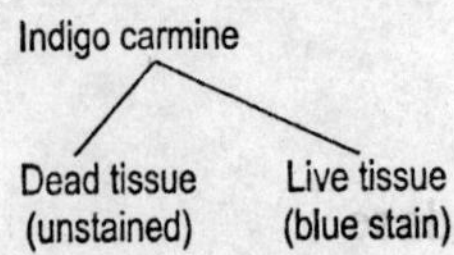

2. **Catalase content:** High content - more viable
3. **Peroxidase:**

   $H_2O_2 + \text{Guaiacol} \longrightarrow \text{Blue, tetraguaiacoquinone}$.

4. **Dehydrogenase:**

   $\text{Colourless TZ solution} \xrightarrow[\text{Reduction}]{\text{Dehydrogenase}} \text{Red formazan}$.

5. **Ferric chloride test:** Soak seeds in 20% $FeCl_3$ for 15 min; Black coloured dead tissue (Damaged seed).

6. **Conductivity test:** Deteriorated seed leachate had high EC.
7. **Excised embryo test:** Quick assessment of germination than normal test.
8. **X-ray analysis:** Nondestructive; Empty, damaged and ill filled seeds are assessed.
9. **Contrast method:** Treat with aqueous $BaCl_2$ - Impregnated dead tissue show lighter on the film than unimpregnated living tissue.

13

Grow Out Test

I. FILL UPS

1. _____ is the official measure for controlling the genetic purity of the seed lot.
2. _____ serves as 'pre-control' as well as 'post-control' for avoiding genetic contaminations.
3. _____ can also be used as a measure to judge the efficacy of the certification agency or the inspector.
4. The minimum population requirement for taking the observations shall be _____ plants.
5. When the maximum permissible off-type plants is 0.2%, the plant required per sample is _____.

II. TRUE OR FALSE

1. Standard sample of cultivar is the official standard sample against which all other samples of the seed of the cultivar judged.
2. For 99.0 (in 100) the reject numbers for sample size 400 is 24.

ANSWER KEYS

I. FILL UPS

1. Grow out test 2. Grow out test
3. Grow out test 4. 400
5. 2000

II. TRUE OR FALSE

1. True
2. False

III. AT A GLANCE

1. Recommended specifications

Crop	Row length (m)	Plant to plant distance (cm)	Space between rows (cm)	Space between plots (cm)
Wheat, barley, oats	6	2	25	50
Pea, cowpea	6	10	45	90
Chickpea, greengram	6	10	30	60
Blackgram	10	25	60	90
Maize	5	10	45	45
Hybrid cotton	6	15	20	45
Paddy				
Very early to medium	6	2	30	60
Late and very late	6	10	60	90
Pearl millet, sorghum	6	10	45	60

2. Reject number for prescribed standards and sample size

	Reject numbers for sample size of	
	800	400
99.5 (1 in 200)	8	*
99.0 (1 in 100)	16	8
95.0 (5 in 100)	48	24
90.0 (10 in 100)	88	44
85.0 (15 in 100)	128	64

* indicates that the sample size is too small for a valid test.

3. Summary

- **Grow out test:**
  - To measure genetic purity
  - Pre-requisite for all hybrids
  - In addition, to check efficacy of Certification Officer
- **Sample size:** Minimum of 400 plants
- **Procedure:**
  - Grow crop as per standard package of practices, but no thinning
  - Grow one standard sample for every 10 sample under test
- **Reporting:**
  - Other crop per cent
  - Off type per cent

14

Seed Vigour

I. FILL UPS

1. Rapid and uniform production of healthy seedling and stand establishment under a wide range of field condition is considered as ______.
2. The sum of those properties of seed which determine the potential level of activity and performance of the seed lot is called ______.
3. Vigour index = ______.
4. Brick gravel test was developed by ______.
5. ______ vigour test is suitable for small grains.
6. ______ was developed by USA to evaluate the seed vigour of maize.
7. GADA stands for ______.
8. GADA test has given valuable results for ______ and ______.
9. Cool germination test is conducted at a constant temperature of ______.
10. In a ______ test, the seed is introduced to a stressful environment unfavourable to seedling development.

II. TRUE OR FALSE

1. A combination of standard germination test with seedling length provides broad evaluation of seedling vigour.
2. Cool germination is for corn.
3. GADA has given valuable results for all types of seeds.
4. Water sensitivity test is a performance test for testing the seed vigour.
5. Vigour index is a performance test for seeds.

III. MATCH THE FOLLOWING

1.	Tetrazolium test	A	Cotton
2.	Paper piercing test	B	Biochemical
3.	Speed of germination	C	Stress test
4.	Seed density	D	Performance test
5.	Cool germination	E	Physical

IV. ONE WORD QUESTION

1. Mention any two physical tests.
2. What are performance tests for seed vigour?
3. Mention any two stress tests.
4. Mention any two biochemical tests.

ANSWER KEYS

I. FILL UPS

1. Seed vigour
2. Seed vigour
3. Germination x seedling length on the day of final count
4. Hiltner
5. Paper – piercing test
6. Cold test
7. Glutamic acid decarboxylase activity
8. Corn and wheat
9. 18ºC
10. Brick gravel test

II. TRUE OR FALSE

1. True
2. False
3. False
4. False
5. True

III. MATCH THE FOLLOWING

1. B
2. C
3. D
4. E
5. A

IV. ONE WORD ANSWER

1. i) Seed density
   ii) Physical soundness
2. i) Seedling length
   ii) Speed of germination
3. i) Cool germination test
   ii) Brick gravel test
4. i) Tetrazolium test
   ii) Respiration and RQ.

V. AT A GLANCE

- **Seed vigour:** Sum total of all properties of seed leading to production of vigourous and healthy seedling under a range of stressful environments.
- **Vigour tests:**

Physical tests	Performance tests	Stress tests	Biochemical tests
Seed size, physical Soundness, seed density	First count, speed of germination, seedling length, seedling dry weight, strong and weak seedling, vigour index, seed metabolic efficiency, mobilization efficiency	Cold test, cool germination test, brick gravel test, paper piercing test, compacted soil test, accelerated aging test, paper-piercing test, exhaustion test, water sensitivity test, osmotic stress.	Glutamic acid decarboxylase activity (GADA test), tetrazolium test, respiration and RQ, mitochondrial activity, ATP level, membrane integrity

- **Seed size:** 100/1000 seeds weight (random samples)

  $$\text{Speed of germination} = \frac{\text{Number of seedling removed daily}}{\text{Days after planting}}$$

- **Vigour index:** Germination percent x Seedling length on the day of final count (Root length and shoot length in cm).
- **Seed metabolic efficiency (SME):** The amount of efficiency determined by the respiration for producing 1 g of dry root and shoot is metabolic efficiency of the seed. Thus, higher the value of SME, lower the efficiency of seed as more seed reserve would be used for producing root and shoot. Amount of food material respired (RESP) is calculated as

  RESP = SDQ – (SHW + RTW + RSW)

  Where,

  SDW - Dry weight of seed before germination

  SHW – Dry weight of shoot

  RTW – Dry weight of root

  RSW – Dry weight of seed after germination

  SME – SHW + RTW/RESP

- **Mobilization efficiency (ME):** Seed with higher mobilization efficiency is considered as vigorous because of its capacity to supply maximum food material to seedling. Weighed seeds are placed on paper towel and kept for germination in a germinator for required period of time at optimum temperature. On the day of final count, seedlings and cotyledons are dried separately at 100°C for 24 h.

- $$ME = \frac{\text{Increase in dry weight of embryonic axis (dry weight of seedling)}}{\text{Decrease in weight of cotyledons}}$$
- **Brick gravel test** (Hiltner test) : Hiltner (1911) to show pathogenic infection, demonstrated the test by spreading 2.5 cm thick layer of moist gravel of 2-3 mm diameter over the sand medium.
- **Accelerated aging test:** Expose seeds at 40±1°C temperature and 99 ± 1% RH.
- **Cool germination test:** Expose seeds at 18°C constant temperature, Eg. Cotton
- **Cold test:** Maize, 70% water holding capacity soil spread on sand for 2 cm thickness; exposed to 10°C for one week and then at 25°C temperature; seedling count on 4th day after 45°C exposure.
- **Exhaustion test:** Cereals and legumes; keep germination roll towel @ 10°C in complete dark and count at 20 days.
- **Water sensitivity test:** 70 g of dry sterilized sand kept at low moisture level, 9 ml; high moisture level, 18 ml at 25°C for 7 days.

$$WST = \frac{I - II}{I} \times 100$$

I – Germination per cent at 9 ml

II – Germination per cent at 18 ml

- **Osmotic stress:** 75 g mannitol / lit of water
- **E.C. test:** Immerse 2-5 g seeds in 100 ml of water @ 25+1°C temperature for 10-12 h; expressed as dSm^{-1}.
- **GADA test:** Corn, wheat
- **Methyl cellosolve test** (TZ test): Extract red formazon in 100 ml methyl cellosolve; read at 480 nm in spectronic 20.
- **RQ test:** Ratio of volume of CO_2 evolved / unit time to the volume of O_2 consumed unit time.

15

Varietal Identification

I. FILL UPS

1. The seed colour of cv COH_2 is _____.
2. The special appendage present in castor is called _____.
3. Modified phenol test was identified by _____ for pearl millet hybrids.
4. _____ test is for the varietal identification of sorghum.
5. _____ test is for the varietal identification of paddy.
6. _____ is used to amplify a short well defined part of a DNA strand.
7. _____ analysis involves the selective amplification of restriction fragments from genomic DNA.
8. _____ markers are otherwise known as microsatellites.
9. _____ involves amplification of DNA segments distance in between two identical microsatellite.
10. _____ markers can be potentially converted into co-dominant markers.

II. TRUE OR FALSE

1. Lablab cultivar CO9 has maroon seed coat colour.
2. Appendages present in pulses are called awns.
3. 2, 4 – D test respond well in rice and maize varieties.
4. Modified phenol test is for corn.
5. Seed coat peroxidise test is specific for soyabean.
6. Hydrochloric acid test is useful to distinguish grain and weedy type millets.
7. Coleoptile colour is a physical test for varietal identification.
8. Appendages is a physiological test for varietal identification.
9. KoH bleach is a chemical test for varietal identification sorghum.
10. Presence or absence of auricle is plant characters for varietal identification.

III. MATCH THE FOLLOWING

1.	Ferrous sulphate colour test	A	Sorghum
2.	KoH bleach test	B	Soybean
3.	Seed coat peroxidase	C	Wheat
4.	Phenol test	D	Rice and maize
5.	GA_3 soak test	E	Paddy

IV. ONE WORD QUESTION

1. Mention any two physical test for varietal identification
2. Mention any two physiological test for varietal identification.
3. Give the chemical tests for varietal identification which are specific to crops.
4. What are the molecular marker tests for varietal identification?
5. Mention any two plant characters for varietal identification.

ANSWER KEYS

I. FILL UPS

1. Yellow
2. Caruncle
3. Halium
4. KoH bleach test
5. Ferrous sulphate colour test
6. Polymerase chain reaction
7. AFLP
8. Simple sequence repeats (SSR)
9. ISSR
10. Sequence characterized Amplified region (SCAR)

II. TRUE OR FALSE

1. True
2. False
3. True
4. False
5. True
6. False
7. False
8. False
9. True
10. True

III. MATCH THE FOLLOWING

1. E
2. A
3. B
4. C
5. D

IV. ONE WORD ANSWER

1. i) Seed size
   ii) Appendages
2. i) Coleoptile colour
   ii) Seedling illumination
3. i) KoH bleach test for sorghum
   ii) Seed coat peroxidase test for soybean
   iii) Ferrous sulphate colour test for paddy
4. i) RFLP
   ii) RAPD
   iii) ISSR
   iv) SCAR
   v) SSR
   vi) AFLP
   vii) SNP
5. Altitude of culm presence or absence of auricles.

V. AT A GLANCE

Approaches

Physical tests	Physiological tests	Chemical tests	Molecular marker tests	Plant characters
Seed size, shape, weight, texture and colour, endospermic characters, appendages	Coleoptile colour, seedling illumination, hypocotyl colour, cotyledon colour, disease resistance, sensitivity to DDT, GA_3 soak, 2,4-D	Phenol, modified phenol, alternate phenol, alkaloid, seed coat peroxidase, sodium hydroxide, potassium dichromate, KOH bleach, ferrous sulphate hydrochloric acid and iodine tests	RFLP, RAPD, SSR, ISSR, SCAR, AFLP, SNP	For example in rice, leaf blade length, width, leaf colour, colour of ligules, auricle and flowers, booting stage, leaf and leaf sheath anthocyanin colouration, presence or absence of auricles, collar ligules and altitude of culm

A. **Seed morphological characters:** Seed size, shape, colour, weight, texture etc; 4 x 100 seeds

- **Seed size:**

Size	Length	Breadth
Short	< 7.5 mm	<2 mm
Medium	7.5 – 1 mm	2 – 2.4 mm
Long	9 – 11 mm	2.4 – 3 mm
Very long	> 11 mm	> 3 mm

- **Seed shape:**
  Example: Long slender – IR 50
  Medium bold – IR 20
  Short bold – ADT 37

- **Seed colour:** Use day light or UV light
  Maize : CO 1 – Orange
  COH 1 – Deep yellow
  COH 2 – Yellow
  Cowpea : CO2 – Mottled colour
  C152 - Light brown
  CO 4 – Greyish black
  Lab lab: CO 9 – Maroon
  CO 10 – Black
  Groundnut : Off white, white rose, tan, red, dark red

- **Endospermic character:** Rice
  - Pearl spot in the center and small
  - Pearl spot in the center and extended
  - Pearl spot in the center and side extended
  - Pearl spot in the center and side slightly extended

- **Appendages / special characters:**
  Groundnut: Beak or reticulation – absent or present (slight, medium, prominent, very prominent).
  Blackgram: Prominent hilum – Vamban 1, T 9; rudimentary hilum – CO 5, TMV 1.

B. **Physiological test:**

1. **Coleoptile colour:**

- Colour is due to anthocynin content
- Sorghum: CO 28 – Reddish stem; CO 27 and CO 25 - Green stem
- Grain amaranthus: Swarna – reddish stem; CO 4 – Green stem

2. **Seedling illumination test:**
- Expose seedling to fluorescent light in dark room
- Oats: White cultivars – Fluorescent type
  Yellow cultivars – Non fluorescent type
- Festuca: Red fescue (*Festuca rubra*) – Yellow root
  Hard fescue (*Festuca lenefolia*) – Green root
- Loliluim: *L.multiflorum* – Fluorescent root
  L.perenna – No fluorescent root
- Alluim: *A. cepa* – Yellow
  A. porrum, A. fistulosum – Bluish

3. **Hypocotyl colour:** Beetroot as white, yellow, light red, red
4. **Cotyledon colour:** Brassica's; immerse seedlings in 85-90% ethanol; lemon or orange colour
5. **Disease resistant test:**
- Wheat cv. Kalyansona – Rust resistant
- Sharmila – Rust susceptible

6. **GA soak test:**
- Rice, maize
- 25 ppm, GA soaking @ 30°C for 4 days

Coleoptile length increase over control	Categorization as response under GA soak test
Less than 25%	Very slow response
26-50%	Low response type
51-75%	Medium response type
76-100 %	High response type

7. **2, 4-D test:**
- Rice, maize
- 5 ppm 2, 4 – D @ 30°C for 4 days

Coleoptile length reduction over control	Categorization as response under 2,4-D test
Less than 30%	High resistant type
30-60%	Medium resistant type
More than 60%	Low resistant type

C. **Chemical test:**

1. **Phenol test:**
- Rice, wheat, barley, oats, rye grass, kenkucky blue grass
- 1% phenol @ 30°C for 4h
- Colour intensity: 0-Negative, 1-9 – light brown to deep black.

2. **Modified phenol test:**
   - Soak seeds in 0.45% $CuSO_4$ or 1% NaOH or 0.6% Na_2CO_3 for 18 h before phenol soak

Cu	Fe	Na
No reaction	Light brown, brown greyish	Bright yellow, yellowish brown deep wine

   - For pearl millet hybrids, 1% phenol solution with a drop of 0.25% ammonia solution @ pH 12 for 24 h.
   - All male shows black colour
   - All female shows intermediate colour
3. **Alternate phenol test:**
   - Soak in warm water for 10 minutes and then in 1% phenol
4. **Lugols solution test/Alkaloid test:**
   - Lupinous varieties
   - Soak in lugals solution (Iodine + potassium iodide + water)
   - Observe for presence or absence of alkaloids
5. **Seed coat peroxidase test:**
   - Soybean
   - Place seeds in 10 drops of 0.5% guaiacol + 1 drop of 0.1% hydrogen peroxidase
   - Reddish brown – high activity
   - Colour less – low activity
6. **Sodium hydroxide test:**
   - Paddy, wheat, garden pea, fodder peas
   - 5% Na_2OH
7. **Potassium dichromate:**
   - 1% for garden pea
8. **KOH bleach test:**
   - Sorghum
   - 1:5 (w/v) potassium hydroxide plus 5-25% NaOCl for 5-10 minutes
   - Presence or absence of tannic acid
9. **Ferrous sulphate colour test:**
   - Paddy
   - 1.5% $FeSO_4$ for 4h

10. **Hydrochloric acid test:**
    - *Cucumis sativus*, *C. melo*
    - 1N HCl
11. **Iodine test:**
    - To distinguish grain and weedy type millets
    - 5% iodine
    - Seeds of weedy type turns black brown in 5-7 minutes.

16

International Seed Testing Association (ISTA)

I. FILL UPS

1. ISTA was founded in _____.
2. ISTA secretariat is located at _____.
3. _____ was founded with the aim to develop and publish standard procedures in the field of seed testing.
4. _____ is one of the leading international journals featuring papers and articles on seed quality and physiology published by ISTA.
5. The technical committees are made up of _____ number of members.
6. _____ certificate is issued when seed sample is drawn officially from seed lot under the authority of a member station and tested for seed quality by the same member station.

II. TRUE OR FALSE

1. ISTA facilitates seed trading nationally and internationally and also contributes to food security.
2. The issuing of the ISTA international seed lot certificates and officially independent ISTA accredited and authorized laboratories.
3. Green certificate is issued when seed sample is drawn from a member station in one country and tested for seed quality in another country by a member station.

III. ONE WORD QUESTION

1. Mention ISTA certificates.

ANSWER KEYS

I. FILL UPS

1. 1924
2. Zurich, Switzerland
3. ISTA
4. Seed Science and Technology
5. 400
6. Orange

II. TRUE OR FALSE

1. True
2. True
3. True

III. ONE WORD ANSWER

1. i) Orange International Seed Lot Certificate

   ii) Blue International Seed Sample Certificate of Public and Private Seed companies for domestic and international trade.

17

Isolation Distance at a Glance

1. VARIETAL SEED PRODUCTION

3 m : Rice, soybean

5 m : Blackgram, greengram, cowpea, field lab lab lab lab

5-10 m : Groundnut

25 m : Tomato

30 m : Cotton CS

50 m : Cotton FS, jute, gingelly CS

100 m : Sorghum variety, redgram, gingelly FS

150 m : Castor CS

200 m : Maize, sorghum FS, pearl millet CS, sunflower CS, castor FS, safflower CS, brinjal FS, chilli CS, bhendi CS

400 m : Sudangrass FS and CS, fodder sorghum FS and CS, pearl millet FS, sunflower FS, safflower FS, chilli FS, pumpkin CS, ashgourd CS, bittergourd CS

500 m : Ribbedgourd CS, snakegourd FS

800 m : Pumpkin FS, ashgourd FS, bittergourd FS

100 m : Ribbedgourd FS, snakegourd FS

2. HYBRID SEED PRODUCTION

30 m : Cotton CS

50 m : Cotton FS

100 m : Rice

200 m : Maize CS, sorghum, pearl millet CS, redgram, tomato

400 m : Maize FS, chilli

600 m : Sunflower

100 m : Pearl millet FS, bittergourd CS, snakegourd CS

1500 m : Bittergourd FS

3. VARIETIES AND HYBRIDS

1600 m for FS and 1000 m for CS of all crucifers except carrot (1000 m for FS; 800 m for CS)

FS : Foundation seed

CS : Certified seed

18

Minimum Germination for Foundation Seed and Certified Seed at a Glance

60% - Bottlegourd, pumpkin, bittergourd, watermelon

65% - Cotton varieties, bhendi

70% - Castor, groundnut, sunflower, soyabean, tomato, brinjal, cluster bean

75% - Sorghum, ragi, pearl millet, redgram, greengram, blackgram, cowpea, cotton hybrids, peas, french beans

80% - Rice, maize inbreds and single cross hybrid, horsegram, safflower, sesamum, niger, jute

85% - Wheat, bengalgram

90% - Maize hybrids, composites, synthetics

UNIT - 5

SEED STORAGE

1

Seed Storage

I. FILL UPS

1. _____ is the maintenance of high seed germination and vigour from harvest until planting.
2. _____ is important to get adequate plant stand in addition to healthy and vigours plants.
3. _____ seeds can be dried to 6-10% moisture depending upon the species.
4. _____ seeds cannot be dried below 30-35% moisture and should be maintained at this temperature.
5. _____ is only a short-term storage and is amenable for fluctuations in temperature and RH.
6. _____ is produced mainly for long term storage.
7. _____ are short lived seeds based on genetic make up.
8. _____ developed a formulae to describe the relationship between temperature, seed moisture content and period of viability.
9. Increase in _____ pressure decrease the period of viability.
10. _____ is the process of filling, weighing and sowing of bag.
11. Seeds undergo _____ due to ageing in storage.
12. For fumigation in seed storage area _____ is used.
13. _____ is an example for intermediary seeds.
14. Rubber is an example for _____ seeds.
15. Pulses are an example for _____ seeds.
16. _____ container is used for long term seed storage
17. _____ spray is used for seed store sanitation
18. _____ fumigation is done to control storage pests.

II. TRUE OR FALSE

1. For every decrease of 5.6°C (10°F) in storage temperature, the life of the seed decreases.
2. For every decrease of 1% seed moisture content, the life of the seed doubles and this rule is applicable between moisture content of 5-14%.
3. Paper bag, aluminium foil pouches are used for packaging flower and vegetable seeds.
4. N_2 and CO_2 atmosphere will decrease the storage life of seeds.
5. In recalcitrant seed, dormancy is absent or weak.
6. Use wooden pallets for stacking upto 7-9 bags height in criss-cross pattern.
7. Polyethylene bag of 700 guage is a moisture impervious container.
8. Sum of temperature and RH in seed storage godown should not exceed 100.

III. MATCH THE FOLLOWING

1.	Cereals	A. Intermediary
2.	Coffee	B. Long term
3.	Neem	C. Medium term
4.	Mesobiotic	D. Orthodox
5.	Macrobiotic	E. Recalcitrant

IV. ONE WORD QUESTION

1. Mention any one difference between orthodox and recalcitrant seeds
2. State one principle of storage.
3. What are types of storage based on genetic make up?
4. What are the types of storage based on storage behaviour with examples?
5. What are the types of storage based on environment?

ANSWER KEYS

I. FILL UPS

1. Seed storage	2. Seed storage	3. Orthodox seeds
4. Recalcitrant	5. Open storage	6. Controlled storage
7. Microbiotic	8. Roberts	9. O2
10. Seed packaging	11. Deterioration	12. Aluminium phosphate @3g/cu.m
13. Neem	14. Recalcitrant	15. Orthodox
16. Moisture vapour proof	17. Malathion	18. Aluminium phosphide

II. TRUE OR FALSE

1. False 2. True
3. True 4. False
5. True 6. False
7. False 8. True

III. MATCH THE FOLLOWING

1. D
2. E
3. A
4. C
5. B

IV. ONE WORD ANSWER

1.

Orthodox seeds	**Recalcitrant seeds**
Can be stored for several years	Can be stored for few days to few months
Contains 10-12% moisture	Contains 30-35% moisture

2. Proper sanitation in seed stores
3. i) Microbiotic
   ii) Mesobiotic
   iii) Macrobiotic
4. i) Orthodox (oilseeds)
   ii) Recalcitrant (Coffee)
   iii) Intermediary (Neem)
5. i) Open storage
   ii) Controlled storage

V. AT A GLANCE

1. Classification of seed storage

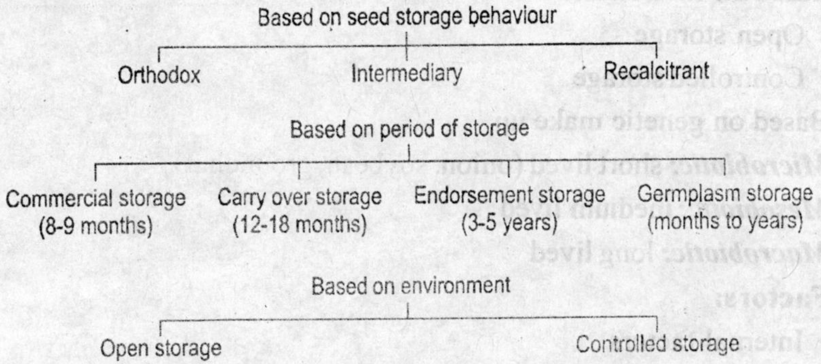

2. Differentiate between orthodox seed and recalcitrant seed with examples

Orthodox seed	Recalcitrant seed
Can be dried to 6-10% moisture depending upon the species	Cannot be dried below 30-35% moisture and should be maintained at this moisture
No decline in germination, if dried	A decline in germination, if dried below this moisture
Tolerant to desiccation (5-7% moisture) and low temperatures (0-5°C)	Intolerant to desiccation (30-35% moisture) and low temperature (12-15°C)
Examples. Cereals, Pulses, Oilseeds etc	Example. Rubber, Coffee, Coconut, Mango, Citrus, Swietenia, Jamun
Prevalent in arid and semi arid environments	Prevalent in warm humid climates
Can be stored for several years	Can be stored for few days to few months
Small to medium size seed often with hard seed coat	Usually medium to large size and heavy seeds
Dormancy often occurs	Dormancy absent or weak
Not metabolically active when shed	Metabolically active when shed
Accumulation of dry weight ceases before maturation	Accumulation of dry weight upto the time of seed dispersal

3. Summary

Seed storage: Maintenance of high germination and vigour until sowing

- **Principles:**
  - Store at dry and cool environment at safe moisture level
  - Proper seed store sanitation for effective control of storage pests and disease
- **Types of storage:**

  Based on storage behaviour
  - Orthodox (cereals, millets, pulses, oilseeds)
  - Recalcitrant (Rubber, coffee, mango, citrus)
  - Intermediary (Neem)

  Based on environment
  - Open storage
  - Controlled storage

  Based on genetic make up
- *Microbiotic:* short lived (onion, soybean, groundnut)
- *Mesobiotic:* medium lived
- *Macrobiotic:* long lived
- **Factors:**
  - Internal factors

- Genetic
- Initial seed quality
- Provenance
- Weather during seed formation
- Pre-harvest infestation
- Seed moisture

- **External factors**
  - RH
  - Temperature
  - **Harrington rules:**
  - For every decrease in 1% moisture, life doubles; this rule is applicable between moisture content of 5-14%.
  - For every decrease in 10ºF (5.6ºC) temperature, life doubles; this rule applies between OºC to 50ºC.
  - Sum of RH and temperature in ºF should not exceed 100. i.e. 50 % RH + 50ºF - 100.
  - Gases
  - Microflora, insects and mites
- **Packaging container:**
  - Moisture pervious container (cloth bag, paper bag)
  - Moisture impervious and vapour pervious container (Polyethylene bags of 100-300 gauge thickness)
  - Moisture impervious and vapour proof container (Polyethylene bags of 700 gauge thickness, aluminium foil pouches)
- **Seed store sanitation:**
  - Pre-cleaning of seed store thoroughly and disinfect it
  - Store should be dry and cool
  - If use old bags, disinfect/fumigate them
  - Use wooden pallets for stacking upto **6-8** bags height in criss-cross
  - Spray malathion 50 EC @ 5 lit/100m^2 for every 3 weeks
  - Aluminium phosphide @ 3 g/cu.m for fumigation
  - In pulses, insect infestation comes from field (e.g.) bruchids.

2

Seed Deterioration

I. FILL UPS

1. _____ is defined as deteriorative mechanism occurring with time that increase the seeds vulnerability and decrease ability to survive.
2. Lettuce seeds develop red necrotic lesions in cotyledons known as _____.
3. _____ morphological changes occur in ground nut due to deterioration.
4. _____ refers to the oxidative degradation of lipids.
5. _____ is an inexorable and irreversible processes.
6. _____ peroxidation results in free radical production.
7. Cell membrane during seed deterioration is disrupted by _____.
8. Delayed _____ is the physiological change during seed deterioration.
9. Loss of _____ integrity is the ultrastructural change during seed deterioration.
10. Swollen _____ decrease respiration which is ultrastructural change during seed deterioration.

II. TRUE OR FALSE

1. A decrease in carbohydrate content is noticed in deteriorated seeds of bamboo which will be utilized for respiration.
2. RQ value of deteriorated seed is low which is due to more CO_2 release and less uptake of O_2.
3. In maize, due to seed deterioration, it develops a peculiar lobed condition in nucleus.
4. A sharp decrease in protein content in aged seeds of maize will lead to decrease in total free amino acids.
5. The general increase in enzyme activity in the seeds increases respirative activity.

III. ONE WORD QUESTION

1. Mention any one morphological changes due to seed deterioration.
2. Mention any one ultra structural changes due to seed deterioration.
3. Mention any one biochemical changes due to seed deterioration.
4. Mention any one physiological changes due to seed deterioration.

ANSWER KEYS

I. FILL UPS

1. Seed deterioration	2. Cotyledonary	3. Darkening
4. Lipid peroxidation	5. Seed deterioration	6. Lipid
7. Free radical	8. Germination	9. Membrane
10. Mitochondria		

II. TRUE OR FALSE

1. True	2. False
3. True	4. False
5. False	

III. ONE WORD ANSWER

1. Darkening / discolouration in groundnut
2. Dissociation of ribosome's results in retardation in protein synthesis.
3. High RQ value
4. Delayed germination and reduced seedling growth.

IV. AT A GLANCE

- **Seed deterioration:** Inexorable and irreversible event in seed
- **Basis of seed deterioration:**
- **Morphological changes**
  - Discolouration (Darkening in groundnut)
- **Ultrastructural changes**
  - Loss of membrane integrity leading to increased leakage of solutes
  - Swollen mitochondria results in decreased respiration
  - Dissociation of ribosomes results in retardation of protein synthesis
  - Degeneration of ER

- **Biochemical changes**
    - Loss of enzymes activity (amylases, proteinases, cytochrome oxidases, glyceraldehyde phosphate dehydrogenases, catalase, peroxidase)
    - Reduced germination
    - High RQ value
    - Increased oxidative degradation of lipids (lipid peroxidation) leading to production of free radicals that damages cell membrane
    - Degradation of food reserves
- **Genetic changes**
    - *Old concensus:* DNA degradation, lesser mRNA production and reduced protein synthesis
    - *New concensus:* Lipid peroxidation results in free radical production that disruptes the cell membrane
    - Mitochondria replication leading lesser mitochondria and respiration
- **Physiological changes**
    - Delayed germination and reduced seedling growth.

3

Seed Treatment

I. FILL UPS

1. _____ refers to the application of pesticides to seeds before sowing or storage to protect the seeds.
2. The chemical gases as fumes are used to control the pests in seed lots is called as _____.
3. The treatments given to the seeds prior to or during storage to protect the seed are called _____ treatment.
4. Application of _____ to seeds before storage as wet or dry treatments will delay ageing.
5. _____ refers to the eradication of fungal spores that have become established within seed coat.

II. TRUE OR FALSE

1. Bavistin is an example for dry or dust form of seed dressing.
2. Seed disinfestation refers to the eradication of fungal spores that have become established within seed coat.
3. Seed fumigation is the process of simply dipping or soaking in chemical solutions.
4. Seed disinfection refers to the eradication of fungal spores have become established within seed coat.
5. The chemicals is applied to the seed with some water to make a uniform coat over the seed surface is called slurry form.

III. MATCH THE FOLLOWING

1.	Seed dressing	A. Surface borne organisms
2.	Antioxidant	B. Aluminium phosphide
3.	Halogenation	C. Bavistin
4.	Fumigation	D. Vitamin A
5.	Seed disinfestation	E. Bleaching powder

IV. ONE WORD QUESTION

1. Give some examples for fumigants
2. Give some examples for antioxidants.
3. Give some examples for halogens
4. Give one example for dry seed dressing.
5. Mention any two types of pre-storage treatment.

ANSWER KEYS

I. FILL UPS

1. Seed treatment 2. Fumigation 3. Pre-storage
4. Antioxidants 5. Seed disinfection

II. TRUE OR FALSE

1. True 2. False
3. False 4. True
5. True

III. MATCH THE FOLLOWING

1. C
2. D
3. E
4. B
5. A

IV. ONE WORD ANSWER

1. Ethylene oxide, ethylene dibromide, calcium cyanide, aluminium phosphide
2. Vitamin A, C, E.
3. Calcium carbonate, bleaching powder
4. Bavistin, activated clay
5. Halogenation, seed fumigation

V. AT A GLANCE

- **Seed treatment:** Application of pesticides to control seed pathogen and insects and for safe storage.

- **Methods of seed dressing:** Dust, slurry, liquid, mist and gaseous form
- **Equipment:** Treatment drum, slurry treater, fumigation chamber
- **Types of pre storage treatment:**
  - **Halogenation:** Expose the seeds to bleaching powder (calcium oxychloride) to dry or vapour from
  - **Antioxidant:** Treat seeds with vitamin A, C, E to quench free radicals
  - **Seed protectants:**
  - Treat seeds with insecticides and fungicides to control seed and soil borne diseases and insects. *E.g.* Bavisin @ 2-4 g/kg of seed
  - **Seed disinfection:** Control of deep seated internally borne pathogen
  - **Seed disinfestation:** Control of surface and externally borne pathogens
  - **Fumigation:** Fumigate the seeds @ 14% moisture with aluminium phosphide @ 2-3 tablets/cu.m. Each tablet weighs about 3 g.

4

Mid Storage Seed Treatment

I. FILL UPS

1. _____ are capable of reducing the age induced damages and restoring the seed vigour by controlling free radical reactions.
2. _____ is the process of soaking the low and medium vigour seeds in water with or without adding chemicals to raise seed moisture and drying back for safe storage of seeds.
3. _____ treatment is similar to the moisture equilibration treatment.
4. _____ treatment causes possible aging effect especially when given for prolonged periods.
5. _____ treatment not only controls free radical reactions, but also improves the seed viability and productivity of stored seeds.

II. TRUE OR FALSE

1. Soaking drying treatment is effective in moist high and high medium vigour seeds of rice.
2. Moist sand conditioning – drying is similar to dipping –drying in its efficacy and suitability.
3. Hydration-dehydration treatment should be given only to stored seeds.
4. Hydration-dehydration will make a seed germinable, which has already lost viability.
5. Direct soaking of leguminous should be avoided.

III. ONE WORD QUESTION

1. Mention any two types of hydration – dehydration treatments.
2. What are the requirements for hydration – dehydration treatments?

ANSWER KEYS

I. FILL UPS

1. Mid storage seed treatment
2. Hydration – dehydration
3. Moist sand conditioning – drying
4. Moisture – equilibrium – drying
5. Mid storage seed treatment

II. TRUE OR FALSE

1. False
2. False
3. True
4. False
5. True

III. ONE WORD ANSWER

1. Soaking-drying and spraying-drying
2. Hydration dehydration is effective in low and medium vigour non leguminous seeds.

5

Germplasm Storage and Cryopreservation

I. FILL UPS

1. _____ is a collection of genetic resources for an organism.
2. The conservation of species in their natural habitats is called _____.
3. _____ is the preservation of components of biological diversity outside their natural habitats.
4. _____ is a type of gene bank that stores seeds as a source for planting in case seed reserves elsewhere are destroyed.
5. _____ is recognised as a UNESCO world heritage site in 2003.
6. _____ is well known repository which will hold up to 2.25 billion.
7. _____ seeds cannot be dried and frozen without damage to DNA.
8. _____ seeds are dried to below 5% moisture and then frozen to -18°C and can be stored for several decades.
9. _____ gene bank where cultures are maintained under slow growth in low / non freezing temperature (1 to 9°C).
10. CIMMYT is an example for_____.
11. The term _____ refers to storage of cells, tissues and organs at the ultra – low temperature of liquid nitrogen.
12. _____ is the process of releasing the vials containing cultures from the frozen state to elevate the temperature between 35 and 40°C.
13. _____ was proposed in 1968 for maintenance of cell culture.
14. *In vitro* conservation of potato is at _____.
15. *In vitro* conservation of cassava is at _____.

II. TRUE OR FALSE

1. The millennium seed bank partnership is the largest *ex situ* plant conservation project in the world.
2. Preservation outside natural habitat is called *ex situ* conservation.

3. Orthodox seeds cannot be dried and frozen without damage to DNA.
4. Seed banks is an example for *in situ* conservation.
5. Seed banks are not typically open to the public.

III. MATCH THE FOLLOWING

1.	Gene bank	A	196°C
2.	Cryopreservation	B	ex situ conservation
3.	CIMMYT	C	Potato
4.	CIP	D	Rubber
5.	Recalcitrant	E	Wheat and maize

IV. ONE WORD QUESTION

1. Give one example for *ex situ* conservation
2. Mention any two examples for protectants.
3. Give any two examples for *in vitro* conservation centres.

ANSWER KEYS

I. FILL UPS

1. Germplasm
2. *In situ* conservation
3. *Ex situ* conservation
4. Seed bank
5. Millennium seed bank lab
6. Svalbard global seed vault
7. Recalcitrant
8. Orthodox seeds
9. 1 to 9°C
10. *In vitro* conservation
11. Cryopreservation
12. Thawing
13. Cryopreservation
14. International Centre for Potato, Peru.
15. International Centre for Tropical Agriculture, Columbia

II. TRUE OR FALSE

1. True
2. True
3. False
4. False
5. True

III. MATCH THE FOLLOWING

1. B
2. A
3. E
4. C
5. D

IV. ONE WORD ANSWER

1. Seed bank
2. Sugar alcohols, polyethylene glycol
3. CIMMYT, Mexico; CIP, Peru
   i) International Wheat and Maize Improvement Centre.
   ii) International Centre for Potato

V. AT A GLANCE

- **Germplasm:** Collection of plant genetic resources
- **Conservation methods:**
  - ***In situ* conservation:** Conservation in natural habitat
  - ***Ex situ* conservation:** Preservation outside natural habitat
- **Seed Bank:**
  - Collection and preservation of seeds of food and other crops
  - Not for exchange
  - Meet out the requirements due to natural disasters
  - Millennium seed bank lab @ Royal Botanical Gardens, Kew, London
  - Svalbard Global Seed Vault, Norway
- ***In vitro* conservation:**
  - Conserve at low/non freezing temperature of 1 to 9°C
  - Paddy – IRRI, Philippines
  - Wheat and maize – CIMMYT, Mexico
  - Cassava – CIAT, Columbia; IITA, Nigeria
  - Potato – CIP, Peru
  - Sweet potato – CIP, Peru; AVRDC, Taiwan; IITA, Nigeria

Cryopreservation:
- Preserve in liquid nitrogen (-196°C)
- Proposed in 1968 for cell culture maintenance
- Conservation of shoot tips in pear, plum, olive etc.

UNIT - 6

SEED HEALTH

1

Seed Pathology

I. FILL UPS

1. The area of science that studies the relationship between pathogens and seeds is _____.
2. The diseases that are caused by fungal pathogens in residues and on the soil surface are defined as _____.
3. The establishment of a pathogens in any part of the seed is referred as _____.
4. _____ pathogen in bean causes infection by penetration through wounds and natural openings.
5. _____ refers to the passive relationship of a pathogens and seeds.
6. _____ type of contamination refers to physical mixing of the seed with pathogen's propagation organ like the sclerotium (or) contaminated plant.
7. _____ is the designated disease of paddy.
8. _____ is the designated disease of cotton.
9. Ear cockle disease of wheat caused by _____ pathogen.
10. _____ is the internally seed borne disease of wheat.
11. _____ is the externally seed borne disease of sorghum.
12. In pearl millet _____ disease is caused by seed contamination and soil contamination.
13. _____ is the externally seed borne disease in tomato.
14. _____ is the seed borne disease of brinjal.
15. _____ is the internally seed borne disease of chilli.
16. _____ is the seed borne disease of cole crops.
17. Wilt is a _____ disease.
18. _____ pathogen causes systemic infection through vascular system.
19. _____ pathogen causes systemic episperm contamination.
20. _____ pathogen causes nonsystemic episperm contamination.

II. TRUE OR FALSE

1. Anthracnose is a designated disease of greengram.
2. Loose smut of wheat is a externally seed borne disease of wheat.
3. Downey mildew of pearl millet is air borne disease of pearl millet.
4. Charcoal rot of potato is a tuber borne disease of potato.
5. Septoria *nodorum* is a non system infection of the episperm.

III. MATCH THE FOLLOWING

(i)

1. *Alternaria brassicae*	A. Penetration through stigma
2. *Rhizoctonia solani*	B. Systemic infection through vascular system
3. *Ustilago tritici*	C. Sticks to surface of seed
4. *Nevossia torrida*	D. Penetration through ovary
5. *Xanthomonas campestris* pv *phaseolina*	E. Contamination of the episperm

(ii)

1. Loose smut of wheat	A Soil borne and air borne
2. Grain smut of bajra	B Fusarium
3. Mosaic virus	C Tuber borne
4. Dry rot of tomato	D Externally seed borne
5. Wilt	E Internally seed borne

ANSWER KEYS

I. FILL UPS

1. Seed pathology	2. Soil borne diseases	3. Seed infection
4. *Xanthomonas campestris* pv. *phaseolina*		5. Seed infestation
6. Accompanying contamination		7. Bunt
8. Black arm	9. *Anguina tritici*	10. Loose smut
11. Kernel or grain smut		12. Ergot
13. Mosaic virus	14. Fruit rot	15. Anthracnose
16. Black leg	17. Soil borne	18. *Xanthomonas*
19. *Ustilago* sp	20. *Neovossia* sp	

II. TRUE OR FALSE

1.	True	2.	False
3.	False	4.	False
5.	True		

III. MATCH THE FOLLOWING

(i)		(ii)	
1.	C	1.	E
2.	D	2.	A
3.	A	3.	D
4.	E	4.	C
5.	B	5.	B

IV. AT A GLANCE

- **Seed pathology:** Study of relationship between pathogens and seeds
- **Types of pathogen:** Fungi, bacteria and virus
- **Nature of infection:**
- **Soil borne diseases:**
    - Caused by fungi only
    - Wilting, yellowing, stunting and plant death
    - Root rot (*Rhizoctonia*, *Sclerotina*)
    - Wilt (*Fusarium*, *Verticillium*)
    - Seedling blight and damping off (*Pythium* , *Phytophthora*)
- **Seed borne diseases:**
    - Internally and externally seed borne
- **Mechanism:**
    - **Systemic infection through seed**
    - Infection through vascular system (*Xanthomonas*)
    - Systemic infection through flower, fruits (*Fusarium*, *Pseudomonas*)
    - Penetration through stigma (*Ustilago* spp)
    - Penetration through ovary wall (*Colletotrichum*)
    - Penetration through wounds and natural opening (*X. campestris*)

- **Seed contamination or infestation**
  - Pathogen sticks on the seed surface (*Alternaria* spp)
  - Accompanying contamination
- **Seed Transmission**
- **Systemic transmission**
  - Infection of embryo (*X. campestris*)
  - Non embryo infection (*Corynebacterium*)
  - Episperm contamination (*Ustilago, Puccinia*)
- **Nonsystemic transmission**
  - Embryo infection (*Ascochyta pisi*)
  - Episperm infection (*Septoria nodorum*)
  - Episperm contamination (*Neovossia* spp)
  - Accompanying contamination (*Sclerotina*)

2

Seed Health Testing

I. FILL UPS

1. _____ refers to the health status of a seed.
2. A group of fungi that infects developing seeds on the plant in the field, but before it is threshed is called as _____.
3. _____ fungi invade seeds at (or) after harvest.
4. _____ method is used particularly for smut and bunt fungi in gramineous host.
5. _____ method is used for detection of karnal bunt of wheat.
6. _____ is a powerful molecular tool, used to detect DNA of microorganisms.
7. _____ is used for a large number of *Xanthomonas* and *Pseudomonas*.
8. _____ tests are based on *in vitro* reactions between antigens and antibodies.
9. _____ is an immune assay system involving polyclonal and monoclonal antibodies for clinical diagnols of seed borne pathogens.
10. _____ is used for examination of presence of acervuli, pycanidia on seed surface and mixed with seed.

II. TRUE OR FALSE

1. Indicator test is used to detect the seed borne disease, TMV in tomato.
2. Dry seed examination is used to determine virus seed transmission.
3. Growing on test has been used successfully for detection of *Xanthomonas*.
4. Washing test is used particularly for detection of loose smut of wheat.
5. *Aspergillus* is an example for field fungi.

III. MATCH THE FOLLOWING

1.	*Alternaria*	A	Karnal smut of rice
2.	*Aspergillus*	B	TMV in tomato
3.	NaOH seed test	C	*Xanthomonas*
4.	Growing on test	D	Field fungi
5.	Indicator test	E	Storage fungi

IV. ONE WORD QUESTION

1. Give one example for field fungi
2. Give one example for storage fungi
3. Mention any two objectives for seed health testing
4. Mention any two methods for detection of seed borne fungi
5. Mention any two methods for detection seed borne bacteria
6. Mention any two methods for detection of seed borne virus.

ANSWER KEYS

I. FILL UPS

1. Seed health	2. Field fungi	3. Storage fungi
4. Washing test	5. NaOH seed soak method	
6. PCR	7. Growing on test	8. Serological technique
9. ELISA test	10. Dry seed examination	

II. TRUE OR FALSE

1. True	2. False
3. True	4. False
5. False	

III. MATCH THE FOLLOWING

1. D
2. E
3. A
4. C
5. B

IV. ONE WORD ANSWER

1. *Alternaria*
2. *Aspergillus*
3. i) Testing for quarantine
   ii) Testing for certification scheme
4. i) Blotter method
   ii) Agar plate method
5. i) Growing on test
   ii) Indicator test
6. i) Dry seed examination
   ii) Indicator test

V. AT A GLANCE

- **Field fungi:** Pathogen infection in the field itself while seed on the plant itself (*Alternaria*, *Curvularia*) @ 90-100% RH and 24-25% moisture
- **Storage fungi:** Invade seeds after harvest and in storage @ 70-90% RH. (*Aspergillus*, *Penicillium*)
- **Methods of testing:**
- **Seed borne fungi detection**
  - Dry seed examination: Presence of *Acervuli*, *pycnidia*, *pericthecia*, *sclerotia* on seed surface and mixed with seed.
  - Seed coat discolouration, reduction in size and weight, shrivelled seed.
  - Blotter method: Incubate in water soaked filter paper @ 22°C and 12h alternate light and dark for 7 days and observe for fungi
  - Agar plate method: Incubate in agar medium and procedure as above.
  - Seedling symptoms test: Observe fungi in the germinated seedling
  - Wash test: For smut and bunt fungi except smut of wheat and barley
  - NaOH test: Soak seeds in 0.2% NaOH for 24h and separate black colour seeds infected by karnal bunt of wheat and kernel smut of rice
  - PCR: Used to detect DNA of microorganisms
- **Seed borne bacteria detection**
  - Dry seed examination: As in fungi
  - Growing on test: To identify *Xanthomonas* and *Pseudomonas*
  - Agar medium: As in fungi
  - Indicator test: Inoculate the water suspension of seed sample into the infiltration of primary leaf node of 10 day old bean seedling and observe for appearance of lesions
  - Serological test: Test the supernatant of a washing of seed sample with antiserum of suspected pathogen
  - ELISA test: Reaction between antibodies and antigen or other microbes is amplified by sandwich method
- **Seed borne viruses detection**
  - Dry seed examination
  - Growing on test
  - Indicator test
  - Serological test

3

Seed Storage Insects

I. FILL UPS

1. _____ is the most important primary pests of cereals.
2. _____ causes serious damage in maize cob.
3. _____ is the field pest of pulses.
4. _____ feeds on already damaged.
5. _____ is the secondary pests of cereals and oilseeds.
6. _____ test method is useful for crops with small seed size.
7. _____ pest attacks seeds of groundnut, cereals and legumes.
8. _____ pest feeds on damaged seeds of cowpea and cocoa.
9. In _____ pest only larva causes the seed damage.
10. _____ pest causes webbing symptom.

II. TRUE OR FALSE

1. Mites causes musty odor and dust symptoms in all seeds.
2. X-ray radiography method is useful for the crops with small seed size.
3. Lesser grain borer causes circular regular holes in spices.
4. *Angoumois* moth reduce the seeds to husk in wheat.
5. Pulse beetle causes circular holes in pulses.

III. MATCH THE FOLLOWING

1.	Circular holes	A Cigaretle beetle
2.	Irregular holes	B Khapra beetle
3.	Seed to husk	C Mites
4.	Webbing	D Pulse beetle
5.	Musty odour	E Indian meal moth

IV. ONE WORD QUESTION

1. What are the methods or tests followed for assessing the damage?
2. Mention any one management practice for storage pest.

ANSWER KEYS

I. FILL UPS

1. Rice weevil
2. *Angoumois* grain moth
3. Bruchids
4. Red flour beetle
5. Saw toothed grain beetle
6. Transparency test
7. Khapra beetle
8. Flat grain beetle
9. Long headed flour beetle or *Angoumois* grain moth
10. Indial meal moth

II. TRUE OR FALSE

1. True
2. False
3. False
4. False
5. True

III. MATCH THE FOLLOWING

1. D
2. A
3. B
4. E
5. C

IV. ONE WORD ANSWER

1. i) Visual inspection
   ii.) X-ray radiography
   iii) Transparency test
2. Fumigate with aluminium phosphide @ 1 tablet (3g) m^2 thrice at 40-60 days interval.

V. AT A GLANCE

- **Storage loss:**
  - Weight loss upto 30 per cent
  - Loss of market value due to discolouration

- Mould attack and caking
- Reduce germination

- **Storage pests:**
  - Rice weevil (*Sitophilus oryzae*) – Make round holes on seeds of rice, maize etc.
  - Angoumois grain moth (*Sitotroga cerealella*) – Larval cause damage on seeds of rice, maize, sorghum and wheat
  - Lesser grain beetle (*Rhizopertha dominica*) – Insect damage seeds of sorghum, maize
  - Larger grain beetle (*Prostephanus truncates*) – Higher weight loss than others
  - Bruchids (*Callosobruchus maculatus*) – Infected pulse seeds in the field itself and eats embryo only by making round holes
  - Indian meal moth (*Plodia interpunetella*) – Damages seed only
  - Rice moth (*Corcyra cephalonica*) – Major primary pests of cereals, groundnut
  - Red flour beetle (*Tribolium castaneum*) – Feeds on already damaged seed
  - Khapra beetle (*Trogoderma granaria*) – Attacks seeds of groundnut, cereals and legumes
  - Saw-tooth beetle (*Oryzaephilus surinamensis*) – Feeds on damaged seeds of cereals, cowpea and cocoa
  - Granary weevil (*Sitophilus granaries*) – Larva and adult damage seed
  - Confused flour beetle (*Tribolium surinamensis*) – Larva and adult damage seed
  - Long headed flour beetle (*Leatheticus oryzae*) – Larva damages seed

- **Management:**
  - Remove infested and old material, and clean and disinfect thoroughly the seed store
  - Spray malathion 50EC @ 5 litres per 100 m^2 area
  - Fumigate with aluminium phosphide @ 1 tablet (3g) per m^2 space thrice at 40-60 days interval

- **Assessment of damage:**
  - **Visual inspection – Examine for discolouration and nature of damage for different pests**
  - **X-rays radiography – Examine to x-rays @ 22KV, 3MA for 10 seconds at 30 cm distance**
  - **Transparency test – Seed coat becomes transparent if boil with laxtophenol for 10-20 min.**

4

Seed Borne Nematodes

I. FILL UPS

1. _____ are also called ed-worms.
2. _____ nematode causes discolouration in groundnut.
3. _____ in rice is caused by *Aphelenchoides besseyi*.
4. The ear cockle disease is caused _____.
5. _____ seed borne nematode causes damage symptoms in pigeon pea.
6. _____ in 1979 listed five nematode genera that are seed transmitted.
7. _____ nematodes are attached externally to the seeds of cereals.
8. _____ nematode causes galls on the roots of bhendi, chilli.
9. _____ nematode damages the flower head of aster in severe causes.
10. _____ nematodes occur as endoparasites in roots, stems and leaves.

II. TRUE OR FALSE

1. Discolouration in groundnut is caused by *Ditylenchus destructor*.
2. Cyst nematode (*Heterodora cajani*) in pigeon pea causes yellowing and stunting.
3. Nematodes are saprozoic and parasitize plants.

III. MATCH THE FOLLOWING

1.	White tip	A	*Aphelenchoides ritzemabosi*
2.	Ear cockle	B	*Meloidogyne incognita*
3.	Pigeon pea	C	*Aphelenchoides besseyi*
4.	Aster	D	*Ditylenchus sipsaci*
5.	Bhendi root galls	E	*Heterodera cajani*

IV. ONE WORD QUESTION

1. Give any two examples for seed transmitted nematodes.
2. Give any two examples for endoparasite nematodes in roots, stems and leaves.

ANSWER KEYS

I. FILL UPS

1. Nematodes
2. *Ditylenchus destructor*
3. White tip
4. *Ditylenchus dipsaci*
5. Cyst nematode *Heterodera cajani*
6. Neergard
7. Ufra nematode
8. *Meloidogyne incognita* (Root knot nematode)
9. *Aphelenchoides ritzemabosi*
10. *Heterodera*

II. TRUE OR FALSE

1. False
2. True
3. True

III. MATCH THE FOLLOWING

1. C
2. D
3. E
4. A
5. B

IV. ONE WORD ANSWER

1. *Aphelenchoides*, *Heterodera*
2. Heterodera, *Rhadinaphelenchus*

V. AT A GLANCE

- **Seed borne nematodes:**
  - May be internal or external
  - Seed gall – *Anguina* sp.
  - Discolouration in groundnut – *Ditylenchus destructor*
- **Seed transmitted nematodes:** *Anguina, Aphelenchoides, Ditylenchus, Heterodora, Rhadinaphelenchus*
- **Management:**
  - White tip (*Aphelenchoides besseyi*) in rice – Hot water treatment @ 55°C for 10-15 min. or carbofuran
  - Ufra (*Ditylenchus augustus*) – Carbofuran

- Ear cockle (*D. dipsaci*) – Hot water @ 54°C for 10 min.
- Cyst nematode (*Heterodera cajani*) in pigeonpea – *Pseudomonas* + *Trichoderma* @ 5+5 g/kg of seed

Detection:

- Dry seed examination
- Desection techniques
- Disection and staining
- Washing and extraction

UNIT - 7

SEED INDUSTRY AND MARKETING

1

Seed Industry

I. FILL UPS

1. RCA stands for _____.
2. Expert standing committee was set up in _____.
3. In _____year, All India Co-ordinated maize improvement programme was started.
4. First maize hybrid was released in the year _____.
5. All India co-ordinated bajra and sorghum improvement programme was started in _____.
6. First sorghum hybrid was released in the year _____.
7. The first five year plan was started in the year _____.
8. NSC was established in the year _____.
9. Seed Review Team was started in the year _____.
10. National Seeds Programme (NSP) was started in the year _____.
11. Seed Control Order was passed in the year _____.
12. STL was started in Tamil Nadu in the year_____.
13. PPVFR was started in the year _____.
14. The New Seed Bill was passed in the year _____.
15. Seed certification was started in the year_____.

II. TRUE OR FALSE

1. Seed Control Order was passed in the sixth five year plan.
2. Association of Official Seed Analyst was started in the year 1908.
3. European Seed Testing Association was started in the year 1919.
4. Seed Act was passed in the year 1969.
5. National Seed Policy was started in the year 2001.

III. MATCH THE FOLLOWING

(i)

1.	New Seed Bill	A. 2001
2.	Seed Act	B. 2004
3.	Seed Rules	C. 1983
4.	Seed Control Order	D. 1966
5.	National Seed Policy	E. 1968

(ii)

1.	Fifth five year plan	A. 1992-97
2.	Sixth five year plan	B. 1980-85
3.	Eighth five year plan	C. 1961-66
4.	Third five year plan	D. 1951-56
5.	First five year plan	E. 1974-79

ANSWER KEYS

I. FILL UPS

1. Royal Commission on Agriculture
2. 1952
3. 1957
4. 1961
5. 1960
6. 1964
7. 1951-56
8. 1963
9. 1908
10. 1975-76

II. TRUE OR FALSE

1. True
2. True
3. False
4. False
5. True

III. MATCH THE FOLLOWING

(i)		(ii)	
1.	B	1.	E
2.	D	2.	B
3.	E	3.	A
4.	C	4.	C
5.	A	5.	D

IV. AT A GLANCE

2

Seed Marketing

I. FILL UPS

1. _____ refers to the actual acquisition and selling packed seeds, intermediate storage delivery and sales promotional activities.
2. _____ entails using marketing information for the purpose of planning.
3. _____ is one of the major channel through which bulk of paddy seeds, pulses seeds and oil seeds are marketed in the state.
4. _____ certificate required for imported seed to ensure that it does not contain a pest or disease.
5. _____ will not normally be issued for seed purchased within a country.

II.TRUE OR FALSE

1. The seed can be held in quarantine at the point of arrival in the country, if deemed necessary.
2. Phytosanitary certificate will be issued for seed purchased within a country.
3. NSC is a multiple window system.
4. Agriculture department is an example for single window system.
5. Stock control and quality assurance entails moving the seeds from point of production to the point of sale.

III. MATCH THE FOLLOWING

1.	Phytosanitary certificate	A. Preferred international transfer
2.	Single window system	B. Department of agriculture to seed producer
3.	Multiple window system	C. Import seed
4.	*In vitro* plantlets	D. Agriculture department
5.	Channel of marketing	E. NSC

ANSWER KEYS

I. FILL UPS

1. Seed marketing
2. Fore casting
3. Seed grower – Agricultural Department - Agriculture department - Seed use farmer
4. Phytosanitary
5. Phytosanitary certificate

II.TRUE OR FALSE

1. True 2. False
3. True 4. True
5. False

III. MATCH THE FOLLOWING

1. C
2. D
3. E
4. A
5. B

IV. AT A GLANCE